Borderless Press is a project of Postcolonial Networks, a global community of scholars, activists and ministers. Our published works reflect a commitment to decolonize knowledge production and distribution. Like all academic publishers, we are committed to rigorous peer-review processes and publication of scholarship that makes important contributions to knowledge. Additionally, we strive for a unique and equitable approach to publishing.

Our authors

- Are from around the world and especially from the Majority World
- Choose the language in which they seek to write and publish their book
- Collaborate with us on all publishing decisions including price of the book
- Share in a significant portion of royalties

The books we publish

- Include a range of authorial voices, from experiential to scholarly
- Are focused on justice concerns from around the world

All author inquiries should be addressed to Dr. Joseph F. Duggan, founder and chief editor of Borderless Press, info@borderless.press.com.

Intercultural Church

Intercultural Church

Bridge of Solidarity in the Migration Context

Agnes M. Brazal

Emmanuel S. de Guzman

Permissions

"Cultural Rights of Migrants" is a revised version of a chapter that originally appeared in the book *Faith on the Move: Toward a Theology of Migration in Asia*, ed. Fabio Baggio and Agnes M. Brazal (Quezon City: Ateneo de Manila University Press, 2008), 68–92. [Republished with permission.]

"The Church as 'Imagined Communities' among Differentiated Social Bodies" is a revised version of a chapter that originally appeared in the book Faith on the Move: Toward a Theology of Migration in Asia, ed. Fabio Baggio and Agnes M. Brazal (Quezon City: Ateneo de Manila University Press, 2008), 118–54. [Republished with permission.]

"Mapping the Church on the Move" is a revised version of the essay published as *Exodus Series 12: A Resource Guide for the Migrant Ministry in Asia*, ed. Fabio Baggio (Quezon City: Scalabrini Migration Center, 2012). [Republished with permission.]

© 2015 by Agnes M. Brazal and Emmanuel S. de Guzman

Published by Borderless Press
www.borderlesspress.com
info@borderlesspress.com

Cover design by Joanna Ruiz
Interior design by Melody Stanford

All rights reserved. No part of this book may be reproduced or transmitted in any form or by any means, electronic or mechanical, including photocopy, recording, or any information storage and retrieval system, without prior permission from the publisher, except by a retriever who may quote brief passages in articles ore reviews.

Although every precaution has been taken to verify the accuracy of the information contained herein, the author and publisher assume no responsibility for any errors or omissions. No liability is assumed for damages that may result from the use of information contained within.

Library of Congress Control Number: 2015904526

ISBN-13: 978-0-9962017-0-4
ISBN-10: 0-9962017-0-X

First edition

Printed in the United States of America

Contents

Acknowledgments ix

Introduction xi
    AGNES M. BRAZAL

I. The Migration Context

1. Looking Backward Toward the Future:
Hopes from Sending Countries
AGNES M. BRAZAL 1

2. The Scent of Marginality: Odorizing Difference
in Migratory Relations
EMMANUEL S. DE GUZMAN 19

II. Theorizing Interculturality

3. Exploring "Interculturality" with Hall, Bhabha, and
Bourdieu
AGNES M. BRAZAL 47

4. Cultural Rights of Migrants: A Philosophical and
Theological Exploration
AGNES M. BRAZAL 69

III. Toward an Intercultural Church

5. Church as "Imagined Communities" among Differentiated Social Bodies
   EMMANUEL S. DE GUZMAN 91

6. Mapping the Church on the Move
   AGNES M. BRAZAL AND EMMANUEL S. DE GUZMAN 117

7. Bridge of Solidarity: Ministries in an Intercultural Church
   AGNES M. BRAZAL AND EMMANUEL S. DE GUZMAN 135

Bibliography 163

Index 185

Acknowledgments

This anthology would not have seen the light of day without the aid of a number of friends and institutions. We would like to thank Jacques Haers, sj for my fellowship at the Katholieke Universiteit Leuven in 2007, and Peter Casarella for the senior research fellowship at the Center for World Catholicism and Intercultural Theology at DePaul University in 2012. These opportunities for sabbatical in Belgium and the United States had provided me with the time to sit down, access invaluable materials for this study, write and edit our manuscript for this publication.

Our peers who critically reviewed this work were crucial toward making this collection of essays more solid, updated, and global in perspective, even as the experience of Filipino migrants are highlighted.

We also profoundly appreciate the support of Joseph Duggan, founder of Postcolonial Networks and Borderless Press, and Jason Craige Harris, Postcolonial Networks board member. We are grateful for each of their genuine desire to help give voice to those in the global South. Special thanks as well to Melody Stanford, Production Editor of Borderless Press, who played a central role in bringing this book to life.

We are thankful to the publishers for permission to reprint a revised version of the following materials: Ateneo de Manila University Press for "Cultural Rights of Migrants" and "The Church as 'Imagined Communities' among Differentiated Social Bodies"; and the Scalabrini Migration Center for "Mapping the Church on the Move."

We owe all of you a debt of gratitude (*utang na loob*) which in Philippine culture is also understood as debt of human solidarity. This is a debt which is recognized and remembered always in the *loob* (inner self) of the recipient.

Lastly, we dedicate this book to our son Nathanael, God's gift of love to us!

Agnes M. Brazal with Emmanuel S. de Guzman

Introduction

This anthology is a collection of articles that were separately written, reflecting a "theology done in fragments." In the two-thirds world, theologians for the most part, could only do theology in "bits and pieces," that is, as we respond to invitations to deliver a talk or write a paper for a pastoral formation program, a conference, an anthology or a journal. Nevertheless, though done in "bits and pieces," these articles are connected by a certain vision—the intercultural [-postcolonial] church.[1]

Various conferences occasioned the writing of the articles in this collection. "Cultural Rights of Migrants: A Philosophical and Theological Exploration" and "The Church as 'Imagined Communities' among Differentiated Social Bodies," were written for a conference in Manila in July 2006, co-sponsored by the Scalabrini Migration Center (SMC), the Episcopal Commission on Migrants and Itinerant People and the Maryhill School of Theology, which culminated in the publication of the book Faith on the Move: Toward a Theology of Migration in Asia.[2] "The Scent of Marginality: Odorizing Difference in Migratory Relations" was a paper delivered at the conference of the Catholic Theological Society of the Philippines (DaKaTeo) on "Marginalization, Exclusion, and Suffering" in October 2006, Tagaytay City, Philippines. The essay "Looking Backward toward the Future: Hopes from Sending Countries" was first presented at the Omnes Gentes Conference on "Migration: Challenges of the Spirit," October 2007, at the Katholieke Universiteit Leuven, Belgium. The essay "Mapping the Church on the Move" is partly based on an essay (with the same title) commissioned by the SMC for

---

1. The meaning of "intercultural" and "postcolonial" will be explained later in this introductory essay.
2. Fabio Baggio and Agnes M. Brazal, eds. *Faith on the Move: Towards a Theology of Migration in Asia* (Quezon City: Ateneo de Manila University Press, 2008).

the Exodus Series: A Resource Guide for the Migrant Ministry in Asia.[3] This article, together with "Bridge of Solidarity: Ministries in an Intercultural Church," was expanded, drawing intentionally from the ecumenical experience beyond that of the Catholic Church in the migration context. All of the above essays have been updated and revised to reduce overlaps.

We decided to put these essays together to: 1) contribute to the development of the concept of interculturality and the related notion of cultural rights; 2) describe and evaluate various models of church operating in the migration context; and 3) elaborate on and propose the intercultural church as a vision and direction toward which other church models can orient themselves.

A View from the Two Poles of the Migration Circuit

This anthology takes cognizance of the situation in both the receiving and sending countries, with a particular focus on the Filipino migrants. Theology of migration is not only that which is constructed at the site of migration or the receiving societies, for this constitutes only one pole in the circuit of migration. The other pole is in the sending country. What happens to the people who stayed behind? One cannot understand fully and theologize on the migration reality without looking at it from the perspective of these two poles. While most of the essays in this anthology focus on the circumstances of migrants in the host societies, the shadow side, the reality back "home" (drawn mainly from the experience of the authors as Filipinos) is recognized to provide a more wholistic picture.

As authors, we have experienced living as migrants when we were licentiate and doctoral students in the Katholieke Universiteit Leuven, Belgium. Because at that time, scholarship stipend was limited, foreign students like ourselves had to look for other sources of finance. As other Filipino students, Manny (Emmanuel) worked in the school cafeteria while I did some cleaning job in the house of a philosophy professor. During his studies, Manny also served as volunteer worker for migrants at the Stella Maris, Ghent, Belgium, and the Filipino chaplaincy in Paris, France. The 353 Stella Maris centers worldwide affiliated with the Catholic Church provide pastoral care, support, and services to seafarers. While in Belgium, I also did an apostolate with

---

3. Emmanuel S. de Guzman, "Mapping the Church on the Move," *Exodus Series 12: A Resource Guide for the Migrant Ministry in Asia*, ed. Fabio Baggio (Quezon City: Scalabrini Migration Center, 2012).

an organization of migrants, the *Samahan ng mga Manggagawang Pilipino sa Belgium* (Association of Philippine Migrant Workers in Belgium). The organization, founded in 1983, aims at promoting the rights and interests of Philippine workers and their families in Belgium. The members are mostly domestic helpers and women married to Belgian nationals. Our other vicarious experiences of "migrancy" would include occasional sabbatical leaves abroad, and as tourists in and outside Asia. While there is a difference between tourists and most migrants,[4] two-thirds world tourists do not necessarily escape being treated as labor migrants or as objects of racist remarks.

Equally important is our experience of living in a sending country where one out of ten families, including our own families, has a migrant relative.[5] In the mid-1970s, the late Philippine dictator Ferdinand Marcos systematized the deployment of labor overseas as a stop-gap measure to address high unemployment rate. In the succeeding administrations, the export of labor was adopted as a development strategy in itself, thus making the Philippines one of the major labor exporters in the global scale. The Philippines which is a sending country is simultaneously a receiving country as well. While home to a large number of Chinese migrants, it also has the largest diaspora community of Koreans in Southeast Asia and the eighth-largest in the world.[6] The number of foreign religious and seminarians studying in the Philippines has also increased in the past decade as the Philippines is becoming a center for theological formation in Asia.[7]

My initial interest, however, in systematically reflecting on the issue of migration was sparked by the 2003 MWI-Institute of Missiology, Missio-Aachen's international academic essay contest for Contextual Theology and Philosophy on the theme "Religious Identity and Migration," where my essay "Beyond the Religious and Social Divide: the Emerging Mindanawon Identity" won the prize.[8]

---

4. On the difference between a tourist and a migrant, see Zygmunt Bauman, "From Pilgrim to Tourist—or a Short History of Identity," in *Questions of Cultural Identity*, ed. Stuart Hall and Paul du Guy (London: Sage Publications, 1996), 30.

5. "Labor Export Policy of Developing Countries: The Case of the Philippines and Indonesia." http://edm.iboninternational.org/component/content/article/413-special-features/250-labor-export-policy-of-developing-countries-the-case-of-the-philippines-and-indonesia (accessed July 2012).

6. "Koreans in the Philippines Explained," http://everything.explained.at/Koreans_in_the_Philippines/ (accessed July 2013).

7. Agnes Brazal, DaKaTeo (Catholic Theological Society of the Philippines): Regional Report, http://theo.kuleuven.be/insect/assets/file/DaKaTeo_Report%202011.pdf (accessed July 2012).

8. *Chakana: Intercultural Forum of Theology and Philosophy* 2, no. 3 (2004): 7–26.

This interest was sustained through our common collaboration with the various programs of the Scalabrini Migration Center in Manila and the Episcopal Commission on Migrants and Itinerant Peoples (ECMI), which includes lecturing at the Exodus Program for pastoral workers with migrants in Asia. We also helped conceptualize and implement their Migration Theology program for the migrant ministry in Asia in 2007. Since then, we have taught migration theology subjects in several theological schools (Loyola School of Theology, Maryhill School of Theology, and St. Vincent School of Theology) in Manila, Philippines.

NAVIGATING THE INTERCULTURAL AND POSTCOLONIAL

As mentioned, the intercultural and postcolonial are two threads or heuristic perspectives that run through the essays in this collection. The meanings of both terms—postcolonial and intercultural—are still fluid thus the need to be clear in what sense we are using these frameworks in relation to migration.

Intercultural communication theories, intercultural philosophy and postcolonial discourses developed separately. The anthropologist Edward Twitchell Hall is regarded by many as the founder of the intercultural communications approach in the 1950s. In the United States, interest in intercultural communication theories heightened in the 1970s as Japan rose in economic power. There was the need for US Americans engaged in business to understand cultural differences in order to facilitate intercultural communication.[9]

For Twitchell Hall, all cultures are unique, homogenous and relatively stable.[10] Intercultural communication[11] opens up a space for dialogue and understanding between different cultures which essentially remained unchanged.[12] This concept of interculturality held by many intercultural communication writers seemingly implies as well the equality of all cultures and of all members of a culture or nation. Hidden, however, is a universalistic tendency in the systematic privileging of Western concepts, such as equality or the categories of individualism vs collectivism understood as valid for all

---

9. Britta Kalscheuer, "Encounters in the Third Space: Links Between Intercultural Communication Theories and Postcolonial Approaches," in *Communicating in the Third Space*, ed. Karin Ikas and Gerhard Wagner (New York: Routledge, 2009), 27.

10. Edward T. Hall, *Beyond Culture* (New York: Anchor Books, 1976).

11. Intercultural communication is the term used by cultural anthropologists to refer to the interaction, oftentimes face-to-face, between individuals from different cultures.

12. Kalscheuer, "Encounters in the Third Space," 26–48.

cultures.¹³ It also ignores the role of power in cultural discourses (e.g. who defines what is the culture? who are its gatekeepers?), as well as, the possibility of hybridization of cultures which has become more apparent with globalization and the phenomenon of massive migration. Some later interculturalists, however, have employed a more discourse-centered approach to culture.¹⁴

Intercultural philosophy, on the other hand, as a way of doing philosophy which dialogues with and integrates other cultural perspectives, emerged in the 1980s mostly from the German speaking parts of Europe. Unlike many intercultural communication theorists, intercultural philosophers like Heinz Kimmerle, Franz Martin Wimmer, Raúl Fornet Betancourt and Ram Adhar view cultures as developing in the process of exchange with other cultures.¹⁵ Our sense of interculturality is more akin to this tradition.

Intercultural philosophy is an attempt to overcome eurocentrism which remains to be a dominant paradigm in the world today. Fornet-Betancourt, a proponent of intercultural philosophy, regards intercultural dialogue as an alternative model to the homogenizing trend in neo-liberal globalization.¹⁶ Even as he recognizes that cultures are ambivalent and produce their own "Babarism," Fornet-Betancourt posits the need to recognize the vision of the world of each culture and what it can contribute toward a common strategy of life for all. The culture of origin is a point of support that can be appropriated in the form of affirmation or overcoming in an exercise of critical reflexivity.

---

13. Britta Kalscheuer and Lars Allolio-Näcke, "Why does the Current Debate on Interculturality Prevent the Development of Intercultural Communication?: A Critical Note on the Interculturality Discourse," http://sietarcongress.wu-wien.ac.at/docs/T6_Kalscheuer.pdf (accessed July 2012); see also Yoshitaka Miike, "Beyond Eurocentrism in the Intercultural Field: Searching for an Asiacentric Paradigm," in *Ferment in the Intercultural Field: Axiology, Value, Praxis* (International and Intercultural Communication Annual vol. 26), ed. William J. Starosta and Guo-Ming Chen (London: Sage, 2003), 243–44.

14. See Joel Sherzer, "A Discourse-Centered Approach to Language and Culture," *American Anthropologist* 89 (1987): 295–309; Srikant Sarangi, "Intercultural or Not? Beyond Celebration of Cultural Differences in Miscommunication Analysis," *Pragmatics* 4, no.3 (1994): 409–27. A discourse, for Michel Foucault, refers to several statements that provide a language to talk about a topic at a particular historical conjuncture. Discourse prescribes what can be talked about and in what way it can be talked about, and rules out ways of speaking or constructing knowledge on the topic. A discourse-centred approach views cultures in a more dynamic way.

15. Samples of their works are as follows: Raul Fornet-Betancourt, *Interculturalidad y globalización. Ejercicios de crítica filosófica intercultural en el context de la globalización neoliberal* (Frankfurt: a.M., IKO: Verlag Interfulturele Kommunikation, 2000); Heinz Kimmerle, *Interkulturelle Philosophiezur Einführung*, vol. 266 (Aufl., Hamburg: Junius, 2002), Ram Adhar Mall, *Intercultural Philosophy* (Lanham, Maryland: Rowman and Littlefield, 2000); Franz M. Wimmer, *Interkulturelle Philosophie* (Vienna: UTB, 2004). "Is Intercultural Philosophy a New Branch or a New Orientation in Philosophy?" http://homepage.univie.ac.at/franz.martin.wimmer/intpheng95.pdf (accessed July 2012).

16. Raúl Fornet-Betancourt, "Philosophical Presuppositions of Intercultural Dialogue," http://them.polylog.org/1/ffr-en.htm (accessed July 2012).

But a genuinely free interaction among cultures can only be ensured if there is equality and social justice at a global level.

Postcolonial criticism, on its part, is a standpoint that is attentive to how colonial/neocolonial interests are represented in cultural texts, for example, migration discourses. While the hyphenated post-colonialism refers to the temporal period after colonization, postcolonialism (without a hyphen) adverts to the resistance to domination both during the colonial period and after,[17] though the term postcolonialism was used to refer to these themes only from the mid-1980s.[18]

Like intercultural philosophy, postcolonial criticism aims to overcome eurocentrism. It highlights however the negotiation/resistance of those in the margins or periphery even within a culture to the dominant discourses of those in the metropolis/center. This does not only include minority ethnicities but also subcultures marked by other differences (e.g. gender, sexual orientations, race) that have become a basis for exclusion and marginalization. Postcolonial theology has been employed as an all–encompassing term for what was also previously known as Third World Theology, though, having extricated "third world" from a specific geographical location, postcolonial criticism now includes as well those in the periphery of First World cultures.[19]

Interculturality, in its emphasis on dialogue, can complement and help balance the postcolonial emphasis on resistance, toward openness to and the creation of alliances between, for instance, women and men against sexism, first world and third world citizens against imperialism, black and whites against racism. Interculturality, as Fornet-Betancourt states, is a "conscious

---

17. R. S. Sugirtharajah, "Postcolonial Biblical Interpretation," in *The Modern Theologians: An Introduction to Christian Theology since 1918*, ed. David F. Ford with Rachel Muers (Oxford: Blackwell Publishing, 2005), 536–37.

18. Arif Dirlik, "The Postcolonial Aura: Third World Criticism in the Age of Global Capitalism," in *Dangerous Liaisons: Gender, Nation, and Postcolonial Perspective*, ed. Anne McClintock, Aamir Mufti and Ella Shohat (London: University of Minnesota Press, 1997), 502.

19. Gerald West, South African theologian, criticizes postcolonial theory's tendency to co-opt homegrown and local discourses (e.g. nationalist resistance during the colonial era, theologies of liberation and inculturation) and its lack of a clear liberation project, having totally divorced itself from or ignored its Marxist roots. Recognizing though that there are elements in postcolonial theory that goes beyond liberation hermeneutics, he sees the potential in developing the hyphen in "liberation-postcolonial." "Doing Postcolonial Biblical Interpretation@Home: Ten Years of (South) African Ambivalence," http://neotestamentica.files.wordpress.com/2009/10/421ggwest-sample.pdf (accessed July 2012). On how postcolonial criticism goes beyond liberation hermeneutics, see Musa Dube , "Postcolonialism and Liberation," in *Handbook of U.S. Theologies of Liberation*, ed. Miguel de la Torre (St. Louis, Missouri: Chalice Press, 2004), 293–94. For a response to West's critique, see Review of Tat-Siong Benny Liew, ed., *Postcolonial Interventions: Essays in Honor of R. S. Sugirtharajah*, *The Bible in the Modern World* 23 (Sheffield: Sheffield Phoenix Press, 2009) by Erin Runions, *Journal of Postcolonial Theory and Theology*, http://postcolonialjournal.com/Resources/Review%20Postcolonial%20Interventions.pdf (accessed July 2012).

Introduction

way of life in which an ethical position in favor of living together (*convivencia*) with difference takes form."[20]

Postcolonial criticism shaped by post-structuralist discourses views cultures as dynamic and hybridized. The concept of hybridity is a useful metaphor in understanding the "in betwixt-and-between" (neither here nor there or both/and) situation of migrants today. Paradoxically, however, postcolonial theorists like Homi Bhabha who come from the literary field, has not been able to theorize adequately the role of power (and significantly of global capitalism)[21] in the hybridization of cultures. He has been criticized for downplaying the violence involved in many forms of hybridities (e.g. production of the mestizo/a in Latin America), in particular, and for regarding language as the "paradigm of all meaning–creating or signifying systems" thus rendering the "World according to the Word," in general.[22]

In this light, toward a more materialist approach to analyzing the dynamics of cultural encounters in the context of migration, most of the essays in this collection have integrated particularly the theoretical framework of the postcolonial theorist Stuart Hall (who has also influenced Bhabha)[23] and the post-Marxist sociologist Pierre Bourdieu[24] for they evidently locate cultural practices in the context of power relations, and are able to steer clear both from rational voluntary subjectivism on the one hand and objective structuralism on the other.

While drawing a lot from Michel Foucault, Hall hesitates to totally abandon structuralist insights (e.g. the structuring forces of capitalism, tendential lines of history) which he deems important in dealing with the complexities and contradictions of late capitalist society. For him, some sense of structure and totality is crucial in summoning resistance in terms of a larger

---

20. Raúl Fornet-Betancourt, *Filosofar Para NuestroTiempo*, cited by Maria Pilar Aquino, *Feminist Intercultural Theology: Latina Explorations for a Just World*, ed. Maria Pilar Aquino and Maria José Rosado-Nunes (Maryknoll, New York: Orbis Books, 2007),15.

21. See critique of Arif Dirlik of postcolonial theorists like Homi Bhabha. Arif Dirlik, "The Postcolonial Aura," 501–28.

22. Ania Loomba, *Colonialism/ Postcolonialism: the New Critical Idiom* (London: Routledge, 1998), 177–83 and Benita Parry, "The Postcolonial: Conceptual Category or Chimera?" *The Yearbook of English Studies* 27 (1997): 12.

23. See Homi K. Bhabha, *The Location of Culture* (London and New York: Routledge, 1994), 32, 41–42, 253, 256–57, 266, 353, and 362.

24. On the relation of Bourdieu's works and praxis to postcolonialism, see Nirmal Puwar, "'Postcolonial Bourdieu': Notes on the Oxymoron," http://eipcp.net/transversal/0308/puwar/en (accessed June 2012).

alliance and more global type of struggle.²⁵ Hall's theory of articulation, as elaborated in the Chapter Three essay in this anthology, is also important in comprehending how identities are formed in the migrant context; that even if identities can be changed, when the lines of tendential force linking identities to particular stereotypes are strong, one has to get through these grooves in order to re-articulate one's identity or "rename" one's self. One cannot just wish away an identity for a person is also hailed into it. This is a corrective factor to the unstable, always shifting perspective on identity in much postcolonial discourses. Employing the image of "suturing," Hall's theory of articulation explains too how, despite the pluralization and fragmentation of identities, a collective identity nevertheless can be forged, which at the same time respects differences.

In turn, Bourdieu's theory of cultural practice—[(habitus)(capital)+field]=practice—is helpful in understanding how the practices of migrants are shaped not only by their cultural unconscious (habitus), but also their capital (social, economic and cultural) and how they employ the latter in the new field (migration context) to maximize their well-being. Bourdieu's framework reminds us that intercultural encounters, whether in the church or the society at large, occur in a field of power relations. The interrelation of the migrants' economic, cultural and social capital determines their position in a field and their right to define doxa or the "good." Genuine interculturality or mutual fecundation in the encounter between cultures in the church or society in general can only happen when asymmetry in power relations has been or is being addressed.

With the above dialogue with developments in cultural studies, we hope we have laid a foundation for theologizing on the intercultural church on solid grounds.

The Collection

Part I of this anthology elaborates on the migration context. "Looking Backward toward the Future," an essay originally prepared for a European

---

25. John Fiske notes: "Hall's constant return to concrete political and social conditions, his insistence that the real effects of ideology and of representation are material, historically specific and available for empirical analysis would appear to have affinities with more of Foucault's work than he is prepared to recognize. This, of course, is the Gramscian or 'culturalist' side of Hall rather than the structuralist one." John Fiske, "Opening the Hallway: Some Remarks on the Fertility of Stuart Hall's Contribution to Critical Theory," in *Stuart Hall: Critical Dialogues in Cultural Studies*, ed. Kuan-Hsing Chen and David Morley (London: Routledge, 1996; reprint ed. 2001), 217.

audience in 2007, establishes a historical and a theological basis for interculturality—our shared journey as strangers or as migrants toward God's reign. It makes use of the notion of anamnestic rationality—remember you were once migrants—to foreground an alternative to the "capitalistic" way of looking at migration. Deploying an intercultural-postcolonial lens, we highlighted how colonial migration and the new migrations today are linked to capitalism. Colonial migration in the past was driven by capitalist need for cheap labor and raw materials, for new market and territories and the desire to arrest the decline in the rate of profit by depopulating Europe. Migration today, though caused by a host of other factors, is partly driven as well by global capitalism's search for cheap labor for services that cannot be devolved in the two-thirds world.

Remembering how Europeans were once migrants (as colonial collaborators and ordinary citizens fleeing famine and poverty) can be a starting point for their solidarity with the migrants of today. The dangerous memory of the migrant experience of the people of God compels all Christians as well to act with greater justice toward the migrants, and to appreciate—as Israel became a blessing to the nations—the gifts that migrants bring.

"The Scent of Marginality" focuses on "difference" in the migration context symbolized as "odor." Odor is a taboo topic but a subject commonly "whispered" in cross-cultural encounters.[26] This article explores the various ways in which the "odor" of the marginalized is politicized and the "odor" or "difference" of the migrant is constructed. It refers as well to how some migrants in turn construct the "odor" of the host culture as a form of resistance. The essay underlines that: "A vision of the [intercultural] church in the perspective of Jesus' proclamation of the kin-dom of God may have to be a multiplicity of smells, not an odorless or odor-free society but, as Paul puts it, a church that is "the aroma of Christ to God among those who are being saved" (2 Cor. 2:15), including perhaps, the odor of dirt which Francis of Assisi, like many of the writers of the early church, regarded as insignia of holiness," a smell that recalls a dangerous memory.

Part II of this anthology consists of articles which propose some theoretical frameworks for understanding interculturality with a postcolonial twist. "Exploring Intercultural Dynamics in the Migration Context" was written for this anthology to further clarify the underlying theoretical framework

---

26. With the possibility of communicating anonymously in cyberspace, the blog of Robert Lindsay on body odor of races, garnered 448 responses. Robert Lindsay, "Do the Races Smell Different?" July 3, 2009, http://robertlindsay.wordpress.com/2009/07/03/do-the-races-smell-different/ (accessed July 2012).

behind the intercultural church model, by engaging with the insights of postcolonial theorists Hall and Bhabha and the sociologist Bourdieu.

"Cultural Rights of Migrants" explores from a philosophical perspective the concept of cultural rights in the migration context, using critically the framework of Bourdieu and the Canadian liberal theorist of immigrant multiculturalism, Will Kymlicka. Based on the document "Cultural Rights: Fribourg Declaration," it defines cultural rights as right to cultural expression, development and identity. Bourdieu's framework helps clarify that cultural right is a right of an individual–in–social relation. Kymlicka, on the other hand, discusses a type of cultural rights of migrants that is group–defined or differentiated but which can be exercised by an individual or a group. He calls this polyethnic rights (e.g. wearing of veil, funding for ethnic art museums). He argues that polyethnic rights should be granted only for external protections and not to control internal dissent. Respect for cultural rights should be integral to the intercultural church. From a theological standpoint, this essay posits that cultural rights can be understood within a Trinitarian social model of relationality and mutuality, equality in diversity, creativity and fecundity.

Part III of this anthology consists of essays expounding on the Church in via, on the way to becoming intercultural. "Church as 'Imagined Communities' among Differentiated Social Bodies" starts by deconstructing popular images of the church—as shepherd, mother and teacher—to show their inadequacy for use in the migrant context. It points to "city life" as one way of re-imaging the church. City life is a form of social relations of "being together of strangers." It is an image that is not new to Christianity (e.g. City of Jerusalem, Augustine's City of God,). Iris Young[27] identified four virtues of city life which may constitute what may be referred to as the ambience of a church with and of migrants: social differentiation, variety of activities, eroticism (an attraction to the novel, strange and surprising) and publicity (a place where anyone can participate and witness).

---

27. The essay "Church as 'Imagined Communities' among Differentiated Social Bodies" is partly based on the theory of Iris Young. Though identified among theorists of multiculturalism, Young does not view group difference in an essentialist sense but rather as "ambiguous, relational, shifting, without clear borders." Iris Marion Young, *Justice and the Politics of Difference* (Princeton: Princeton University Press, 1990), 171. For Young, "social groups" are affinity groups with similar cultural practices or way of life. While social groups sharing a common experience of oppression can fade away when the group for instance overcomes marginalization, there are also social groups that emerge resulting from the "freedom of city life." Young would, however, be more skeptical than Hall regarding the production of a collective will amidst differences. De Guzman's essay though, in re-imagining the church, focuses on her concept of relational difference and "affinity" to argue for the need for respect for various cultural groups and for dialogue among these social groups within the church.

Introduction

"Mapping the Church on the Move" draws an itinerary of the church in the migration context. Four models of the church are described: monocultural host church, monocultural migrant church, multiculturalist church and the intercultural church, with their pastoral features, premises and assumptions, biblical and theological anchors. While recognizing that divergent circumstances in the migration context may lead to the formation of other church models, we regard the intercultural church as a vision and orientation toward which the other models can direct themselves.

The final essay "Bridge of Solidarity: Ministries in an Intercultural Church" elaborates on the metaphor of the intercultural church, that is, the community of Christ's disciples, as bridge of solidarity. It explores the distinctive characteristics of pastoral ministries in this church model—ministry of welcome, worship, table fellowships and story-telling, dialogue with peoples of other faiths, teaching, advocacy and networking, theologizing—and the kind of ministers needed. It also posits that even churches in sending countries are called to become intercultural, and identifies some facets of these ministries in the originating country.

Agnes M. Brazal

I
The Migration Context

1

LOOKING BACKWARD TOWARD THE FUTURE
Hopes from Sending Countries

There is a Philippine proverb which states: "One who does not look back at the past can never arrive at his place of destination." Two central images expressed in this proverb will provide the framework for this essay: 1) image of remembering (looking back at the past) and 2) image of movement (toward a "destination" or a "future").

Memory has often been viewed as fundamental to our characterization of the future. The first part of this paper will underline the importance of remembering the past—Europeans' own experience of migration on the one hand and Christian's identity as "migrants" on the move toward the "promised land" or the 'reign of God" on the other. This remembering will hopefully serve as a foundation for the second part of the paper—a plea for a "forward-looking" solidarity with migrants and sending countries.[1]

DANGEROUS MEMORIES

The German theologian Johannes Baptist Metz elaborates on the significance of dangerous memories for our characterization of the future. "In what sense can memory function as a practical and critical, and even dangerous emancipatory force?"[2] Metz notes that there are memories where the past

---

1. This is an updated version of the paper first presented at the Omnes Gentes Conference on "Migration: Challenges of the Spirit," October 18–20, 2007, Katholieke Universiteit Leuven, Belgium.
2. Johannes B. Metz, "The Future in the Memory of Suffering," *Concilium* 6, no. 8 (June 1972): 14.

is stripped of its danger and oppression. Going back to the past can become a form of romantization—"the good old days," a source of refuge from the present. We can give the myth of a Western Europe that never experienced emigrating as an example.³ Another form of memory is, however, dangerous because they uncover new insights for the present and makes a demand on us today. They question our presuppositions. "They are memories we have to take into account; memories, as it were with future content. Because some memories are subversive for the present, the erasure of certain historical memories is a common measure of totalitarian regimes."⁴

Remember You were Once Migrants!

Can the story of European migration be remembered as a "dangerous memory" that can be a starting point for charting the future? Even in the pre-Columbian period, migration had already marked the history of Europe: the Poles migrated to Germany, the Scots to Ireland, and the Greeks to Asia Minor. The colonial expansion of Europe to new territories, however, is significant, in ushering a new wave of intercontinental migration, within the sphere of capitalism that was starting to become global.

According to Pieter Emmer, between two to three million peoples from Europe moved to other continents like the New World (America) and the southern part of Africa before 1800. This number rose dramatically to 61 million after 1800. The Europeans were then migrating as well to North Africa, Kenya, Rhodesia, Australia and New Zealand. Only about 20 percent of this number returned home.⁵

Were the migrants from Europe during the period of colonial expansion any different from the migrants of today? A closer look at the European migrants to the Americas can help traverse the seeming distance between the migrants before and now.

Many of the European migrants to Latin America likewise migrated in search for a better life than what they had in their homeland. They were

---

3. See Pieter Emmer, "'We are Here, Because You were There': European Colonialism and Intercontinental Migration," in Migrants and Refugees, ed. Dietmar Mieth and Lisa Sowle Cahill, *Concilium* (1993/4) (London: SCM Press, 1993): 42.

4. Metz, "The Future in the Memory of Suffering," 15.

5. Emmer, "We are Here, Because You were There," 44.

fleeing poverty and hunger.[6] Migration of Europeans to North America, mostly bound for the United States from 1789–1924, was propelled too by the search for land and money, as well as, freedom of religion and better opportunities.[7] It is estimated that more than half of white emigrants to the English colonies of North America in the 17th and early 18th centuries were indentured servants. They sold themselves to merchants and ship captains in exchange for transportation to the colonies. Similar to slaves, indentured servants could be traded, were required the permission of owner to get married, and could be physically punished. Unlike slaves, they could be freed after a fixed period of time, usually three to seven years.[8] In the 18th and early 19th century, many Europeans travelled as redemptioners who negotiated their indenture only at the end of the arduous voyage thus putting them at a greater disadvantage.

Thus, similar to many migrants today, the European migrants risked their lives in search of greener pastures. Colonial migration provided the "land-hungry Europeans" easier possibility of owning agricultural lands and to grow and market new products such as coffee, tea, and cotton. Those who went to the moderate climactic zones like North America benefited from prolonged life expectancy, capacity to have bigger families, security from epidemics and deadly diseases, as well as, undernourishment which they would have experi-

---

6. The Spaniards who left for Argentina from 1850–1920 were poor and from the rural areas. Eighty percent of Portuguese who went to Brazil from 1850–1900 were unskilled workers looking for a place in the Brazilian job market. In 1750–1815, Germans migrated to Brazil after a famine in Germany. The massive exodus of northeastern Italians to Brazil from 1876–1945 can be characterized too as "a desperate flight from hunger." "Migration to Latin America," http://www.let.leidenuniv.nl/history/migration/chapter53.html (accessed August 2007). Brazil was receiving immigrants even after its independence in 1822.

7. A potato famine triggered the diaspora of small Irish tenants and agricultural workers fleeing from hunger, from 1845–1853, with around 2 million emigrants leaving the United Kingdom and around a million more in the next decade. In a period of a hundred years, the Germans went to North America because of low wages, high food prices, and their small peasants' dwarf landholdings. A potato blight in 1840 occasioned the departure of people, often encouraged by local German authorities. Due to agricultural crises, the Dutch emigrated from 1847–1857 and 1880–1893. The Portuguese migrating to North America at the turn of the 20th cen., as with those who migrated to Brazil, were mostly unskilled with very poor financial resources. In south Italy, economic and political crises from 1870–1945 triggered an exodus of Italians. Population growth and widescale proletarianization in Eastern Europe led to the migration of millions of people to the USA between 1870 and 1914. Less than 200,000 gypsies were among the 20 million Eastern Europeans who went to the USA before 1914. "Migration to North America," http://www.let.leidenuniv.nl/history/migration/chapter52.html (accessed August 2007).

8. Nathan W. Murphy, "Origins of Colonial Chesapeake Indentured Servants: American and English Sources," http://pricegen.com/immigrantservants/origins.htm#intro (accessed November 2009); originally published in the *National Genealogical Society Quarterly* 93, no. 1 (March 2005): 5–24.

enced more were they at home.⁹ Migration also depopulated parts of Europe like UK and Germany, which were suffering from overpopulation. Emmer noted that the primary advantage Europe got from the colonial expansion was not so much the products or trade but the migration escape hatch which benefited not only the migrants but also those left behind.¹⁰ At the underside of this story were the victims of colonization—the colonized peoples, the African slaves, the indigenous peoples that have been massacred, etc.

At the end of the Second World War, another stream of intercontinental migration occurred; this time, that of returning colonial administrators and their collaborators. This likewise proved beneficial to Europe because the return of trained professionals, both Europeans and emigrating peoples, helped to rebuild post-war Western Europe. Europe needed this extra labor to attain the growth rates it had achieved in the 1950's and 1960's.

Remembering that the foreparents of the European peoples were once migrants themselves, fleeing hunger and poverty, searching for better opportunities and freedom, can indeed be a dangerous memory! It poses a challenge to the current generation to be one with the sufferings and hopes of their foreparents in a "backward-looking solidarity," as well as, with migrants and the sending countries today in a "forward-looking solidarity."¹¹ Metz underlines that the memory of humankind's history of suffering "offers inspiration for a new form of solidarity of responsibility towards those most distant from us, inasmuch as the history of suffering unites all men like a 'second nature'."¹²

Remember We are God's People on the Move Toward God's Reign

For us Christians, in particular, a dangerous memory is likewise revealed in a reading of the Judaeo-Christian tradition where the "migration" or the "movement from the known to the unknown promised land" is not just a historical accident in the life of our religious fore parents but central to the

---

9. Emmer, "We are Here, Because You were There," 43.
10. Ibid., 50.
11. See Metz, "The Future in the Memory of Suffering," 19–20.
12. Ibid., 13.

identity of Israel and of Christians.[13] (*Erga Migrantes Caritas Cristi* 14-15; EMCC hereafter)

In his article, "What are you talking about to each other as you walk along?" (Lk 24: 17), Giovani Zevola argued how the vocation of Abraham to journey from the "known" toward the "unknown" or the "promised land" signifies as well the vocation of all Christians; that is, to be a migrant on the move toward a homeland.

The very identity of the people of Israel is hinged on this: "A wandering Aramean was my ancestor; he went down into Egypt and lived there as an alien… (Dt. 26:5).[14] But God has blessed Israel, delivering them from oppression while they were living as aliens in Egypt, providing food and dress for them as they were wandering in the desert, and leading them to the "promised land," where they too lived as aliens among the inhabitants of the land.[15] Israel's narrative, Frank Crüsemann points out, never portrayed the land as empty, but recognized that they have to live, that is, as "aliens" with other inhabitants in the land God promised. For the most part of its history, there was also no sedentary Israel: "The land is promise and largely remains a promise";[16] they never really "arrived," but were always in perpetual movement or departure.

The prescription not to molest or oppress an alien thus stands at the centre of Old Testament law, with the oldest law book of the Bible containing the injunction twice.

> Ex. 22: 21 "You shall not molest or oppress a resident alien, for you were aliens in the land of Egypt."
>
> Ex. 23: 9 "You shall not oppress a resident alien; you know the heart of an alien for you were aliens in the land of Egypt."

Anamnestic rationality, which integrates reason and memory, characterizes biblical traditions. It is the historical memory of their suffering as aliens that compel Israel to be in solidarity with the strangers among them. Zevola puts

---

13. Giovani Zevola, "What are you Talking About to Each Other as you Walk Along?" (Lk 24: 17): Migration in the Bible and our Journey of Faith" in *Faith on the Move: Toward a Theology of Migration in Asia*, ed. Fabio Baggio and Agnes M. Brazal (Quezon City: Ateneo de Manila University Press, 2007), 94.

14. The context of the book of Deuteronomy is the end of the Northern Kingdom of Israel in 722 which gave rise to a refugee problem. Frank Crüsemann, "'You Know the Heart of a Stranger" (Exodus 23:9): A Recollection of the Torah in the Face of New Nationalism and Xenophobia," *Concilium* (1993/4): 98. For a critique of the notion that *gher* simply refers to landless peoples not belonging to another ethnicity, see ibid., 101–104.

15. Ibid., 106.

16. Ibid., 105–107.

it succinctly: "In the foreigner's face, Israel comes closer to seeing its own face."[17]

The ethical dimension of treating the alien well is further grounded on a theological belief that God is a friend of and cares for the alien: "For the Lord, your God, befriends the alien, feeding and clothing him. So you too must befriend the alien, for you were once aliens yourselves in the land of Egypt." (Dt 10: 17-19)

This remembering passes on into the New Testament, in particular in the gospel of Matthew, where Jesus himself is presented as someone with "foreign blood" (Mt. 1) from Tamar an Aramean, Rahab who is from Canaanite Jericho, Ruth from Moab[18] and Uriah, a Hittite, and mother of Solomon. The Matthean gospel also represented the family of Jesus as having gone to exile in Egypt until King Herod died and it was safe for them to return to Galilee.

In continuity with this tradition, in the epistle to the Hebrew, the patriarchs beginning with Abraham were seen as a typology of the Christian identity: "pilgrims in search of a homeland." (Heb 11:14). A "continual exodus"[19] is in fact suggested in the 2nd century letter to Diognetus:

> ... But, inhabiting Greek as well as barbarian cities, according as the lot of each of them has determined, and following the customs of the natives in respect to clothing, food, and the rest of their ordinary conduct, they display to us their wonderful and confessedly striking method of life. They dwell in their own countries, but simply as *sojourners*. As citizens, they share in all things with others, and yet endure all things as if foreigners. Every foreign land is to them as their native country, and *every land of their birth as a land of strangers*.[20] (Emphasis mine.)

This last line calls to mind what Yhwh expressed to Israel in Leviticus 25:23: "[T]he land is mine; with me you are but aliens and tenants." To conclude this section, we pose again the question: Can the memory of our common religious identity as a people on the move in search for "God's reign," and the shared historical experience of migration of our peoples, link us in a "forward-looking solidarity" with migrants and sending countries today?

---

17. Zevola, "What are you Talking about to Each Other, as you Walk Along?" 101.

18. See Diane Bergant, csa, "Ruth: The Migrant who Saved the People," in *Migration, Religious Experience and Globalization*, ed. Gioacchino Campese, cs and Pietro Ciallella, cs (New York: Center for Migration Studies, 2003), 49–61.

19. Ibid.

20. "Letter to Diognetus," http://www.crossroadsinitiative.com/library_article/344/Letter_to_Diognetus.html (accessed August 2007).

"Forward-looking Solidarity": From Global Capitalism to a Socially Sustainable and Ethical Model of Development

Solidarity, for John Paul II, is the correlative response to the fact of interdependence in our world today. He defines it as "a firm and persevering determination to commit oneself to the common good; that is to say to the good of all and of each individual, because we are all really responsible for all. This determination is based on the solid conviction that what is hindering full development is that desire for profit [capitalism] and that thirst for power already mentioned."[21]

A common factor linking colonial migration to the new migrations today is capitalism. While a number of other structural forces causing or reinforcing migration had been identified in various studies, one cannot adequately

---

21. *Sollicitudo Rei Socialis*, no. 37, henceforth referred to as SRS. We have focused here on solidarity as the virtue that goes with anamnestic rationality, as we are dealing with the migration context not only in the receiving but also in the sending countries. Hospitality as a Christian imperative is more associated with or called for in the host society, even as the guests become hosts and the hosts become guests. See William O'Neill's use of the parable of the Good Samaritan as paradigm of anamnestic solidarity in "Christian Hospitality and Solidarity with the Stranger," in *And You Welcomed Me: Migration and Catholic Social Teaching*, ed. Donald Kerwin and Jill Marie Gerschultz (New York, NY: Lexington Books, 2009), 150. For the virtue of hospitality as practiced by the early Christians, see Wayne A. Meeks, *The First Urban Christians: The Social World of the Apostle Paul* (Yale University Press, 1983), 109 and Donald Senior, "Beloved Aliens and Exiles: New Testament Perspectives on Migration," in *A Promised Land, A Perilous Journey: Theological Perspectives on Migration*, ed. Daniel G. Groody and Gioacchino Campese (Notre Dame, Indiana, University of Notre Dame, 2008), 29–32; in the patristic era, Peter C. Phan, "Migration in the Patristic Era: History and Theology," in *A Promised Land*, 49–54; in different periods of church history, Jean-Pierre Delville, "Migrations and Christianity," paper presented at Omnes Gentes conference on "Migration: Challenges of the Spirit," October 18–20, 2007, Katholieke Universiteit Leuven, Belgium; Fabio Baggio, "History of the Pastoral Care of Migrants," *Exodus Series 5: A Resource Guide for the Migrant Ministry in Asia*, ed. Fabio Baggio (Quezon City: Scalabrini Migration Center, 2005). For discussions on hospitality to the stranger/migrant, see the following: Christine D. Pohl, *Making Room: Recovering Hospitality as a Christian Tradition* (Grand Rapids, Mich.: Eerdmans, 1999); Idem, "Responding to Strangers: Insights from the Christian Tradition," *Studies in Christian Ethics* 19 (2006): 81–110; Lucas Chan Yiu Sing, "A Model of Hospitality for our Times," *Budhi: A Journal of Ideas and Culture* 10, no.3 (2006): 1–30; Ilsup Ahn, "Economy of 'Invisible Debt' and Ethics of 'Radical Hospitality': Toward a Paradigm Change of Hospitality from 'Gift' to 'Forgiveness,'" *Journal of Religious Ethics* 38 (2010): 243–67.

For another alternative to the capitalistic view of migrants and the security discourse regarding migration, see Kristin Heyer, "Reframing Displacement and Membership: Ethics of Migration," *Theological Studies* 73 (2012): 188–206.

respond to the contemporary issue of migration without considering its central link to global capitalism.[22]

Colonial migration can be described as a product of imperialist expansion, to look for new territories where the surplus labor (population) of Europe can migrate. To arrest the decline in the rate of profit, British merchants encouraged the migration of their surplus population.[23] While a reserve army of labor was needed to keep wages low, too much excess becomes a burden to the State and threatens to be a source of political discontentment. European emigration helped resolve high unemployment rates in Europe while at the same providing labor power to exploit the natural resources in the colonies.[24]

The forced migration of Africans during the period of colonial expansion was also propelled by the need for laborers in the plantations in the tropical colonies. Shipping firms engaged in the snatching and selling of about eleven million Africans from the African continent. "Against the anti-slavery agitation, the planters in the Caribbean, in Brazil and in the US South pointed out how important slavery was for the economy of the colonial mother country."[25] When the slave trade was banned and slavery abolished in the 19th cen., the shipping companies turned to Asia, particularly China and India for indentured laborers. This migration of contract workers (which involved kidnapping and selling of workers as well) was eventually halted in China and India because of pressures from the public in UK, US and France and from Indian nationalists respectively.

In today's global context, the widening gap between rich and poor nations, brought about by colonial and neo-colonial policies as unequal trade relations and irresponsible lending of capital to dictatorial governments in the 70's that had led to the third world debt crisis,[26] has prepared the way

---

22. For a bibliography of authors that have elaborated on this, see Edna Bonacich and Lucie Cheng, eds., *Labor Immigration Under Capitalism: Asian Women in the United States Before World War II* (Berkeley: University of California, 1984), 1. Other structural forces reinforcing migratory movements are as follows: 1) the development of means of instantaneous communication technology and mass transportation; 2) political and economic linkages between sending and receiving societies such that receiving countries like Korea can also be at the same time sending countries; 3) the need for highly skilled workers in the main metropolitan centers of the world, and for providers of services which cannot be devolved in two-third world countries. See Saskia Sassen, *Globalization and its Discontents: Essays in the New Mobility of People and Money* (New York: The New Press, 1998), 37–45.

23. Alejandro Portes, "Migration and Underdevelopment," *Politics and Society* 8, no. 1 (1978): 1–48.

24. Bonacich and Cheng, *Labor Immigration Under Capitalism*, 15.

25. Emmer, "We are Here, Because You were There," 47–48.

26. Part of the IMF's structural adjustment program imposed on indebted third world countries is the promotion of an export-led development, so they can earn more dollars to repay their debts. See Sassen, *Globalization and its Discontents*, 43 on how export led-development fosters migration.

for labor emigration. While huge income gap may be insufficient by itself to produce mass emigration, it is a strong push factor.

New Industrial Reserve Army

Metropolitan capital benefits from labor emigration especially from a pool of exploitable workers or source of cheap labor that would serve as a reserve army and help arrest capital's cyclical fall of rate of profit. As Karl Marx argues: "the whole form of the movement of modern industry depends, therefore, upon the constant transformation of a part of the labouring population into unemployed or half-employed hands."[27] The presence of a reserve army controls the rise in wages of nationals. If on the other hand, the reserve army is reduced and wages rise, profits and capital accumulation decrease leading to a fall in investment and to retrenchment.

(Im)migrants, therefore, according to Stephen Castles, are the new industrial reserve army that cushions the effects of cyclical crises in a capitalist economy. They are mostly relegated to 3 D (dirty, dangerous and difficult) jobs. Their entry into these types of jobs has allowed the promotion of nationals to more skilled, white-collar jobs or into supervisory positions.

On the other hand, the "guest worker" type of migrant in Western Europe before the 1970's, which is currently coming back in the form of migrants from the new and candidate member states (NCMS) of the European union, is especially advantageous for employers, because it is flexible and mobile. The State does not need to shoulder their full "reproduction costs" (i.e. their own education and that of their children, etc.) as their families are left behind and the wages are largely spent in the countries of origin. Furthermore, migrants who relatively lack political voice[28] can do the 3 D jobs which nationals would not want to do.[29] Those with short-term residence and work permits

---

27. Karl Marx, *Capital: A Critique of Political Economy*, vol. 1: *The Process of Production Capital*, ed. Frederick Engels, trans. Samuel Moore and Edward Aveling (Moscow: Progress Publishers, reprint ed, 1984), 593.

28. European states vary in the extent they recognize migrants' freedom of assembly and demonstration and of association. Since the 1970's, foreign citizens and workers have participated in various degrees in protests and advocacies to better their social conditions. In certain cases, they have been granted voting rights and representation at the local level. Tomas Hammar, "The Civil Rights of Aliens," in *The Political Rights of Migrant Workers in Western Europe*, ed. Zig Layton-Henry (London: Sage Publications, 1990), 89.

29. Manuel Castells underlines that nationals do not opt for these jobs because they are dirty, dangerous, and difficult; rather, it is because these jobs are badly paid in relation to "what would be unacceptable to a working class which had the necessary strength to impose better working conditions and higher wage levels." Manuel Castells,"Immigrant Workers and Class Struggles in Advanced Capitalism: The Western European Experience," *Politics and Society* 5, no. 1 (1975): 33–66.

and discretionary decisions about prolongation of permits may find it more precarious to join unions and other associations. The lack of political voice of migrants serves the interest of capitalists who benefit from a divided working class composed of nationals on the one hand and migrants on the other. Racism[30] and xenophobia further benefit the cause of capitalists, because they provide ideologies that deepen this divide between national and migrant workers and prevent them from uniting to fight for their common concerns.

The role of irregular migrants as reserve army is not that different, except that they are the most vulnerable group of migrants. European states have implemented a very restricted migratory regime whereby labor force quotas are below the amount that the economies need or can absorb.[31] Restrictive migration policies vis-à-vis job availability and difficulties in the process allowing regular admission contribute to the rise of irregular migration.[32] Yet governments do not deal squarely with the problem because, as Fabio Baggio argued in the context of East and Southeast Asia,

> [e]ven though it is not admitted at the official level, the dynamics of many flourishing local and national economies 'require' the contribution of cheaper unauthorized foreign workers, whose work is not supported by taxes, health insurance and social security. It is a hidden stock of workers extremely submissive to and controllable by employers.[33]

Considering the decline in population growth in many parts of Europe, the reserve army of migrant labor (regular or irregular) is very important for the European economy since rise in labor supply is necessary for capital accumulation.[34] Castles qualifies that: "The effect of abundant labour supply in the long run was not to keep wages down absolutely, but to keep down

---

30. Discrimination in Europe in the early 1970's was not based specifically on race. Italian migrant workers in Switzerland and black workers in Britain were discriminated to the same degree. In the late 1980's, as a result of the emergence of a "European consciousness" and the decline in individual European nationalism, European white migrants became more acceptable than immigrants of other color or phenotype. Stephen Castles, *Ethnicity and Globalization: From Migrant Worker to Transnational Citizen* (London: Sage Publications, 2000), 87.

31. Laura Zanfrini, "The Ethics of Migration: Reflections on Recent Migration Policies and 'Non-policies' in Italy and Europe," in *Migration Management and Ethics: Envisioning a Different Approach* (Corso Milano: Polimetrica, 2006), 82–85.

32. Other factors include the emergence of aggressive recruitment machineries (regulated and unregulated ones) and trafficking in persons. Graziano Battistella, "The Human Rights of Migrants," *Exodus Series* 11, 7.

33. Fabio Baggio, "Migration Politics and Ethics in East and Southeast Asia," in *Migration Management and Ethics: Envisioning a Different Approach*, ed. Fabio Baggio and Laura Zanfrini (Corso Milano: Polimetrica, 2006), 44. For a similar phenomenon in the US, see William T. Cavanaugh, "Migrant, Tourist, Pilgrim, Monk," *Theological Studies* 69 (2008): 344.

34. Castles, *Ethnicity and Globalization*, 73.

their relative share in national income, allowing profits and investments to remain high."[35]

On the part of the sending countries, while indeed they benefit from labor emigration through contract workers' remittances, it is important to consider that they also lose a lot because the years of investment in education and skills training given to their citizens do not primarily benefit the country but rather the metropolitan centers. Brain drain has become a serious problem in a sending country like the Philippines which has experienced a shortage of experienced doctors, nurses, teachers and other professionals due to emigration. The country simply becomes a training ground for fresh graduates who eventually leave when they have obtained some experience. This is compromising the country's potentials for economic growth and development, because of the current shortage of skilled professionals. Brain drain in the sending countries, on the other hand, translates into brain waste in the receiving countries. Due to the presence of racial and ethnic discrimination in the receiving countries, the education of the migrant is oftentimes not given equal value and recognition as that of the national.[36]

A New Service "Class"

Even before Europe stopped accepting non-European migrant labor in the 1970's due to the oil crisis and the threat of a world recession, the process of family reunification was already under way. Many of the "guest workers" did not return to their countries of origin where in many cases, the conditions have deteriorated. They instead started bringing their spouses and children thus initiating the process of family reunification which was already well established by the time labor migration stopped. Initially meant to be a temporary labor system, the "guest workers" became permanent settlers. As this was an unplanned process, owing to governments' lack of foresight, and it occurred at a time of economic crisis, the migrants' need for housing, education, health and social services were not met adequately leading to urban decay and social tensions.[37]

While migrants and their families began to be blamed for these problems and were collectively represented as parasites to the welfare system and a threat to socio-political stability, it was through this same family reunification

---

35. Ibid., 74.
36. Zanfrini, "The Ethics of Migration," 89.
37. Castles, *Ethnicity and Globalization*, 75.

that Europe got additional supply of labor from the 1970's to the second half of the 1990's when Europe opened up again to accepting "guest workers." Furthermore, these families' female migrant population also provided the domestic and care services which have been considered increasingly useful and necessary with the end of the European welfare system and the changes in the way the family is organized in Europe.[38]

In states like Italy and Spain where care work continues to be delegated to women but with no adequate state support or welfare structures, governments were willing to relax migration policies for domestic workers. Special provisions were made for domestic workers so they can still enter legally or be regularized through the amnesty program.[39]

Focusing in particular on Italy, Jacqueline Andall states that normally only higher income families are able to access the services of a migrant domestic worker. Since the expense for employing a domestic worker can be as much as the average salaries of an Italian woman, many families resort to employing irregular migrants who can be paid half the legal rate and without social security insurance. This leads to the proliferation of irregular domestic workers, an exploitable pool of labor. Within a patronage relationship, the employers, in return, help find work for the relatives of the irregular migrant. While these workers are eventually regularized by their employers, they can still be without pension even after forty years of work, because of the years they served as undocumented migrant.

Domestic work for migrants in Italy has also been transformed from a short-term into a long-term employment, even if one in ten migrant domestic workers had attained a university degree.[40] It is difficult to move out of this sector not only due to the rigidly racialized labor market but also

---

38. Zanfrini, "The Ethics of Migration," 79. For a discussion of various models of welfare and employment structures in Europe that influence women's choices vis-à-vis family work, see Jacqueline Andall, "Hierarchy and Interdependence: The Emergence of a Service Caste in Europe," in *Gender and Ethnicity in Contemporary Europe*, ed. Andall (Oxford: Berg, 2003), 44.

39. Zanfrini, "The Ethics of Migration," 72. See also Linda Bosniak, "Citizenship, Noncitizenship, and the Transnationalism of Domestic Work," in *Migrations and Mobilities: Citizenship, Borders and Gender*, ed. Seyla Benhabib and Judith Resnik (New York: New York University Press, 2009), 127–56.

40. The study of Christina Ho of Chinese migrants in Australia likewise shows a "brain waste," especially among wives accompanying their husbands. Economically independent before, they had for the first time become dependent on their spouses. She remarks: "I encountered dozens of women cleaning hotel rooms or sewing clothes in their living rooms and garages, who had previously worked as teachers, engineers and in other professions." "China's Brain Drain is our Brain Waste," 2004, http://www.smh.com.au/articles/2004/09/20/1095651256166.html?oneclick=true/#, quoted in Susie Jolly, with Hazel Reeves, "Gender and Migration: Overview Report," BRIDGE, 27 http://www.bridge.ids.ac.uk/reports/CEP-Mig-OR.pdf (accessed July 2012).

because of the live-in character of the job which, though allowing them to save more money leaves domestic workers with very little free time to explore other possibilities. The live-in and long-term nature of the job all the more becomes problematic considering that the domestic workers have families either with them, in the countries of origin or even in a third country. While facilitating the care of other women's children, migrant domestic mothers are unable to provide the proximate care their own children need.

A special concern in the sending countries is the children left behind. A study of the Scalabrini Migration Center in Manila in 2003 showed that while the extended family assists in taking care of the children, those with migrant mothers tend to slightly score higher in anxiety and loneliness scales.[41] What is more worrisome however is the development of a migration mentality among the children of migrants. A 2003 survey in the Philippines revealed that sixty percent of children of overseas foreign workers expressed of their plans to work abroad and of taking courses that are needed in the countries of the North. We also have the paradoxical reality of parents migrating to give their children a better future; and these children, after getting a university degree in the Philippines, end up nevertheless as domestic workers in Europe (although receiving a salary that may be six times more than what an average professional earns in the Philippines).

The continuing need for a pre-modern employment like domestic work in post-industrial societies, show how work structures continue to reflect patriarchal frameworks; reproductive work is delegated primarily to women,[42] and treated as a private rather than a public responsibility. What is needed, as Andall underscores, are "accessible welfare structures that enable all women to reconcile their productive and reproductive roles."[43] It is also crucial that migrant domestic workers are able to organize and protect their rights to transform their working and social conditions.

Siphoning out Highly Skilled Workers

A contemporary trend in the restructuring of the world economy is the increasing concentration of management, communication, research, develop-

---

41. Maruja Asis, *Hearts Apart: Migration in the Eyes of Filipino Children* (Manila: ECMI-CBCP, Scalabrini Migration Center and Overseas Workers Welfare Administration, 2004), 54–55.

42. While reproductive work is primarily a responsibility of the Italian woman, 24.3 percent of domestic workers are male migrants. Caritas di Roma, Immigrazione. Dossier statistico 1999, Rome: Anterem, cited by Andall "Hierarchy and Interdependence," 47. On Filipino domestic workers in Hong Kong, see Gemma Tulud Cruz, *An Intercultural Theology of Migration: Pilgrims in the Wilderness* (Leiden: Brill, 2010).

43. Andall, "Hierarchy and Interdependence," 54.

ment and finance, referred to as "global control capability" in major metropolitan cities like London, New York, Frankfurt, Paris, Tokyo, Sydney and Singapore.[44] Highly skilled specialists, researchers and knowledge workers are thus being attracted to migrate and work in such centers.

Aside from this, there are specific needs for which there is lack of native supply. European countries, in the second half of the 1990's have started attracting highly-skilled migrants from the developing world in these fields. While the presence of these highly trained migrants can help improve the collective representation of non-European ethnic groups, this would have the negative effect of siphoning out some of these countries' best minds, and together with the exodus of other professionals, can seriously undermine the capacity of developing nations to improve their economies. We are however aware that some countries like Ireland, South Korea, and Taiwan are experiencing a strong return migration or a net "reverse brain drain." India is following suit.[45] But such a return migration would not happen unless a certain level of development has been achieved by the home country, meaning, there was a critical mass of skilled professionals who stayed behind to push forward their country's development.

HOPES FOR THE FUTURE

Migration impacts both the receiving and the sending countries. While considering the needs of both sides, it is primarily from the perspective of a sending country, that we have identified the following as some of the major areas which require attention and action.

First, migrant labor force quotas set up by the Western countries should reflect more accurately the demand for labor. This will help curb the rise in irregular migration, and migrants' vulnerability to exploitation.

---

44. Castles, *Ethnicity and Globalization*, 75–76.

45. Michele R. Pistone and John J. Hoeffner, *Stepping Out of the Brain Drain: Applying Catholic Social Teaching in a New Era of Migration* (New York: Rowman and Littlefield, 2007), 102. Pistone and Hoeffner propose the alternative term "step-out migration" instead of "brain drain," since the former is more neutral. With improvements in global communication and transportation, they underline that it is now easier for skilled migrants to contribute as well to their originating countries' development through investments, contact-building, remittances, or via a return migration, etc. Parvati Raghuram argues, however, that in contrast to the work of IT experts or scientists for example, complete and frequent transference between medical systems is more difficult in addition to the greater investment of the state and professional bodies in this field thus making return migration of medical professionals more unlikely. Studies have also shown how the exodus of medical professionals have negatively affected directly the provision of health services in the originating country. "Caring about the Brain Drain Migration in a Postcolonial World," *Geoforum* 40, no. 1 (January 2009): 25–53.

Secondly, there is a need to strengthen migrants' voice in enhancing migration policies through their participation in unions and voluntary associations. It is important for national workers to unite with migrants on common issues to dispel the notion that migrants are competing with them and stealing their jobs.

Thirdly, there is a need to educate the citizenry on the mutual exchange in migration such as the contribution of migrant labor to the economy and the savings of the receiving countries in the "reproduction costs" of workers since it is the sending country that invested in the education and rearing of these able-bodied workers. Anamnestic rationality (in the longue duree) and a sense of mutuality should balance the conception that migrants are a burden to the welfare system.

Fourthly, the barriers to mobility of the (im)migrant labor force should be removed. This may include access to subsidized childcare, language courses and recognition of the cultural capital (education, skills) of the migrant regardless of race or ethnicity.[46] Labor mobility prevents the racialization of low paid jobs. In relation to this, Andall surfaces the need to examine how, in their active participation in the recruitment or placement process, religious organizations and voluntary sector associations assisting migrants, may be unwittingly helping racialize domestic work particularly in Italy.[47]

A fifth concern is the brain drain that results from migration. Can the countries of the North, in the spirit of solidarity and global justice, help promote brain circulation, to curb brain drain? Brain circulation aims at encouraging immigrants to return regularly, not to extract local knowledge and have this patented by foreign corporations, but rather, to genuinely contribute to their country's development. In cases of "brain strain hotspots," they can likewise limit large-scale recruitment and instead help promote retention and return of highly skilled workers.[48] With regard medical professionals, Raghuram argues for the need to locate the concern for medical provision not only within the nation but transnationally. In this context, restitution which includes financial compensation to countries for their medical per-

---

46. Dhananjayan Sriskandarajah, "Migration Madness: Five Policy Dilemmas," *Studies in Christian Ethics* 19, no. 1 (2006): 30.

47. For the role of the church in the recruitment of domestic workers in Egypt, see Amira Ahmed, "'I need work!': The Multiple Roles of the Church, Ranking and Religious Piety Among Domestic Workers in Egypt," *The Asia Pacific Journal of Anthropology*, 11, nos. 3 and 4, (September-December 2010): 362–77.

48. Ibid., 33. For its part, the Philippine government is trying to boost medical tourism to motivate local doctors to stay. There were some in the government who were proposing to temporarily ban the migration of doctors.

sonnel who migrated should be viewed as an act of redistributive justice.[49] On their side, the debt of solidarity of highly skilled immigrants should not simply be confined to sending remittances,[50] but more importantly, in their participation in a "brain circulation."

Sixth, the increasing difficulty for citizens of countries with large migratory flows, in getting visas for Europe and North America and the use of external border controls (e.g. via the airlines in various connecting flights),[51] aimed at curbing irregular migration, make the journey of an ordinary two-third world student, tourist or conference participant so arduous. Is it right to collectively punish a social group for individual violations of visa regimes?[52]

Lastly, at the risk of sounding "utopic" but which nevertheless needs to be expressed for this is the "future" we are aiming at, is the vision for a more just and fair global economic order, so that people from the developing world will no longer be forced to leave their families behind, and all women and men can participate freely in both productive and reproductive work.

Conclusion

The dangerous memories of European migration and our vocation as Christians to be a people on the move toward God's reign poses a challenge to the church to respond not only to the issue of exploitation and racial-ethnic-gender discrimination of migrant workers, but also the neo-colonial policies that have contributed to the widening chasm between the countries of the North and the South. In the past two centuries, the State, Church and public opinion in Europe have worked to curb the evil effects of capitalism through

---

49. Raghuram, "Caring about the Brain Drain Migration in a Postcolonial World."

50. Among the moral hazards of overseas migration, as experienced in the Philippines, is the development of dependency on remittances. The other members of the family do not work anymore and simply rely on the remittance coming from abroad. Remittances were also able to insulate the economy from economically unwise but politically popular decisions of government leaders. Thus while the migrants and their families have benefited from the remittances, this has not translated into long-term development for the country. See also Fabio Baggio, "The Migration-Development Disconnect in the Philippines," in *Moving Out, Back and Up: International Migration and Development Prospects in the Philippines*, ed. Maruja M.B. Asis and Fabio Baggio (Quezon City: Scalabrini Migration Center, 2008), 109–26. In China though, their economic growth has been fuelled by foreign investment 70 percent of which came from the Chinese diaspora. Susie Jolly, with Hazel Reeves, "Gender and Migration: Overview Report," BRIDGE, 16. http://www.bridge.ids.ac.uk/reports/CEP-Mig-OR.pdf (accessed July 2012).

51. Zanfrini, "The Ethics of Migration," 65–66.

52. See also, Miroslav Marynovych's discussion of the difficulties faced by Ukrainians in getting a visa. "Citizenship," in *Catholic Theological Ethics: Past, Present and Future. The Trento Conference*, ed. James F. Keenan (Quezon City: Ateneo de Manila University Press, 2013), 268.

consciousness-raising, advocacy and legislation. A similar challenge faces us today: how can we help re-structure the global and local economies, and migration policies, in particular, so that they become more ethical and socially sustainable from the perspective of both sending and receiving countries?

One may say that the Church in Europe has already become a minority and possesses little impact on the bigger society. The church can indeed either retire into self-seclusion and degenerate into a sect or respond to and be reinvigorated by this new sign of the times.[53] Being themselves "strangers in their own land" can hopefully make the European Christians identify more with the plight of migrants. Thus, the solidarity of the European Church with the migrants will no longer be based on an abstract solidarity of shared humanness,[54] but rather on a shared journey as "strangers."

Agnes M. Brazal

---

53. Pontifical Council for the Pastoral Care for Migrants and Itinerant People, *Erga Migrantes Caritas Christi* (The love of Christ towards migrants), 1 May 2004, no. 14.

54. Richard Rorty, *Contingency, Irony and Solidarity* (Cambridge: Cambridge University Press, 1989), 189–98.

2

THE SCENT OF MARGINALITY
Odorizing Difference in Migratory Relations

To enter the world of migratory relations is to venture into what Sarah Whatmore describes as modes of traveling through the heterogeneous entanglements of social life.[1] Most of us who studied abroad know the life of a transnational migrant, what it means to live and find meaning in "hybrid geographies." To reword a biblical wisdom: "You know the scent of marginality, because you once smelled of difference" (Ex 3:9).

In this essay, we shall use smell or odor[2] interchangeably as the olfactory activity, a cultural category for social relations, and as a metaphor for the construction of reality and meanings. I shall deal first with the role of smell in human interactions and offer a rather succinct analysis of the marginalization of the olfactory sensorium in the social, as well as, academic world. This provides the horizon for a discussion of the situation of international migrants. Lastly, I offer some *"in-scents"* on how odor can be a fruitful resource for sniffing the biblical tradition so as to inspire and challenge us today in odorizing difference that respects and promotes the cause of migrants.

---

1. Sarah Whatmore, *Hybrid Geographies: Natures, Cultures, Spaces* (London: Sage Publications, 2002).

2. Technically, the sense of smell or olfaction is the ability of humans and animals to perceive odors. Odor, what is smelled, refers to the property or quality of a thing that affects, stimulates, or is perceived by the sense of smell.

The Power and Marginality of Smell in Social Life

The olfactory activity is perhaps the least recognized experience, yet it probably plays a much greater role than we commonly think in human interactions. It is said that a healthy individual can distinguish 10,000 different odors. For smelling is an irrepressible sense; odors cannot be contained; they escape and travel wherever they want to go. They intrude upon our bodies against our will, invading our privacy, affecting our emotions, and sometimes triggering memories that we have thought were long forgotten.[3] They reach into all aspects of our life. To reword Michelle Murphy, experiences pass through our noses, and they do not pass through without verdict.[4] The immediacy of smell is mediated by our nose that other senses may lack. Like the air we breathe, we just have to inhale or exhale odors. Of course, one can cover his or her nose but not for long, and odor has a penetrating ability to make its presence recognizable. Odors are indeed in the nose of the beholder. Our nose opens unique possibilities of perception, emotion, and imagination.[5] Though they seem to lie below the conscious thought, odors suggest, stimulate, evoke, warn, frighten, and arouse us.

While the experience of smell is personal and subjective, it is also a social event. Odors, according to anthropologists Constance Classen and colleagues, are "essential cues in social bonding."[6] We communicate by smell even without knowing it. Various cultures, however, use odors for communicating messages,[7] such as through the use of different incenses to establish

---

3. This phenomenon of odor-evoked memories have been subsumed under the catch-all label of the "Proust effect," named after the French novelist, Marcel Proust (1871–1922) whose memory was famously and productively stimulated by an olfactory, as well as, gustatory experience. One of odor-evoked memories I have is that of a strong cleaning detergent. Whenever I smell that odor, I am led back to my first trip overseas in 1981 when I was housed temporarily in the Provincial House of a religious congregation in Brussels. Wherever I was inside that place, and even when I first entered the main entrance, I smelled that odor of detergent. It evokes emotions of excitement and anxiety, but especially of strangeness, loneliness and of being lost in a different land, different people, different customs, and different time zone.

4. Michelle Murphy, "The 'Elsewhere within Here' and Environmental Illness; or, How to Build Yourself a Body in a Safe Space," *Configurations* 8 (January 2000): 96–97, cited by Joy Parr, "Smells like?: Sources of Uncertainty in the History of the Great Lakes Environment," http://www.historycooperative.org/journals/eh/11.2/parr.html (accessed September 2007).

5. "The FEAR of smell – the smell of FEAR," http://www.grandarts.com/exhibits/STolaas.html (accessed September 2007).

6. Constance Classen, David Howes, and Anthony Synnott, *Aroma: The Cultural History of Smell* (London/New York: Routledge, 1994), 2.

7. For a discussion of cross-cultural studies on the most salient uses of odor, visit "The Smell Report: An overview of facts and findings," http://www.sirc.org/publik/smell.pdf; and "Smell: Early Research & Culture: Early Odour Research in the West," nicks.com.au/admin/externalviewer/.../file/file_20079291640545471.pdf (accessed September 2007).

channels of communication with different spirits; as a means of attraction, whether of members of the opposite sex, game animals, or spirits; as a means of repulsion, whether of enemies, animals or evil spirits; and for enhancing one's chances for success at a particular endeavor, as in playing games of chance. The Ongee of the Andaman Islands, when greeting someone, do not ask "How are you?", but *"Konyuneonorange-tanka?"* meaning "How is your nose?" Etiquette requires that if the person responds that he or she feels "heavy with odor," the greeter must inhale deeply to remove some of the surplus. If the greeted person feels a bit short of odor-energy, it is polite to provide some extra scent by blowing on him or her. In India, the traditional affectionate greeting—equivalent of the Western hug or kiss—was to smell someone's head. An ancient Indian text declares "I will smell thee on the head, that is the greatest sign of tender love."

A whole multitude of smells elicit different reactions in different cultures. The bodily trail of a person may be caused by diet, environment, or emotional state, but how another person would judge it is also conditioned by cultural norms. Odors do not have a single given meaning but are interpreted quite differently by distinct groups of people. In many societies, odor is a means of and a model for speaking about how people see their selves and other people. For example, among the Serer Ndut people of Senegal, they consider themselves as clean, while they assign milky or fishy odors to neighboring tribes, and rotten odor to cadavers. Europeans are accustomed to thinking of the natives as unwashed, and themselves as clean and innocuous-smelling, but from the standpoint of the Serer Ndut, Europeans are urinous.[8] Raw onions for the Serer Ndut are fragrant, something that other cultures will never consider as a perfume.

Scientists debate whether this ability to detect odors is something innate in humans but Rachel Herz who has been working on the psychology of smell suggests that odor preferences are also largely the result of learned responses, of which models of interpretation derived from culture are one of its key factors.[9] The old axiom applies here: what is smelled is smelled according to the mode of smelling of the smeller. Various people have their distinct ways of knowing a particular person by his/her odor and how he/she stands or rather smells in the world. That odorial activity is something we learn by experience implies also that the odors we like or dislike are not fixed

---

8. Classen et al., *Aroma*, 103–104.

9. "Scent and Emotion Linked through Learning," http://www.jyi.org/news/nb.php?id=110 (accessed September 2007).

but can undergo changes or revisions. Odors are not static in the individual, any more than they are in the environment.[10]

Unlike the sense of sight which is panoramic and linear yet restrictive, smell is boundary-transgressing and multi-directional. Odors are difficult to measure scientifically because they are largely intuitive, elusive, and inexact. This can be the reason for the reluctance of academia – including theological disciplines – to study smell seriously. I suspect that a topic on smell or odor will raise eyebrows for those who stand in the tradition of theology as "systematic," "rational," and "unequivocal" in thought and language. Odor is viewed as a sensitive topic and is best whispered in private conversations, as there is also the reservation to speak of it in formal public gatherings. One can therefore be faulted for making an issue of something which is not even rationally discursive, or perhaps be accused of unsolicited advice on a potential socially divisive theme.

The disdain for odors among Christian intellectuals is actually not new. Clement of Alexandria in the second century C.E. warned that "(a)ttention to sweet scents is a bait which draws us into sexual lusts." Origen even condemned incense as "food for demons."[11] Antipathy to perfumed scents was also common among martyred Christians who refused to burn incense to honor the image of the Roman emperor. These images of early Christianity are a bit surprising because peoples of the biblical world were not deficient in their use of fragrances to appease God. But reflective of the Greco-Roman, Neoplatonic worldview, Christians under the empire assigned odor to the world of the senses, the homeland of evil, and many ceased washing themselves and were proud to reek of honest dirt and sweat.

In its far-reaching effect till today, a treatise on smell, if it can be considered theology at all by mainstream scholarship, is labeled "populist," or in churchy jargon, "pastoral," which seems to imply that it lacks intellectual substance. I am reminded also by a colleague that to use smell even as a figure of speech runs the risk of exaggeration that verges on truth and falsehood, reality and imagination, existent and non-existent. Besides, when one opens up his or her nostrils, the speech is often anecdotal than scientific. Indeed, the unmentionable can make intellectuals uncomfortable; the absorbing homogeneous atmosphere evaporates as people find themselves gasping for something outside of the rational or seizing that which cannot be grasped. The nasal reception and rejection of the topic then is itself part of its being

---

10. Classen et al., *Aroma*, 115.
11. Cited in ibid., 51.

a social event. The ambiguity of the sense of smell may lead us to insights, or better still, *in-scents* about our assumptions about ourselves and the world we live in.

The marginalization of the sense of smell in the academia and in society has its own social history.[12] While other cultures give physical, psychological, even medicinal, and social value to the olfactory sense, Western cultures tend to diminish its importance in human and social life. During the enlightenment period, philosophers downplayed smell as neither a significant means of acquiring knowledge nor of aesthetic enjoyment. Smell was relegated to the epistemological cellar, in the dust heap of the senses according to Kant. The sense of sight had become the pre-eminent means and metaphor for discovery and knowledge that were associated with men who as explorers, scientists, doctors, politicians, or industrialists, claim to be discovering and dominating the world through their keen gaze.

Smell's function in conveying or acquiring truths had increasingly been devalued. Smell was considered the sense of intuition and sentiment, of home-making and seduction. Perfume was said to encourage vanity and licentiousness, all of which were associated with women (example, in the 18th century, menstrual odor was once considered seductive). There emerged what can be called as the "gendering of smell," in which a whole hygiene industry has been built on the perception that women smell. Moreover, boundary-transgressing odors upset patterns of social relations and social ranking, as well as, patterns of economic transactions in the larger social body. Pungent bodies represent madness and savagery on the evolutionary scale of civilization, as Charles Darwin, Sigmund Freud and others explained. The suppression of odor became one of the defining characteristics of "civilized man." Anthropologists seeking to understand other cultures focused on the olfactory processes of non-Western, 'primitive' cultures, not to be enlightened about the richness of those cultures as much as to devaluate these people. It was believed that the higher the civilization, the lesser people smell and ultimately they lose their olfaction.

The relative unimportance of the sense of smell in the West may explain the paucity of the English language for aromatic experiences. Often, references to odor are borrowed from gustatory terms in the form of similes ("it smells like…"), which are also limited in the scale of sweet, sour, salty, and bitter. Sometimes odors are designated by reference to the things from which they emanate, for example, the smell of coffee, the smell of paint, the

---

12. The foregoing summary is based on Classen et al., *Aroma*, chapters 2 and 5.

smell of grass. A rich olfactory vocabulary suggests the power of smell in everyday living. Filipinos, for instance, have ample resource of terms for, let's say, unpleasant odor, some of which are untranslatable in English—*mabaho* (bad smell), *mabantot* (bad smell), *mapanghi* (smells like urine), *masangsang, maalingasaw, maangi, maanggo, maanghit* (smells like the underarm), *malansa* (fish-smell).

In English societies, terms for unlikable odor have been employed for the different "other." The aspiration for odor-free or unscented world also arose out of the class distinctions of the agrarian and industrial economies. As George Orwell so succinctly wrote, "the real secret of class distinctions in the West can be summed up by four frightful words ... *the lower classes smell.*"[13] The Puritan ethic of "cleanliness is next to godliness" is said to have resulted to some Western cultures' greater difficulty in detecting odor. Individual persons may suffer this inability but projected onto the cultural realm, groups may also carry social anosmia (lack of ability to smell) or selective or specific hyposmia (a reduced, inhibited, or impaired olfaction). What some people experience, at least for those who think that they have anosmia, is a selective or specific hyposmia. This means that some people unconsciously are selective in what they smell; there are odors that they receive but there are other odors that do not enter into their olfactory system.

Class and gender relations became impregnated with smell and odor. Accordingly, on the marketing front, advertising agencies have focused their attention on identifying—and often inventing—personal anxieties about odor that could be resolved by the purchase of specific products. For example, in 1919, a deodorant for women called Odo-Ro-No came out in the U.S. market. The company was the first to invent the "B.O." (for "body odor"), which brought a taboo topic to public awareness and promoted the product for "daintiness" and "sweetness" which women could achieve. Odo-Ro-No even had an "Armhole Odor Test" to help previously ignorant potential customers learn the socially destructive dangers of B.O. In the same decade, the Lambert Pharmaceutical Company developed an antibacterial liquid to be sold as a general antiseptic. This was Listerine. As in Odo-Ro-No, Listerine's famous campaign featured a woman (again!) named Edna, who was "often a bridesmaid but never a bride." It tells the sad tale of how she was approaching her "tragic" 30th birthday, still unmarried due to her affliction: halitosis,

---

13. George Orwell, *The Road to Wigan Pier* (London: Victor Glooancz, 1977), 159, as quoted in Classen et al., *Aroma*, 166.

which the ad explains, "you, yourself, rarely know when you have it. And even your closest friends won't tell you."

AUTODYSOMPHOBIA[14] FOR THE STENCH OF THE STRANGER

The foregoing discussion tells us that not only smell has been placed in a marginal status, but societies and cultures too have classified people according to "social odors." When particular odors are associated with particular people, places and events, it leads to narratives, and stories in turn give shape to identities of people, positively perceived or otherwise. To borrow from Mary Douglas, in smell as in matters of food, the message about odor is really about different degrees of hierarchy, inclusion and exclusion, boundaries and transactions across the boundaries.[15] The unfamiliar odor of people is inherently suspect. People sensed with a different odor are perceived as dangerous and threatening, precisely because those who perceive them are unsure of just how to classify them. What causes class and ethnic opposition is a perception that the other person is not-one-of-us, in other words, a stranger or an alien.

Some researchers try to explain "racial odors" through anatomical differences. In 1914, Havelock Ellis (1859–1939), a British doctor and sexual psychologist, claimed that there is some association between greater hairiness of ethnic groups and their marked odor. Black people, Ellis claimed, have stronger odor than other social groups due to the hairiness of their bodies, and it becomes stronger with bathing or washing because this opens the pores of their skin.[16] In a recent study, clinical laboratory scientists James Kohl and Robert Francoeur explain that differences of odor correlate with

---

14. *Autodysomphobia* is a persistent, abnormal, and unwarranted fear of one with vile odor. It can cause panic attacks and keep people apart from loved ones and business associates, but it also causes distress on the part of the person suffering from it. Symptoms typically include shortness of breath, rapid breathing, irregular heartbeat, sweating, nausea, and overall feelings of dread, although everyone experiences autodysomophobia in their own way and may have different symptoms. In our paper, we use the term in a symbolic way to describe the fear of the other who is different.

15. Mary Douglas, *In the Active Voice* (London: Routledge&Kegan Paul, 1982), 82–124.

16. Havelock Ellis, *Studies in the Psychology of Sex: Sexual Selection in Man*, vol. 4 (Philadephia: Davis, 1914), 59, 60, as cited in James Vaughn Kohl and Robert T. Francoeur, *The Scent of Eros: Mysteries of Odor in Human Sexuality* (New York: Continuum, 1995), 161.

difference in the development of sweat or apocrine glands.[17] They argue that, racially, the most striking fact about apocrine glands is their weak development in the underarm area of Orientals. Approximately half of the Korean population has no apocrine glands under their arms. Similarly, underarm apocrine glands are sparse and do not touch one another in the Japanese.[18]

Classen and colleagues, however, challenge the view that social groups, particularly ethnicities, have distinct odors. Such a claim is still a scientifically untenable proposition, or at least a controvertible question even among scientists and those who want to make a big issue out it. What exists is how people use smell or odor in a symbolic way to include or exclude others. Smell or perceived social odors particularly provide a potent symbolic means for creating and enforcing class, ethnic, gender, and even religious boundaries. Through social contact, the scent of the other is not so much the real issue as the feeling of dislike transposed into the olfactory domain. An example of a racist olfactory discourse comes from an unemployed youth in Birmingham, England, who made the following remark about Pakistani immigrants in the U.K.: "I just don't like Pakis. They stink. Pakis really reek. You can tell one in the street a mile away …." This remark about odor differences cannot be explained by biological or dietary reasons. What comes out strongly in the youth's statement is the perception of others who are different as having a smell. Odors seem to be intrinsic to group of "outsiders" or of "foreigners"; that they have odorial traits as inalterable as skin colors. "Rather than a cause of ethnic antipathy, olfactory aversions are generally an expression of it."[19]

Perceptions of smell, thus, can place people in the margins, and sometimes in a fatal way. In 14th-century France, for example, lepers and Jews were vio-

---

17. Kohl and Francoeur, *Scent of Eros*, 161. Apocrine glands are found in areas with hairs such as around the nipples, the genital area, armpits, and the navel, also in the scalp, forehead and cheeks, under the nose, base of eyelashes, bearded portion of the face, and in several other areas. These specialized glands secrete a milky substance with properties that allow bacterial action to convert the substance to pheromones, which are chemical messages or odors that convey information subliminally between individuals of the same species. When an individual interacts with another individual, it causes changes in hormone levels and in behavior. Humans have a "social odor" that allows us to smell each other's odor.

18. An American soldier relates this anecdote during his tour of duty in the Vietnam War: "I am alive today because of my nose. You couldn't see a camo banker if it was right in front of you. But you can't camouflage smell. I could smell the North Vietnamese before hearing or seeing them. Their smell was not like yours or mine, not Filipino, not South Vietnamese either. If I smelled that smell again, I would know it." (As quoted by Boyd Gibbons, "The Human Sense of Smell," *National Geographic* 170 (1986), 348–349.) If laboratory research on the relationship between hairiness and odor is true, why then were the Americans defeated by the North Vietnamese? Could it be that American soldiers, because of greater hairiness in the body, were more odorous such that the Vietnamese knew their enemy more than the invaders? Just a naughty thought.

19. Classen et al., *Aroma*, 165.

lently attacked and dispersed by shepherds and peasants.[20] Lepers and Jews were thought to be getting more economic privileges from the monarchy. To get back at them, the people spread the rumor that lepers particularly were poisoning the water system in the kingdom. Viewed morally, lepers were infecting and corrupting French Christian society. Lepers and Jews smelled the same putrid odor of avarice (particularly the Jews who were accused of killing Jesus), and they need to be cleansed away from society. Their decaying odor was symbolic or metaphorical of the social ills that had plagued France, with the lepers and Jews as convenient scapegoats. Centuries later, the same argument against the Jews would be used by Hitler in the expulsion and extermination of Jews.[21]

The abstract reality of odors is likewise made tangible, physical, and specific through the spatial dislocation and relocation of people. Place, writes Philip Sheldrake, has become "a concrete and symbolic construction of space that serves as a reference for all those to whom it assigns a position."[22] By containing odors in particular places for particular groups of people, it also seeks to control and regulate their geographic movements. For people of different odors, to cross places not of your own is seen as intruding into stable, fixed locations and disturbing its inhabitants. Places thus become landscapes of exclusion. "Power is expressed in the monopolization of central places by socially strong groups and the relegation of weaker groups in society to less desirable environments."[23] This makes "spaces of odor" a political, as well as, an economic issue, with the paradox of belonging and non-belonging.

In the contemporary world, international migrants appear most vulnerable to the invidious equation of odor and poverty, along with moral filth. Despite the seemingly borderless flow of capital and ideas in our globalized world, political borders continue to circumscribe the physical location and relocation of populations. For example, Jacques Chirac, former mayor of Paris, then later Prime Minister of France, trying to win votes from electorates unsympathetic to immigrants, declared that the state's "threshold of

---

20. David Nirenberg, *Communities of Violence: Persecution of Minorities in the Middle Ages* (Princeton: Princeton University Press, 1996), 56–68.

21. Hitler wrote in *Mein Kampf*: "The cleanliness of [Jews], moral and otherwise, I must say, is a point in itself. By their exterior you could tell that these were no lovers of water, and to your distress, you often know it with your eyes closed. Later I often grew sick to my stomach from the smell of these caftan-wearers....All this could scarcely be called very attractive; but it became positively repulsive when, in addition to their physical uncleanliness, you discovered the moral stains on this 'chosen people'." Quotation taken from Classen et al., *Aroma*, 172–73.

22. Philip Sheldrake, *Spaces for the Sacred* (London: SCM Press, 2001), 9.

23. Ibid., 21.

tolerance" has been passed, and illustrates with the comment that "the French worker goes nuts" having to live next to "the noise and odor" of immigrants.[24]

Discrimination often takes the form of racist olfactory discourses, which are usually ordered based on the interconnecting hierarchies of class, race, nationality, and gender, and sometimes religion as well. Consider the following that appear in various places in the internet: Korean households smell like mothballs; a European tourist felt like throwing up in trains crowded with Indians; within European cultures, "working class Italians smelled of fried peppers, and Greeks smelled of garlic and brilliantine, and, when they sweated, their underarms smelled of yogurt." Chinese Muslims of West Asian/Central Asian descent, "even when they bathe, still stink," and Filipinos are described to be smelling of coconut oil, fish, or worse, like a dead rat.

In Australia, racial discrimination is prohibited and very high fines—including jail terms—can be imposed on the offenders. John Howard, during his term as Prime Minister, even proposed a regulation to help the migrants integrate into the continental lifestyle. The tone of the proposal though is far from benign. All migrants must take an English test, according to Howard, "regardless of their skin colour, body shape, *body odour* and all sorts of thing." (Italics mine). The former Prime Minister remarked that, "We feel that it is the best time to apply this rule, since we have had more and more Asians in the country."[25] Howard may have forgotten that his ancestry, as the rest of the Whites, come from outside Australia, and that the original inhabitants of the place are the Aboriginal people. Australia had a very racist past which included the practice of apartheid. Indigenous peoples have lost almost all their land and suffered from discrimination and prejudices. The institutionalized attempt to prevent Aboriginal children (and thus future generations) from being socialized into Aboriginal culture resulted in the "Stolen Generation."[26]

Moreover, the Global Commission on International Migration reports the heightened interest—in the context of terrorism and control of irregular migration—in biometric technology for identity checks, which can tend to discriminate against migrants:

> Long used in the realm of criminal proceedings, as well as, in the private and commercial sector, biometrics have received a great deal of attention as a

---

24. Wade Graham, "The French Immigration Debate: The Short, Hot Summer of '91," http://www.thesocialcontract.com/pdf/two-one/Wade.pdf (accessed September 2007).

25. http://uncyclopedia.org/wiki/UnNews:"Fair_dinkum"_for_Aussie_migrants (accessed September 2007).

26. See Michael J. Shapiro, "Triumphalist Geographies," in *Spaces of Culture: City, Nation, World*, ed. Mike Featherstone and Scott Lash(London: Sage Publications, 1999).

way of "filling the gaps" in traditional methods of border control. Biometrics refers to the identification of a living person through their physiological or behavioral characteristics. Physiological characteristics include fingerprints, hand geometry, iris shape, face, voice, ear shape, and body odor. Behavioral characteristics include hand-written signatures and the way a person walks. (Italics mine.)[27]

Thus, in less conspicuous yet powerful ways, odors have been used to mark the "differences that make a difference," to use Gregory Bateson's handy phrase.[28] Traits and values are established based on olfactory symbolism, such as characterizing certain odors as good or bad, and in assigning them to different beings or states in order to signify moral goodness or badness. In other words, odor can be a marker of class, gender, race or ethnicity, even religion, and other constituents of social identity. For many migrants, especially those coming from the two-thirds world, there is the feeling that they are permanently under surveillance because they are of a different body—in shops, at work, at home, and in public spaces. They try to learn the language, adapt the ways of dressing and eating, but they cannot hide their skin and physical features, and their odors as well. There is always the suspicion that their malodorous body upsets the aesthetic, political, social, cultural or moral, and even sanitary orders of the societies they are in.[29]

ODIFEROUS TACTICS: WE ARE WHAT WE SMELL!

I remember some summer break in 1995 while studying in Belgium when I worked as a bartender in Stella Maris, a center for seafarers in Ghent. I noticed how Northern Europeans drank the strongest beer, either alone, by themselves or chatting in low voice while thick cigarette smoke cloud their heads. They would be joined by Polish and Russians who despite the language barrier understood the language of vodka. The Chinese crowded the bar counter, privy at almost everything, asking the prices of the stamps and everything else. Korean seafarers stood and watched, shifted places to have a vista of the club from various angles, leisurely but quietly strolling around

---

27. Rebekah Thomas, "Biometrics, Migrants, and Human Rights," www.migrationinformation.org/Feature/print (accessed September 2007).

28. Gregory Bateson, *Steps to an Ecology of Mind: Collected Essays in Anthropology, Psychiatry, Evolution, and Epistemology (Chicago: University of Chicago Press, 1972)*. British anthropologist Bateson famously defined information as "the difference that makes a difference." When it stops making a difference, it's no longer information.

29. Abdelmalek Sayad, *The Suffering of the Immigrant*, trans. David Macy (Cambridge: Polity, 2004), 205–206.

and about. Then there were the South Asians who asked for tea in a land known for over 800 kinds of beer! They would settle for juice but would compare that their fresh fruit drinks in their native land is delightfully refreshing than the canned beverage they paid dearly. The Filipino seafarers would rush inside Stella Maris and instantly turn the usually dull place into a festive hall. Sprinting toward the billiard table, they got hold of cue sticks and played with six or as much as ten players. They loved playing the guitar and singing on top of their voices. There were also local customers who frequented the place after work. With better knowledge of beers, they chattered on people's lives other than their own.

When all these diverse colored people crossed paths in a shared space, exchanged stories and cursed their authorities, laughed, sang, and simply have fun, and where odor provides the ambience, I began to understand how the Tower of Babel crumbled to the ground. There is little of homogeneity and univocity that marks the guarantor of settled life and routine schedule, a life which is built on the backs of others—the exploited labor of the conquered and exiled people.[30] In the belly of the empire is a flourishing of colors and narratives, and where people find courage and wisdom to name their pain and articulate their vision of life. Learning from Mikhail Bakhtin, the experience can be described with a healthy dose of aromatics, almost carnivalesque in performance—chaotic, and at the same time, liberating.

It is not easy to live at the margins. Marginalization is a structural dimension that "involves the deprivation of cultural, practical, and institutionalized conditions for exercising capacities in a context of recognition and interaction."[31] Migrants experience prejudice or discrimination based on skin color, gender, social class, religion, etc. There are gradations of marginalization within groups in the margins. Women, for example, are marginalized in many countries, though white women themselves can discriminate women of other colors, ethnicities or nationalities.

At the margins, life nevertheless is not totally powerless or helpless. Constructively and productively, marginal people use resources and tactics familiar to their marginal status in order to survive the harsh realities of life, as well as, to resist domination and exploitation, and to reinvent their identities, history and relationships. In this sense, power, to borrow from

---

30. I have drawn this insight from Eleazar S. Fernandez, "From Babel to Pentecost: Finding a Home in the Belly of the Empire," *Semeia* nos. 90–91 (2002): 29–50.

31. Iris Marion Young, *Justice and the Politics of Difference* (Princeton: PrincetonUniversity Press, 199), 55.

Michel Foucault, is mobile and contingent as it flows through social actors as they negotiate, form alliances or compete with one another in different circumstances.[32] Looking at marginality with its creative aspect (but not only that because there is also its dehumanizing aspect) enables us to move out of the restricted view of power as simply between "those who have it, and those who don't." Migrants thus are not hapless victims of centrist, dominating, totalizing groups. They are able to negotiate with the resources they have, no matter how limited these may be, to survive amidst difficult or harsh realities of domination, and to assert their humanity, as individuals and collectives. How?

In olfactory relations, marginal groups can "attempt to gain respectability by dispelling or masking their presumed ill odor."[33] The founder of a Korean-American association suggests that Korean migrants "should control (their) ethnic odors such as the smell of kimchi." They also "should maintain a good appearance." In order to counter the negative conceptions of Filipinas as husband-stealers, Filipino women married to Japanese men try to work diligently, practice self-discipline, and strive to keep their marriages intact—ideals that fit the understanding of Japanese womanhood. In the process, they create and claim spaces for themselves and their families in Japanese society. Evinced by cultural activities of numerous Filipino associations throughout Japan, many migrants also pool their energies to counter adverse notions about Filipinas, and proactively supplant these with the so-called 'tasteful difference' that are in keeping with their own self-descriptions.

Migrants can also wear perfumes or deodorants that are acceptable to dominant groups in society. Using these products, however, could do little in dispelling a prejudice which is fundamentally cultural. Deodorizing oneself, or bathing in perfume, reinforces the perception that their social group is smelly, not to count the remarks that the cosmetic remedy one wears is cheap. This only reinforces their classification as low-cost workers who are mere bodies that circulate in global labor markets to be drafted and discarded, exchanged and replaced, even assaulted and dismembered. "Not having the cultural means (because [the migrant] does not have the material means on which cultural means depend) required to take possession of the individuation of his (sic) body, he discovers his individuation only to lose possession

---

32. H. Dreyfus and P. Rabinow, *Michel Foucault: Beyond Structuralism and Hermeneutics* (Brighton: Harvester Press, 1982).

33. Classen et al., *Aroma*, 161.

of his body."[34] As Algerian migrants say of their experience in France, they are "stealing their (own) presence" by becoming somebody else's bodies. Seen from another angle, the turn to perfumes is the migrants' way of countering the predicament of marginalization by restoring their self-esteem.

I once asked a migrant why Filipino workers still feel nice after a day of cleaning three to four houses. She replied that scrubbing toilets, vacuum-cleaning carpets, deodorizing rooms with Lysol can be suffocating to one's dignity. Perfuming herself after work gives her back the sense of who she is, that "I *am* my body and not just *having* a body compensated for its labor." She then reached something from her bag, splashed it in her hands, her neck, and blouse, and remarked: "*O, amoy-baby ulit, di ba?*" (See, don't I smell like a baby again?"). Migrants strive to make their marginality meaningful amidst the harsh realities of life in affluent societies that try to deodorize difference.

Ironically, returning migrants in search of home find themselves alienated in their homeland. Working overseas even in lowly jobs offers new pleasures, new excitements, new freedoms, and new sense of personhood. This liberation of the self, even if it is only partial, may be experientially profound and empowering as to make it impossible for the migrant to remain the same as before migration. Smelling good for their kin and neighbors, they are seen as sources of power and wealth, treated as "kings and queens" as Filipino returnees would say. *Jovan* and *Brute* were popular colognes once preferred by migrants. Never mind the fact that they are inexpensive, *Jovan* and *Brute* became the trademark of a changed person who is superior in status. Coming home, migrants project their new situation through boxes of goods which when opened emit strong fragrance of success, literally and metaphorically. Kin and neighbors begin to see models in the returning migrants and would like to follow the trail of their body fragrance in the international workplace. Sooner or later though, the scent of "home but not at home" dissipates as migrants feel estranged in their own culture. Experiencing newly found or regained self-esteem for what they have achieved overseas, migrants return to old structures of inequity and social relations that are basically feudal in character.[35] Consequently they leave again and repeatedly engage in contractual work overseas, making their pilgrimage a narrative of multiple openings and endings.

---

34. Sayad, *Suffering of the Immigrant*, 206.

35. Mai Dizon-Añonuevo, "Migrant Returnees, Return Migration and Reintegration," in *Coming Home: Women, Migration and Reintegration*, ed. Estrella Dizon Añonuevo and Augusto T. Añonuevo (Manila: BalikbayanFoundation, Inc., 2002), 136–51.

The Scent of Marginality

Speaking of product scents, a thesis has been put forward by Koichi Iwabuchi in his book *Reentering Globalization*.[36] The Japanese scholar on pop culture advises that marketing and consumption of goods internationally is influenced by what he calls "cultural odor." This refers to the detectable imprint of a particular culture that is left behind on a product or export. Iwabuchi argues that 'cultural odor' is rooted in the creator culture, and can potentially be a problem for exportation (in Filipino, *"kumakapit daw ang amoy ng tao sa produkto"*). Just as a person's smell clings to the clothes he or she wears, the odor of a particular cultural group sticks to the product it manufactures. Iwabuchi seems to be playing with concepts as he speaks of "cultural odor" both as physical and symbolic realities. A product which smells too much like the odor of the culture that created it will not be very attractive to foreign buyers. It is thought that the success of selling Japanese products internationally, like Pokemon and the samurai, was because they focus on "cultural fragrance," which as opposed to a "cultural odor," is a socially and culturally acceptable smell that does not derive primarily from the product but with the image of the country of origin. It is culture re-packaged—Japan's projection of itself as the best example of the fusion of Western and Asian cultures.

Another way by which migrants deal with marginality is with redolent tactics that "declare their own olfactory norms, evaluate their olfactory identity as positive, and denounce the false olfactory identity foisted on them" by those in centrist social locations.[37] If it is true that Filipinos are highly sensitive to smell (though all cultures in some ways are odor sensitive), migrant workers can use this unique gift to their advantage. We have mentioned already that Filipinos do not seem to have the paucity of language to convey aromatic experiences. We tend to use smell as well to criticize or put down other ethnicities: *amoy-Arabo; amoy-Instik; amoy-Bombay; amoy-Italiano; amoy-Belga* (Arab-, Chinese-, Indian-, Italian-, Belgian-smell)—whatever these mean. While their olfactory discourse may express biases or prejudices (we can also be accused as racists), Filipino migrants use this as a tactic of refusal to go along with the norms of dominant groups, especially when the critique is also meant to make fun of dominating groups. Though they do not directly articulate it in front of the principal addressee, migrant workers joke a lot about their employers such as their odors. Stay-in domestic

---

36. Koichi Iwabuchi, *Recentering Globalization: Popular Culture and Japanese Transnationalism* (Durham, NC: Duke University Press, 2002). Iwabuchi argues that the lack of cultural odor was what led to the success of products like Sony Walkman, which conveyed ideas about sleekness and portability.

37. Classen et al., *Aroma*, 161.

workers, in particular, get to know intimate details not only in the house but more so in the private lives of their employers. Debased in the public sphere when employers impose rules covering such matters as curfews and dress codes, the migrants' proximity of presence in the household allows them to have a peek into the privacy of the locals' lives. Such intimate information is exchanged with other migrant workers, partly for entertainment and partly as way lessening the overbearing impact of marginalization.

The word "humor" itself is related to odor since its origin derives from the humoral medicine of the ancient Greeks. It is said that a balanced mix of fluids known as the four humours or internal bodily fluids (blood, phlegm, black bile and yellow bile), will give people distinctive personalities and organic essences, including odor. Socially, "humor is a means of dealing with contradictions or tensions in cultures and the human condition that are fraught with anxiety."[38]

Moreover, migrants make their bodily presence felt by being themselves through many ways of ethnic assertions, such as wearing their ethnic attire in public, speaking in their own language, and cooking their preferred food. We have also heard anecdotes of Filipinas who taught their European husbands in matters of cleanliness, like taking care of their bodies and hygiene. Further, in resourceful ways, migrants take elements from two or several worlds, fusing these elements as they negotiate their partial citizenship.[39] The fusing of cultural elements is evident particularly through cooking. Actually, 80 to 90 percent of what we call taste or flavor is actually smell. A study among some European countries informs us that migrants are becoming influential social agents who through food and meals help revise and redefine the hosts' images of migrants more positively, as well as, change the eating habits of the host society.[40] Though it cannot be scientifically measured, it is possible to speak also of changes that occur in the way of smelling of Europeans. We can see the change on their dining table, not only in the kind of food they eat but also with whom they eat.

---

38. Michael E. Harkin, "Things the Nose Knows," http://www.chass.utoronto.ca/epc/srb/srb/nose.htm (accessed September 2007). This article appeared in Volume 9 of *The Semiotic Review of Books*.

39. The concept is developed by Rhacel Salazar Parreñas, "Transgressing the Nation-State: The Partial Citizenship of 'Imagined (Global) Community' of Migrant Filipina Domestic Workers," http://www.iuoui.edu/-anthkb/a104/philippines/migrationfilipinas.htm (accessed September 2007). Parreñas refers to "partial citizenship" as "the stunted integration of migrants in receiving nation-states."

40. Dean Harper, *Living in Two Cultures: The Socio-Cultural Situation of Migrants and their Families* (Aldershot, UK: Gower and the UNESCO, 1982), 321.

Migrants also create alternative odor zones to promote their personal and communal wellness, and through negotiating alliances with co-migrants. Perhaps the most noted form of odiferous assertion of migrants is when they occupy the public spaces during Sundays and holidays. By coming out to the open, migrant workers reject invisibility that is associated with negative marginality. The streets, parks, plazas, and train stations have become their space in places.[41] Local citizens may find this scandalous, almost insane. In these places, odors cannot be restricted anymore; people of different odors have reclaimed as it were their rightful place in the global market economy, which they are building with their sweat and blood. Applying here Michel de Certeau's thoughts, the circulation of odor of difference, as in walking in these cityscapes, is a way of imposing a local and personal narrative on the city; one which operates behind or despite the official maps and routes, as a way by which "ordinary people" resist the mechanisms of power, control, and surveillance.[42]

It is in these places where spatial connections of human life that meanings of existence are deeply encountered. Their bodies have exceeded the reach of symbolic representations, and it is more visceral than any kind of visual experience with the walls and pavements becoming painted with collective traces of the global community. The migrants seem to be exuding with honor: We are what we smell! The odorless capitalist market economy is being filled with the air of "common sense and uncommon scent"[43] of labor migration.

Sniffing Odor-evoked Dangerous Memories

For those with the nose to smell the Hebrew and Christian Scriptures are filled with olfactory experiences for theological in-scents (or insights, if you still wish) that is both inspiring and challenging for us today. I do not aim to be comprehensive in my olfactory discourse; instead, I will just give hints at certain possibilities for understanding and speaking of God. My attempt

---

41. I have discussed elsewhere the use of public spaces as pivotal in the construction of the migrants' collective identity and history. See Emmanuel S. de Guzman, "The Laity in the Ministry to the Migrants," *Exodus Series 6: A Resource Guide for the Migrant Ministry in Asia*, ed. Fabio Baggio (Quezon City: Scalabrini Migration Center, 2005), especially 6–12; and idem, "The Church as 'Imagined Communities' Among Differentiated Social Bodies," in *Faith on the Move: Toward a Theology of Migration in Asia*, ed. Fabio Baggio and Agnes M. Brazal (Quezon City: Ateneo de Manila University Press, 2008), 118–54.

42. Michel de Certeau, *The Practice of Everyday Life,* trans. Steven F. Rendail(Berkeley: University of California Press, 1984).

43. The phrase is taken from American TV gourmet Julia Child, recipient of honorary doctorate in Harvard University.

is not exegetical and I dispense with the complexities surrounding historical questions. I will do "scent-talking" in an experimental, free-wheeling manner and thus will engage at times in free translation of Scripture texts. My hermeneutical key to the sacred texts is to sniff the odors that are invisible to the reading eye. Hence, not only in a few pages can we find the world of odors but in every narrative, therefore also in every page, the revelatory odor of God is "prescient."

God, after all, as expressed in the God-talk of Israel, has nostrils that breathed life to the clay to make it a living human, a *nephesh* (Gn 2:7). That second creation story (or, actually the earlier tradition) reminds us that humans are made out of clay from the ground (from *adamah* to *adam*), signifying our earthly roots, that we are tied to the earth including the odor of *geosmin* (earth smell). No wonder the human chemoreceptors are extremely sensitive to the smell of earth, including fellow earthlings. The *nephesh*-ness of the humans means that they are essentially and entirely oriented to relationships. Smelling quite piquant, the human is appealingly provocative (we can also say, provocatively attractive!). Their scent is so strong that God was even able to track them; the humans hiding in Her garden (Gn 3: 8). Influenced by Davidic ideology, the etiological narrative seeks to explain the human condition of intimacy and estrangement; it also serves as a critique of civilization with its anti-human values of greed, strife, cruelty, and callousness in a time of prosperity and abundance.

Together with the natural world which is fragrant with life, humans have the same origins and are to relate with one another as good guests in God's garden. In a sense, we are all foreigners in God's land, a people of different but interrelated aroma.[44] But as the story goes (Gn 3:1–4:26), disaffection governed the relationships of humans who disdained each other's odors, rupturing their communal limbic system and thus their relationship with God too. Becoming strangers to one another, humans became strangers to themselves. Noah to befriend God again offers grilled food after the flood (Gn 8:21).When God smelled the delightful burnt offering, She said to Herself, "Never again will I doom the earth because of humans, since their desires at heart are malodorous from the start; nor will I again strike down all living beings, as I have done." Humanity is rescued to the fact that Yhwh is seized with pity.

---

44. Maurizio Pettaná instructs us that in the Hebrew Bible, the semantic field of "foreigner" includes *zar, nokri, toshabh,* and *gher*. They refer to different realities, depending on the relationship of the foreigner to Israel. See Maurizio Pettaná, "Migration in the Bible: The Commandment of Hospitality," *Exodus Series 6*.

Thomas Staubli and Silvia Schroer, in their examination of the use of body symbolism in the Bible, point out that the belly with all the entrails is one of the central images Israel used to speak of the compassion of God. In humans, the entrails with its putrid odor contain vital organs for the well-being of the person. Together with the heart, the entrails and belly fill the entire space within the torso, the central part of the body. "Heart and entrails, thinking and feeling compose a common space of human inwardness out of which we react and make decisions." Comparable to the Japanese *hara*, the belly, entrails and heart are the basis of human well-being and psychic impulses. The English term "compassion" comes close to express the sense of deep awareness of the suffering of another coupled with the wish to relieve it. In Hebrew there is a group of words with the same root as the Arabic *rahman* or *rahmat*, compassion. The Hebrew *rahem* means "to have compassion" or "to have mercy," and *rahamim* is compassion or sympathy. All these words contain a still simpler and earlier word namely, *rehem*, the female lap, uterus, or womb. Together with the heart the *rehem* is the internal organ most commonly mentioned in the First Testament."[45] The *rehem* thus is the seat of empathy and sympathy, and God's name is merciful and graciousness (Ps 116:5).

For how could God abandon humanity? Giving Her name to Moses as "I am the odor with you" (*ehyeh aser ehyeh*), God knew the suffering of Her people with their cry for liberation. She gave her word to Moses to bring the exiled people to a good and spacious land of sweet-smelling milk and honey (Ex 3: 4–17). The connotation of the phrase "land of milk and honey" could have been taken with wry humor by the herders and farmers of that rough and craggy land. For many centuries after the Israelites had settled, the place was scarred by bloody wars of conquest or its resources drained by rival local elites. Israel was a land tattooed with invaders' boot. God's liberating action upon Israel (and upon the whole humanity for that matter) need not always be pleasant smelling; it could be fusty as in the belly, not because God smells bad but because God suffers with Her people. Deutero-Isaiah beautifully depicts the *rahamim* of God who scents the malaise condition of humanity: "Can a mother forget her infant, be without compassion for the child in her womb? Even should she forget I will never forget you" (49:15). Israel, the rebellious yet beloved people, is compared to a child to whom the mother offers her unwavering love. "Wrath and a sense of justice urge divine

---

45. Thomas Staubli and Silvia Schroer, *Body Symbolism in the Bible* (Collegeville, Minn.: The Liturgical Press, 2001), 71–72.

punishment on Israel, but then sympathy burns in Yhwh's belly, so people are once again spared."[46]

When it comes to how God wanted to be adored, at times She seemed to prefer the costly ketoret used in the temple (e.g., Ex 25:1, 2, 6; 35:4, 5, 8, 27–29). At other times though, She was adamant that neither burnt rams nor myriad streams of oil can make Her happy. Rather, as the prophet Micah tells us, She demanded that true worship be a matter of bodily conduct: to act justly, love tenderly and walk humbly with her (Mic 6:6–8). This demand is made in the context of a dehumanizing situation of the lives of the excluded in the countryside while the elite groups of leaders, merchants, landowners, judges, priests and prophets based in the cities had their wealth and power burgeoning through exploitative, corrupt, and fraudulent practices. For the prophet, the musty conditions of the poor are the result of oppression that is entrenched in the structures of society. Prophesying on behalf of Yhwh, Micah envisions a society in which the powerholders who have poor social sense of smell and taste, or have lost it entirely, will be overwhelmed by God's power and the unclean and all those perceived to be polluted with dirt will be vindicated. The day of the Lord, as in Amos and the other prophets, is the day of justice and redemption—the peasants will regain their land and smell again the freshness of their harvest, the homeless will build their well-ventilated homes, the women and children will smell of danger of abuse no more, the workers of vineyard will savor the wine they have grown, the dignity of the lame and all the afflicted will be restored, and the outcasts will be oozing with confidence in new relationships.

God's soothing and life-giving essence became embodied and expressed in that man from Nazareth, who Luke says is a prophet of the kin-dom, strong in odor before God and Her people, that is to say, he smelled like God and acted the way God would have acted (Lk 24). The fourth evangelist describes his coming to human history as God's odor becoming tangible in flesh and blood, and moved into the neighborhood to walk with us (Jn 1). Jesus of Nazareth made his presence felt at a time of restlessness and ferment in Palestine. Far from being a gentler and kinder empire, *pax Romana* was experienced as disorder with a climate of instability and insecurity by many urban and rural subject peoples. Circumstances of turmoil and agitation, repression and persecution marked the life of people, already burdened by structures of Roman imperial rule and overstrained by local elites advancing their own interests and wanting to preserve their places in society. The

---

46. Ibid., 79.

burden of double taxation, imposed by the Roman colonial power and by aristocratic elite, especially by the priests of the Jerusalem temple, was almost unbearable. Adding to the pressure of injustice, the Pharisees spelled out the conditions for righteousness under the law. It resulted to intra-cultural differentiation or intense social division, as people were separated between the clean and unclean. For the *am ha'aretz* or "people of the land," the way of fidelity to God was clear, but often that way was permanently sealed. The peasant majority who were poor and non-literate had nothing to benefit from this entire situation. Their air of hope for God's promise of liberation was diminished by oppression and despair.[47]

It was in this context that the Galilean Jew invoked the prophet Isaiah's words. In a programmatic and paradigmatic text, Jesus understood his mission as bringing God's aroma of justice especially to the rejected and abused malodorous bodies (Lk. 4:16–19). This God is not remote and aloof to the poor and the suffering but the One who is so near to them (Mt 3:2, 17; Mk 1:15), for God's reign of compassion and solidarity can finally be inhaled by those whose noses have been stuffed with oppressive odors. It is striking that Mark portrays Jesus' ministry as taking place in Galilee most of the time. It was there that Jesus launched his project of odorizing difference by proclaiming God's reign as all-inclusive and comprehensive. He discharged God's caring authority over the whole of life and broke down barriers to include all in God's space. The stories narrated in the Gospels are one in saying: humans are liberated from all forms of decaying servitude and are reborn for goodness and total wellness. The coming of Jesus was truly a savoring joy for all peoples, even as some would regard him more than a prophet; he was God-scent to the world, the oil-anointed one expected to bring deliverance.[48]

Jesus was mostly perceived by his contemporaries in the tradition of the prophets of the old—"God's intoxicated advocate of social justice," in the words of Marcus Borg.[49] The festive table of royal banquet or wedding feast was Jesus' central symbol of God's offer of inclusive wholeness.[50] I will not explain the following texts but I invite the readers to put themselves in the

---

47. Donald Senior, *Jesus: A Gospel Portrait* (Mahwah, N.J.: St. Paul's Publication, 1997).

48. Consult the divergence of studies by contemporary scholars such as Marcus J. Borg and N.T. Wright, *The Meaning of Jesus: Two Visions* (San Francisco, C.A.: HarperSanFrancisco, 1989).

49. Marcus J. Borg, *Meeting Jesus Again for the First Time: The Historical Jesus and the Heart of Contemporary Faith* (San Francisco, CA: HarperSanFrancisco, 1995); *Jesus, A New Vision: Spirit, Culture, and The Life of Discipleship* (San Francisco, CA: HarperSanFrancisco, 1987).

50. See Elizabeth Schüssler Fiorenza, *In Memory of Her: A Feminist Theological Reconstruction of Christian Origins* (New York: Crossroads, 1992).

events and open up their nostrils to snuff the odors exuding from the participants in the stories: the feeding of the multitudes in a barren, dusty place; his physical contacts with the leper, the blind, and the crippled; the sermon on the plain (or mount); the chat with the two sisters near the kitchen; the dinner with the Pharisee and with the woman with alabaster vial of perfume; and the raising of Lazarus who has been dead for four days.

Consider also the amalgam of substances diffused in the air in his close encounter with the woman ill of hemorrhage; his conversation with a Syro-Phoenician or non-Jewish woman, who challenged Jesus' stereotypes and prejudices; the Passover when the air was filled with the odor of burning flesh and the reek of blood; and the temple cum marketplace in Jerusalem; and the washing of the feet of the disciples. Or, we can just be with Jesus as he walked on foot from Galilee to Jerusalem; with his itinerant followers who come from various occupations and geographical backgrounds; among the *ptochos* (dispossessed peasants, day laborers, beggars, and cheap prostitutes) with whom he shared table fellowship without the presence of perfumed patrons and brokers,[51] who eventually accused him of being a glutton and a drunkard; beside him as cold sweat was pouring out in anguish and the smell of death while praying to his Abba at Gethsemane; watching his violent execution on the cross, even from afar as his disciples did; and with Mary and other women who smelled his risen odor at his tomb.

Insofar as people at the margins are concerned, Jesus healed out of compassion. He set no preconditions and made no demands on them but only to live a life of righteousness. To them who were reeking with the stench of mundane life, with their putrid odor of suffering that was infecting and corrupting the artificially perfumed temple guarded by the elites, Jesus offered his body that cleanses, a body which in fact emitted the tang of a sunbaked Galilean peasant yet whose *dunamis* invokes Sophia's scent. His were simply acts of gratuity of restoring the dignity of humans and being accepted again in the company of God. To his disciples, both men and women, Jesus made demands to be prophetically sensitive to the death dealing ideologies that have marginalized people. It has been pointed often by scholars that, when speaking about what following him means or about the reign of God, Jesus employed metaphors taken from the Galilean environment, such as the sower, the birds of the air, the lilies of the field, the foxes with no holes, the salt, the barns crammed with the harvest, the net filled to the breaking point,

---

51. See John Dominic Crossan, *The Historical Jesus: The Life of a Mediterranean Jewish Peasant* (San Francisco, CA: HarperSanFrancisco, 1992).

the goats and sheep, the bread and fish. Each of these metaphors also convey particular scents that he wanted his disciples to embody, for membership in his company was not a guarantee for entering God's space but the living out of a new relationship with God that leads to a revitalized relationship with co-humans.

To those who turned up their noses at the malodorous Jews and Gentiles, Jesus turned their noses inside-out: "Those who say they do not have odors cast the first stone!" He wanted the elitist center to sniff the world from the side of the odorous marginal and demanded to give to these people the privilege of insight about life, the world and God borne of their suffering. The rich and the elite will have a place in God's space if they adopt a life of integrity that favors the interests of the marginal.[52] His announcement of God's pleasurable kin-dom that knows no boundaries went together with his acrid denunciation of social norms that were killing people, especially those whom society has assigned with fetid marginality. That denunciation reached its peak when Jesus drove out the sellers and buyers around the Jerusalem temple which Jesus also threatened to destroy. The temple had ceased to be the holy place of God but the symbol of religious, economic, social, and cultural degeneration. Jesus was not indifferent to the acerbic conditions of the marginalized but he could also not stand the corrosive hypocrisy of the power-holders. In N.T. Wright's view, God's Kingdom is "the victory of God" over injustice, cruelty, and deception.[53] Jesus' action in the temple, as we know it, reached its limit in the eyes of the elite. In particular, Jesus predicting the destruction of the temple may have threatened the aristocratic priests who occupied a high place in society.

His violent crucifixion was clearly judged as related to a perceived political threat to the Jewish and Roman leaders. In later decades after his death, some of his followers would tone down the role of Roman authorities by depicting Pontius Pilate as a benign leader who washed his hands upon affirming the judgment of death on Jesus. Such interpretation is perhaps understandable given their situation as a nascent community seeking to avoid head-on collision with authorities (for example, see Rom 13:1–7 and 1 Pt 2:13–15).[54] Nonetheless, the Roman imperial rule was neither secondary nor accidental to the execution of Jesus. He was charged with serious disruption of the "new world order" and the verdict came immediately. On the side of Jesus,

---

52. See Juan Luis Segundo, *The Historical Jesus of the Synoptics* (Maryknoll, N.Y.: Orbis, 1985).

53. N. Thomas Wright, *Jesus and the Victory of God* (Minneapolis: Fortress, 1996).

54. E.P. Sanders, *The Historical Figure of Jesus* (London: Allen Lane, The Penguin Press, 1993), 273–74.

his death can only be understood as the ultimate consequence of what he stood for in service to God's kin-dom. The possibility of death was always there as there had been patterns in the past when prophets were rejected and martyred. The smell of death was real and Jesus saw this as part-and-parcel of the salvation-offered-by God (Mk14:25; Lk 22:15–18; cf. 1 Cor11:26; also Mk 10:42–45; Lk 22:24–27; Jn 13:1–20; Lk 22:29–30). The public display of his naked body at a prominent place expressed utmost humiliation of the crucified. This had been done many times by the Roman colonizers not only in order to deter others from rebellion and crime but also to magnify their power. The victim's fresh wounds, with blood oozing out and its musty odor, are attractions to birds of prey and scavenger dogs. It took the courage of a few friends to take his body down from the cross and cleansed it for a decent burial.

Johann Baptist Metz aptly describes the passion, death and resurrection of Jesus as dangerous memories for us today.[55] Dangerous memories consist of experiences of suffering that make demands on us, in the present, to "interrupt," unsettle and question our present values and ways of living. They contain insights that subvert our world, turning it upside down. To live by the dangerous memory of Christ is not to forget the cause of his life. In contemporary time, the dangerous memory of Christ cries out in the history of suffering of society's victims, the forsaken ones. Critically remembering what Jesus lived for, prevents the privatization and internalization of suffering and the reduction of the Gospel to purely religious or spiritual message, without its social and political dimension. Christian praxis is a *memoria passionis* that opens up a new vision of future, a *memoria resurrectionis*, on behalf of the suffering people. This way, the Risen Jesus can be proclaimed in the praxis of Christ's followers.

Not Quite an Ambrosial Conclusion

In the Christian medieval tradition, we have the so-called "odor of sanctity" that we associate with men and women of exceptional holiness, whose bodies, during their lifetime or after death, are said to emit sweet odor or divine

---

55. Johann Baptist Metz, *Faith in History and Society*, trans. David Smith (New York: Seabury Press, 1980). According to Metz, the theologian in current times has three primary duties. They are: to protect the narratives from distortion; to decode dogmas into once again dangerous memories (challenging, critical, hopeful); to use methods of inquiry that highlight the political toward social transformation.

perfume.[56] It is believed that they are living now in a state of grace, eternally. These persons were only few, for it appears that the life of holiness while available to all is achieved only by those who were truly faithful to God through often a life of asceticism, and later in our historical tradition, to those who were also faithful to the teachings of the church. The odor of sanctity and the smell of orthodoxy came into play with politics that even Kings were thought to derive their authority from God, as a sign of which they were anointed with holy oil. It appears thus the odor of sanctity has been confined to centrist locations of power, maybe not the doings of the saints but by those who smelled their fragrance, religiously and politically.

Contemporary migration brings diversity of bodies in a shared space, where odorial difference is not to be eradicated but to be recognized, cherished, and perhaps even celebrated. Odors thus can bring people together without necessarily deodorizing difference. Theology can no longer ignore the world full of exiles, displaced people, minorities, diaspora communities, disputed borders, and the struggles by indigenous peoples. In this line, Pope Francis exhorts priests in a 2013 Chrism Mass homily, "This I ask you: be shepherds, with the 'odor of the sheep', make it real, as shepherds among your flock, fishers of men."[57] For us Christians and our churches, Jesus' praxis is at the core of the dangerous memory for us to remember and to give witness to. God's promise of odor of sanctity for the saintly church, then, can truly be shared for the world. A vision of church in the perspective of Jesus' proclamation of the kin-dom of God may have to be a multiplicity of smells, not an odor-less or odor-free society but, as Paul puts it, a church that is "the aroma of Christ to God among those who are being saved" [2 Cor 2:15].

Emmanuel S. de Guzman

---

56. During the European Christian medieval period, "(t)he fragrance exuded by the bodies of saints offered a striking contrast with the customary putridity of corpses, especially in an age when most people were all too familiar with the reek of death. The bodies of the well-to-do were sometimes buried with spices and herbs, but this could only supply a temporary antidote to bodily corruption. In order to forestall any suspicions that the odour of sanctity might be due to such burial practices, reports of its occurrence emphasize that no spices, ointments or balms had been used to treat the saint's body. The odour of sanctity demonstrated the power of God to place mortals outside the seemingly universal decay of death." Classen et al., *Aroma*, 53–54.

57. "Chrism Mass: Homily of Pope Francis," http://w2.vatican.va/content/francesco/en/homilies/2013/documents/papa-francesco_20130328_messa-crismale.html (accessed April 2014).

II

Theorizing Interculturality

3

EXPLORING INTERCULTURAL DYNAMICS
in the Migration Context with Hall, Bhabha and Bourdieu

The high unemployment rate of 2nd generation immigrants, the 2005 immigrant youth riot in Europe, the phenomenon of homegrown terrorism, the rise of xenophobia and anti-immigrant sentiments—these are just some of the issues that foregrounded the question of immigrant integration (or lack of it) in receiving countries.

Coming from a liberal country that espoused multiculturalism, Frans Wijsen notes that just a few decades earlier, the ideal envisioned in the Netherlands vis-à-vis immigrants is that they integrate while retaining their identity. The government actively endorsed education in their own language and they were not even required to speak the Dutch language. Today, however, the increasing segregation of immigrant groups in the country has led scholars to speak of a "multi-cultural tragedy" or a "multicultural illusion."[1]

European writers usually distinguish between interculturality and multiculturalism. Multiculturalism refers to the policy of peaceful co-existence of different cultural communities in one nation-state, with neither intention nor vision of interaction to create a larger community of bonding. Interculturality

---

1. Frans Wijsen, "'The Future of the Church is in our Hands': Christian Migrants in the Netherlands," in *Postcolonial Europe in the Crucible of Cultures: Reckoning with God in a World of Conflicts*, ed. Jacques Haers, sj, Norbert Hintersteiner and Georges De Schrijver, sj (Amsterdam: Rodopi, 2005), 101. See, "Multiculturalism in the Netherlands and the Murder of Theo Van Gogh," http://findarticles.com/p/articles/mi_m2242/is_1669_286/ai_n13661901 (accessed August 2007).

on its part not only respects differences but creates a space for the interaction of diverse cultural groups within a society.[2]

The term "interculturality" was first used in the 1970's in the South and North Mediterranean of Europe in relation to these countries' experience of strong immigration. While the understanding of what interculturality means continues to develop, among its main elements, as identified by the International Network on Cultural Policy, are the creation of spaces for interactions among diverse cultures, the call for mutual listening and dialogue and a consequent positive transformation in the view of the other.[3]

Interculturality has also oftentimes been employed in theology or religious studies to describe the dialogue between different religions. Robert Schreiter refers to interculturality as "the ability to negotiate or cross a cultural boundary"[4] while Raimund Pannikar focuses on the resulting "mutual fecundation" which is a characteristic of an authentic encounter between cultures.[5] The term *inter* implies mutuality and reciprocity in the relationship with the other.

Wolfgang Welsch refers to this mutual fecundation not as interculturality but as "transculturality." Welsch criticizes a type of intercultural discourse which still views cultures as islands or homogenous spheres. He thus prefers the term transculturality to focus on the mixtures of and permeations between cultures.[6] However, the term "transculturality" can also lend itself to being misunderstood as "supracultural" and thus we prefer to retain the term interculturality while nuancing its meaning.

From a critical appropriation of insights from the postcolonial theorist Stuart Hall and Homi Bhabha and the post Marxist sociologist Pierre Bourdieu, we hope to further clarify the following about our understanding of interculturality: 1) It presupposes that cultures and identities are negotiated;

---

2. Raúl Fornet-Betancourt, "Hermeneutics and Politics of Strangers: A Philosophical Contribution on the Challenge of Convivencia in Multicultural Societies," in *A Promised Land, A Perilous Journey: Theological Perspectives on Migration*, ed. Daniel Groody and Gioacchino Campese (Notre Dame, Indiana: University of Notre Dame, 2008), 219; Ram Adhar Mall, *Intercultural Philosophy* (Lanham, Maryland: Rowman and Littlefield Publishers, 2000), 9.

3. Annual Ministerial Meetings, "Interculturality Moving Towards a Dialogue among Nation," International Network on Cultural Policy, http://incp-ripc.org/meetings/2003/theme3_inter_e.shtml(accessed May 2005).

4. Robert Schreiter, "Communication and Interpretation across Cultures," *International Review of Mission* 85 (1996): 229.

5. Raimund Panikkar, "Religion, Philosophy and Culture," http://them.polylog.org/1/fpr.en.htm (accessed May 2005).

6. Wolfgang Welsch, "Transculturality: The Puzzling Form of Cultures Today," in *Spaces of Culture: City-Nation-World*, ed. Mike Featherstone and Scott Lash (London: Sage, 1999), 194–213.

2) that it recognizes an in-between space or third space of enunciation that is also the site of the in-beyond; 3) that the negotiation of cultures and identities occurs in fields of power relations; 4) that it is reflexivity which allows for the transformation of the cultural unconscious.

Cultures and Identities as Negotiated

Interculturality, as understood here, presupposes that cultures are dynamic and heterogeneous. Culture, posits Stuart Hall, is primarily concerned with the practice of "the production and exchange of meanings—the 'giving and taking of meaning'—between the members of a society or group."[7] To be part of the same culture is to have a shared way of classifying or interpreting the world as well as a common language to express oneself and communicate with others.

Hall, however, rejects both the tendency in what is referred to as culturalism toward a naive view of experience and its notion of society as a totality.[8] Culturalism is characterized by adherence to certain correspondences. Social identity=particular experiences=set of particular political interests, roles and actions, as well as, a set of what is considered authentic cultural practice=position in the economic sphere. Most versions of multi*culturalism* view cultures, identities, and differences as given through an already authenticated cultural tradition.

In line with the thoughts of the Italian neo-Marxist philosopher Antonio Gramsci (1891–1973), and in critical dialogue with structuralist and poststructuralist thoughts, Hall stresses the heterogeneity and complexity of societies.[9] Society is not to be conceived as a unified totality or as homogenous. It is to be analyzed as a differentiated and complex totality with multiple and contradictory determinations that are historically particular. Each level of articulation or special form of practice (economic, political, ideological, etc.)

---

7. Stuart Hall, "Introduction," in *Representation: Cultural and Signifying Practices*, ed. Stuart Hall (London: Sage, 1997).

8. Idem, "Cultural Studies: Two Paradigms," *Media Culture and Society* 2, no. 1 (January 1980).

9. Paul du Gay, Stuart Hall, Linda Janes, Hugh Mackay and Keith Negus, *Doing Cultural Studies: The Story of the Sony Walkman* (Keynes: The Open University, 1997), 12.

has its own relative autonomy. Many systems and currents of philosophical thought can thus exist in a given society.[10]

Globalization processes such as migration and the compression of time and space brought about by developments in information and transportation technology, further reinforce the pluralization of cultural codes and fragmentation of identities. Due to external cultural influences, it has become more difficult for national identities to remain 'intact'. Through media and other communication systems, we are bombarded by a variety of identities, appealing to different parts of ourselves from which it seems possible to choose. Globalization processes are producing hybrid identities not only in the centers of the global system but even in the peripheries.[11]

Even as identities get fragmented in a global society, identity remains important, according to Hall, because it defines a place or space from which people speak. Identities, however, should no longer be understood in the sense of a unified stable core. Cultural identity is not the "collective or true self hiding inside the many other, more superficial or artificially imposed 'selves' which a people with a shared history and ancestry hold in common and which can stabilize, fix or guarantee an unchanging 'oneness' or cultural belongingness underlying all the other superficial differences."[12]

Hall links identity with identification viewed as an articulation, a construction, and a continuous process. A term Hall used to describe the process of identification is that of 'suturing'. 'Suture' is a surgical term meaning to 'stitch'. Identification is our 'stitching' into the story by means of which identities arise (e.g. myths of ancestry), thus operating partly in the realm of the symbolic and the imaginary and always partially constructed.[13] Identities are thereby "points of temporary attachment to the subject positions which

---

10. Hall rejects as well the "dominant ideology thesis" which posits that there exists one unified wholistic ideology which permeates everyone. The "dominant ideology thesis" is announced in Marx and Engel's *Communist Manifesto* (1848): "the ruling ideas of each age have ever been the ideas of its ruling class." Culturalism is likewise opposed to the idea that the superstructure (politics and world of ideas) simply reflects the base (economic).

11. While identity choices is more extensive in the West, the pluralizing effects of globalization is felt too in the peripheries, albeit, at a slower and more uneven manner. Stuart Hall, "The Question of Cultural Identity," in *Modernity and its Futures*, ed. Stuart Hall, Tony McGrew and David Held (Polity Press, in association with Open University, 1992), 305.

12. Stuart Hall, "Cultural Identity and Diaspora," in *Identity: Community, Culture, Difference*, ed. Jonathan Rutherford (London: Lawrence and Wishart, 1990).

13. See Peter Brooker, *A Glossary of Cultural Theory* (London/New York: Oxford University Press, 2002, 2nd ed.), 245–46 for an elaboration of how the meaning of "suture" as employed in film theory is derived from Jacques Lacan's psychoanalytic theory.

discursive practices construct for us. They are the result of a successful articulation or chaining of the subject into the flow of discourse."[14]

This entails a two way process. First, suturing necessitates that the subject is 'hailed' or 'interpellated' into place as social subjects of a particular discourse. Interpellation is a term used by Louis Althusser to refer to the process by which a subject is addressed and positioned in relation to an ideological discourse.[15] To illustrate this, Althusser noted that when a policeman calls out "Hey, you there!," nine out of ten individuals would turn around thinking that they are the ones being addressed. In turning around, the individual becomes a subject, re-positioned in relation to an ideological code of law and criminality. Secondly and importantly, the subject must invest in this position or identify with this discourse for the suturing to be effective. For example, the migrant community or the receiving society can hail us into these discourses (colored, Moslem, Hispanic, Latino, etc.), obliging us to take positions either to reject, appropriate or negotiate with them. Thus, identities are "points of temporary attachment to the subject positions which discursive practices construct for us. They are the result of a successful articulation or chaining of the subject into the flow of discourse."[16]

A disturbing aspect of identity is that it is only constructed "through the relation to the Other, the relation to what it is not, to precisely what it lacks, to what has been called the *constitutive outside* that the 'positive' meaning of any term—and thus its 'identity'—can be constructed."[17] The process of identity formation is thus integrally related to the process of exclusion, leaving out, rendering others outside. As produced in or through difference, it is not fixed but always challenged by that which it excludes.

Identities nevertheless remain important vis-à-vis the question of agency and politics. "[I]dentities are about questions of using the resources of history, language and culture in the process of becoming rather than being: not 'who we are' nor 'where we came from' so much as what we might become, how we have been represented and how that bears on how we might repre-

---

14. Stuart Hall, "Introduction: Who Needs Identity?" in *Questions of Cultural Identity*, ed. Stuart Hall and Paul Du Gay (London: Sage, 1996), 6.

15. Ibid., 145.

16. Ibid., 6.

17. Ibid., 4–5.

sent ourselves."[18] Though overdetermined by various forces (social, linguistic, psychic, etc.),[19] the subject is capable as well of active agency. And even if identities are multiple and fractured, a collective will, Hall posits, can be forged through a hegemonic process that does not obliterate, but rather, works through differences, by successfully rearticulating the interests of other social groups within its framework.

INTERCULTURALITY: RECOGNIZING THE SPACE IN-BETWEEN AS SITE OF IN-BEYOND

Interculturality focuses on dialogue and interaction between cultures toward a praxis of *convivencia*. While not discounting the importance of the transgression model of oppression and resistance (e.g. minority groups' resistance to the cultural majority), advocates of interculturality need to look for other models that are more open to the creation of alliances (e.g. *between* ethnic minorities and ethnic majority against racism and xenophobia, *between* women and men against sexism, *between* first world and third world citizens against imperialism, *between* black and whites against racism, and so on).[20]

Hall: Politics of Constituting "Unities-in-Difference"

In the words of Hall, this would entail "a politics of articulation" or a politics of constituting "unities-in-difference." Difference on the one hand, can be understood either as a 'radical and unbridgeable separation' or on the other hand, as 'positional, conditional and conjunctural'. A politics of articulation does not entail the dissolution of difference but rather, goes *beyond* difference via "the construction of a collective will through differences ...."[21]

The development of the Mindanawon identity in Mindanao-Sulu, Philippines, a major site of internal migration in the early 20th century till the 1960's, is an example of a "politics of constituting unities-in-difference." Various communities (grassroots, NGOs, members of the academe and church peoples) have fostered the construction of this transcendent identity in lieu of promoting a culture of peace. This movement which is gaining momentum

---

18. Ibid.,4.

19. Ibid., 2.

20. Lawrence Grossberg, "Identity and Cultural Studies: Is that All there Is?" in *Questions of Cultural Identity*, 87–107.

21. Stuart Hall, "Old and New Identities, Old and New Ethnicities," in *Culture, Globalization and the World System*, ed. Anthony D. King (London: Macmillan, 1991; reprint ed., 1993), 58.

refers to the inhabitants of Mindanao-Sulu as Mindanawons. The term is based on geographical location and stresses the concept of a shared territory. It first originated in what is called the 'tri-people' perspective, that is, that Mindanao-Sulu, as a result of social and historical forces, is now home to three distinct groups of peoples – the Lumads (non-Islamized indigenous groups), Moros, and Christians. The term 'tri-people' was meant to give equal recognition to the three groups that now populate Mindanao regardless of population size. 'Tri-people' according to some, however, tends to divide rather than unite by overstressing the distinctness of the three groups of people. Mindanawon consciousness goes beyond a tri-people perspective because it not only respects differences but also stresses the linkage and similarities of the three peoples, their shared problems, as well as, their common link to the land. Islamic fundamentalists, on the other hand, tend to reduce Moros and Christians into two "totally distinct and entirely separate peoples" in conflict with each other since time immemorial. In terms of nationhood, the Mindanawon perspective rejects the homogenous or mono-cultural concept of nation-state in favour of a type of multi-nation federalism that would allow for one or several Islamic States, as well as, indigenous peoples' right to their ancestral domain.[22]

Hall makes use of the theory of articulation to explain the process by which a collective will can be produced while still respecting differences.[23] Articulation describes how relatively autonomous practices get linked. Articulation involves the linking or joining of parts that are not necessarily connected (e.g. Lumads, Christians, Moros) to make a unity. "The unity which matters is a linkage between that articulated discourse and the social forces with which it can, under certain historical conditions, but need not necessarily, be connected. Since there is no necessary correspondence among the elements, it is important to analyze why connections are established at a particular historical moment.[24]

Certain "lines of tendential force" articulating the Moros as a "totally distinct and entirely separate" ethnicity from the Christians may exist but these

---

22. Agnes M. Brazal, "Beyond the Religious and Social Divide: The Emerging Mindanawon Identity," *Chakana: Intercultural Forum of Theology and Philosophy* 2, no. 3 (2004): 7–26.

23. The term "articulation" seems to have originated from Antonio Gramsci who posits that cultural forms and practices are not simply determined by socio-economic processes but rather, possess relative autonomy.

24. John Fiske, "Opening the Hallway: Some Remarks on the Fertility of Stuart Hall's Contribution to Critical Theory," in *Stuart Hall: Critical Dialogues*, ed. David Morley and Kuan-Hsing Chen (London: Routledge, 1996), 53.

are not essentially fixed.[25] Tendential historical relations define the historical structuring of a given terrain.[26] One cannot therefore just separate Moros from this particular historical embeddedness. If you want to re-articulate Moros in another way (i.e. as Mindanawon as well), you are going to come across all the grooves that have articulated them already. This just shows that cultural texts are not simply free-floating; no text is free of its previous structure of encoding or articulation or what we can call its ideological history.[27] While not determining future articulations, it is important to learn how to read previous encodings if we are to take seriously ideology[28] as a contested terrain.

In his theory of articulation, Hall negotiates between two extremes—culturalism and post structuralism. On the one hand, in line with a poststructuralist approach, he deconstructs culturalism's structural unity and identity and instead views society as a "network of differences" operating on the micro level. Similarly, the subject is fragmented and decentered. On the other hand, in line with structuralism,[29] Hall recognizes the importance and in a sense, determining pressure of linguistic structure (e.g. shared codes), even as he underlines that these are subject to changes as well.[30]

Bhabha: Third Space

Homi Bhabha, another cultural theorist, speaks of a "Third Space of enunciation"[31] where cultural statements and systems are constructed. Third Space is a concept which Edward Soja, a postmodern cultural geographer has introduced. It is 'an-Other set of choices' which goes beyond binary

---

25. See Thomas McKenna, *Muslim Rulers and Rebels: Everyday Politics and Armed Separatism in the Southern Philippines* (Berkeley: University of California Press, 1998), 82–83.

26. Stuart Hall, "The Problem of Ideology: Marxism without Guarantees," in *Critical Dialogues*, 42–43; Idem, "Reconstruction Work," Ten-8: 16, cited by Lawrence Grossberg, "History, Politics and Postmodernism," in *Critical Dialogues*, 160.

27. Stuart Hall, "On Postmodernism and Articulation: An Interview with Stuart Hall," in *Critical Dialogues*, 142–43.

28. Ideology here does not refer to false consciousness but rather the "means constituting concrete individuals as subjects, the subject denoting both subjectivity and subjection." Benita Parry, "The Postcolonial: Conceptual Category or Chimera?" *The Yearbook of English Studies* 27 (1997): 6.

29. Structuralism analyzes the interlinkage of some fundamental elements on which are based mental, linguistic, social, and cultural structures, and by means of which meaning is produced.

30. Fiske, "Opening the Hallway," 217.

31. Homi K. Bhabha, "Introduction," in *The Location of Culture* (London/New York: Routledge, 1994; reprint 2010), 54.

pairings (e.g. migrants' culture vs receiving country's culture).[32] Third Space, for Bhabha, is an 'in-between' space of cultural meaning and identity. "These '*in-between*' spaces provide the terrain for elaborating strategies of selfhood—singular or communal—that initiate new signs of identity, and innovative sites of collaboration, and contestation in the act of defining the idea of society itself."[33] The "in-between space" is a site for negotiating nationhood, community interest and cultural values, thus also the site of the in-beyond or of hybridity.

A hybrid in biology is a result of the cross-breeding of two species to produce a third specie. This is extended in cultural theory to refer to the mixed or hyphenated identities of persons (immigrants for instance) or of texts studying this phenomenon. Hybridization thus can be linguistic, cultural, political, etc.[34] Bhabha first developed the concept in relation to the construction of culture and identity in the colonial context.[35] The colonial government hopes to reproduce in the colonized their culture but fails by producing instead a hybrid, an in-between. The production of a hybrid in itself questions any notion of an essentialist cultural identity.

The term "hybridity" though is limited by its connotation of inter-species grafting and the Victorian extreme right view of different race as different species, which postcolonial theorists reject.[36] Using the terms of Hall, hybridity needs to be de-articulated from these meanings and re-articulated within a postcolonial perspective.

Bhabha's cultural theory has been criticized, however, for downplaying the violence involved in many forms of hybridities (e.g. production of the mestizo/a in Latin America)[37] in particular, and for regarding language as the "paradigm of all meaning-creating or signifying systems" thus rendering

---

32. Brooker, *A Glossary of Cultural Theory*, 252.

33. Bhabha, "Introduction," in *The Location of Culture*, 2. A contemporary emerging example of a third space is Mexifornia which is neither Mexican nor American. See Karin Ikas, "Crossing into a Mexifornian Third Space," in *Communicating in the Third Space*, ed. Karin Ikas and Gerhard Wagner (New York: Routledge, 2009), 123–45.

34. Examples of hybrid identities would be the creole (of French lineage but from the West Indies or Southern part of the USA), mulatto (mixture of black and white lineage) and mestizo or mestiza (mixed Spanish and Native American lineage).

35. Bhabha, *The Location of Culture*, 168–69, 296.

36. Robert Young, *Colonial Desire: Hybridity in Theory, Culture and Race* (London: Routledge, 1995), 10.

37. Ania Loomba, *Colonialism/Postcolonialism: the New Critical Idiom* (London: Routledge, 1998), 177–83.

the "World according to the Word,"[38] in general. His concept of hybridity can gain greater depth if complemented by Hall's more materialist concept of articulation where discourse is not divorced from social, economic, and political structures.

To describe hybridity, Guillermo Gomez Peña, a performance artist residing between Mexico City and New York, replaces the "bankrupt notion of the melting pot" with the image of the menudo chowder. Menudo is a dish which is common too in the Philippines. In the menudo dish which consists of meat, peas, carrots, potatoes and bell pepper, "most of the ingredients do melt, but some stubborn chunks are condemned merely to float."[39] The chunks that remain persist, however, not because they form the essential unchangeable core of the culture's identity; rather, these are products of negotiations in a certain field of power relations.

Bourdieu: Negotiations in a Field of Power Relations and Reflexivity

Pierre Bourdieu's theory of [cultural] practice situates the intercultural dynamics within the context of power relations: [(habitus) (capital) + field] = practice.[40] Habitus for Bourdieu refers to "a system of lasting, transposable dispositions which, integrating past experiences, functions at every moment as a *matrix of perceptions, appreciations and actions*."[41] Habitus is inculcated through socialization especially from childhood (e.g. table manners) and is inscribed in the body such as in one's way of talking or walking or taste (e.g. the Koreans like kimchi, the Chinese, stinky tofu and the Europeans, blue cheese). These dispositions become second nature to a person and operate largely in a pre-conscious manner.[42] Habitus orients individuals on how to act and respond in their everyday life without strictly determining them. It provides them with a "feel for the game," a practical sense as to what is

---

38. Parry, "The Postcolonial: Conceptual Category or Chimera?" 12.

39. G. Gomez-Peña, "The New World (B)order," *Third Text* 21, no. 9 (Winter 1992–3), 74, cited by Bhabha, *The Location of Culture*, 312.

40. Pierre Bourdieu, *Distinction: A Social Critique of the Judgment of Taste* (Cambridge, Mass.: Harvard University, 1984), 101.

41. Idem, *Outline of a Theory of Practice*, trans. Richard Nice (Cambridge, Mass.: Cambridge University, 1977; reprint ed. 1998), 83.

42. John B. Thompson, "Introduction to Bourdieu's Language and Symbolic Power," in *Pierre Bourdieu*, ed. Derek Robbins, vol. 3. (London: Sage, 2000), 184.

appropriate or not in a particular circumstance. Bourdieu also used the term "cultural unconscious" to refer to habitus.[43]

For Bourdieu however, members of the same ethnic grouping do not necessarily possess a similar or homogenous habitus. Class distinctions get embodied in the habitus. In contrast with Karl Marx, he does not identify a social class solely in economic terms. Gender, race, ethnicity, place of residence and age are all inseparable features of class habitus, which can enhance or restrict access to economic, social, and cultural capital. He defines classes in terms of "'similar positions in social space' that provide 'similar conditions of existence and conditioning' and therefore create 'similar dispositions' which in turn generates similar practices."[44]

Bourdieu further notes that, on the one hand, habitus is a "structured structure"; what individuals view as reasonable or unreasonable for people of their status in the social world, stems from habitus. In this way habitus perpetuates existing opportunity structures/conditions. On the other hand, habitus is also a "structuring structure"; it has an inventive or creative dimension. The durable dispositions can generate or produce a variety of practices and perceptions in fields beyond those in which the habitus was initially acquired.[45] Gary Bouma's study of religion and migrant settlement in Australia, for instance, showed that Muslims in Australia do not simply take overseas models as normative; they search for what it means to be a Muslim in Australia, thus creating an in-beyond religiosity. "As Muslims gather to establish mosques and schools, they are forging a new form of Islam one which is true to its ancient heritage but one which is also true to Australia."[46]

One Haitian student in my seminar on "Interculturality and Migration" also related the improvization and inventiveness of the Haitians in New York City, who developed a strong devotion and pilgrimage to the Black Virgin. While pilgrimage is an important practice in Haiti, the patron saints to which the migrants went changed. For example in Haiti, pilgrims used to go to St. James, St. Joachim, St. Marie Madeleine and Our Lady of Mt. Carmel shrine. Since the migrants in New York could not find those saints there, they substituted the Polish Black Virgin and famous Corpus Christi which they do not have in Haiti. According to Karen McCarthy Brown, the

---

43. David Schwarz, *Culture and Power* (Chicago: University of Chicago, 1997), 101.

44. Pierre Bourdieu, "What Makes a Social Class? On the Theoretical and Practical Existence of Groups," *Berkeley Journal of Sociology* 32 (1987): 6, cited by Schwarz, *Culture and Power*, 153–54.

45. Bourdieu, *Outline of a Theory of Practice*, 72.

46. Gary Bouma, "Religion and Migrant Settlement," *Asian Migrant* 18, no. 2 (April–June 1995): 41.

Haitian immigrants see in the Black Virgin, Ezili Danto, a female spirit, single independent mother who fought with her children in the Haitian slave revolution.[47] The Haitian immigrants are thus generating a hybrid faith expression or a reconceptualization of their faith, which can sustain their hope in their migration ordeal.

In general, in the case of migrants who are physically and culturally displaced from their original setting, their actions or perceptions, in Bourdieu's concept of practice, will not simply be determined mechanically by their habitus (cultural unconscious) but is a fruit of the encounter between the habitus and the field (also called champ or game) or particular social context within which they act. Their practice will be a strategic response to the new field(s) within which they now find themselves.[48]

A field can be described as a structured space of positions of status or stakes; a site of struggle for the right to speak or the power to legitimate. The interrelation of one's capital—economic (what you have), cultural (what you know) and social capital (who you know)—affects one's position in the field and right to define doxa or the truth.[49] Capital, for Bourdieu thus is broader than its common economic connotation. In identifying culture as capital, Bourdieu underlines the "power dimensions of cultural dispositions and resources in market societies."[50] For instance, how the culture of a migrant is evaluated in the host country (the new field) affects one's status in that country and how the migrant will negotiate and try to survive in this new field.

For Bourdieu, cultural practice possesses logic; it is a response that maximizes one's economic, cultural and social capital in the field of power. This should not simply be interpreted in an economistic sense but rather, approximates more the person's search for dignity and recognition. Ethnonationalism/ fundamentalism is an example of a strategic response of Muslim

---

47. Karen McCarthy Brown, *Mama Lola: A Vodou Priestess in Brooklyn* (Berkeley: University of California Press, 1991).

48. For an example of how second-generation Korean Americans are reinventing their churches, see Sharon Kim, "Shifting Boundaries within Second-Generation Korean American Churches," *Sociology of Religion* 71 (2010): 1 98–22.

49. Susan Thieme, for instance, showed how Nepalese migrants in India have mobilized their social capital to form a credit association which provides them with access to financial capital. *Social Networks and Migration: Far West Nepalese Labour Migrants in Delhi* (Münster: Lit Verlag, 2006).

50. David Schwarz, *Culture and Power* (Chicago: University of Chicago, 1997), 80. See UmutEril for her case studies of skilled Turkish and Kurdish migrant women in Britain and Germany, showing how women of the same ethnic group do not possess homogenous cultural capital and how they convert this capital to other forms of capital. "Migrating Cultural Capital: Bourdieu in Migration Studies," *Sociology* 44, no. 4 (2010): 642–60.

minorities/migrants who find themselves at the margins of a field or society in an attempt toward increased social recognition.

Using Bourdieu's theory as a heuristic guide, it is therefore important that interculturality includes addressing structures of asymmetrical power relations so that mutual fecundation really occurs. Bourdieu is particularly sensitive to the use of symbolic violence. Symbolic violence is a "soft" violence which largely goes unnoticed, because it has been internalized and is part of the everyday social habits. Sexism and racism are examples of symbolic violence. Supported by other dominant discourses, symbolic violence is "misrecognized" and becomes acceptable. Bourdieu links this violence to symbolic capital (prestige, honor, recognition) accrued to somebody and on the basis of which the person engenders a sense of duty to or inferiority in others. It goes without saying that colored people and women are the first victims of symbolic violence, which can be expressed in stereotypes, prejudices and discriminatory practices.[51]

Interculturality or mutual fecundity can only truly happen in the context of a mutually empowering relation. To know whether mutuality exists in a relationship entails a power analysis. Who or which group possesses greater economic, cultural and social capital? Who possesses symbolic capital or the power to define doxa? Is power being used to dominate or "is there an active commitment on the part of all parties to become increasingly mutual? Is a mutually empowering relational dynamism at work transforming the relationship? If not, it is not a right relationship."[52] Interculturality as a mutually empowering relation must thus lead to changes in objective conditions such as, the dominant societies' recognition of other ethnic groups' cultural capital, as well as, the latter's right to increased access to economic capital (e.g. through fair trade relations).

There is a danger in many postmodern discourses today to focus on celebrating cultural diversity and forget how the result of cultural encounters is very much dependent as well on power relations and thus on the current extensive effects of global capitalism.[53] Interculturality as a mutually empow-

---

51. Bourdieu regards gender domination as "the paradigmatic form of symbolic violence." Pierre Bourdieu and Loïc J. D. Wacquant, *An Invitation to Reflexive Sociology* (Chicago: The University of Chicago Press, 1992), 170. He notes that gender is different from class in having rooted itself in "certain indisputable natural properties" thus naturalizing itself more effectively than other forms of differences. Pierre Bourdieu, *Masculine Domination*, trans. Richard Nice (Stanford, California: Stanford University Press, 2001), 22–23.

52. Carter Heyward, "Mutuality," in *A-Z of Feminist Theology*, ed. L. Isherwood and D. McEwan (Sheffield: Sheffield Academic press, 1996), 155–56.

53. Terry Eagleton elaborates on this critique in *The Idea of Culture* (Oxford: Blackwell, 2000).

ering relation is integrally linked with liberation from oppressive structures on the local, national, and global level.

Otherwise, the encounter between cultures simply leads either to the domination of one culture by another (the assimilation of the minority culture into the dominant culture) or the formation of enclaves of ethnic minorities. But such ethnic enclaves are, in the context of unequal power relations, strategic responses of peoples to maximize their economic, cultural and social capital. In migration cities in the US or France, you find colonies of Moroccan, Algerian, Chinese or Indian communities in certain suburbias or temporary hostels. These communities live at the "borders" of the receiving societies; in ghetto communities from the perspective of the dominant groups, or in independent territories from the perspective of the migrants. "This is our place." "We are on our own territory." "The estate belongs to us." "Here we can be ourselves and practice our ways!" These communities co-exist with minimal interactions with the host communities outside the sphere of labor relations.

In Betwixt-and-Between Situation of Migrants[54]

Using the concepts of habitus and field as heuristic device, we can say that the newly-arrived migrant finds himself/herself in the midst of peoples sharing a different habitus. S/he is transported to another field(s), with less social, cultural or economic capital. From a spatial perspective, to be in betwixt-and-between means to be at the margin, the periphery or the boundaries of the field. This can literally mean not having a permanent and stable residency or if one has a residency; it is residing in a colony that has been stigmatized. In the field of power, being in-betwixt-and-between means not being situated at the center of power; it is not having any voice in matters of public interest or not possessing the right to speak and define *doxa*. For example, in many European Union nations, you cannot normally be a citizen unless you are married to a national; as a non-citizen, you cannot vote no matter how long you have been staying in the place.[55]

---

54. See Peter Phan, "The Experience of Migration as a Source of Intercultural Theology in the United States," in *Migration, Religious Experience, and Globalization*, ed. Gioacchino Campese, cs and Pietro Ciallella, cs (New York: Center for Migration Studies, 2003), 149–51.

55. Some countries like Sweden, Norway, Denmark, Ireland and the Netherlands have extended voting rights on the local level to denizens. Denizens are foreign citizens with a permanent resident status. Zig Layton-Henry, "Citizenship or Denizenship for Migrant Workers?" in *The Political Rights of Migrant Workers in Western Europe*, ed. Zig Layton-Henry (London: Sage, 1990), 190.

Being in betwixt-and between can also mean "to be neither here nor there," to be neither fully in a "field" in the home nor the host country. It is to live in transit, especially for the contract workers; the body is here but their life is back there in the home country. A mother can be working in Singapore and Hong Kong while managing long distance the household here in the Philippines through the cellphone. The Algerian sociologist Abdelmalek Sayad likewise writes of Algerian immigrants to France: "Their country is back there, their house is back there, their wives and children are back there, everything is back there, only their bodies are here (in France) ..."[56] Sayad notes of Algerian migrant contract workers who go to France as young men and come back, middle aged; they marry at the age of 55 or 60 ... then they start having children; life hangs or stand still until they get back to Algeria to live their life ... the period of contract work in France is just a period in transit.

Being in betwixt-and-between can mean not being fully integrated into and accepted by either cultural systems. The migrants' cultural capital may not be regarded as possessing the same value as it has in one's home country. A minority or a marginalized group is usually apriori regarded as less educated with the degrees in the home country not being considered to be on par with the equivalent diploma in the host country. Linguistically, an in betwixt-and-between person may speak both the language of the country of origin and host country, but oftentimes do not have a mastery of any of the languages and usually speaks with a distinctive accent.

To be in betwixt-and-between is "to be neither this thing nor that." This is more acutely experienced by immigrants especially by the 2nd generation children.[57] Born in a foreign country, they are for instance neither Mexican nor Americans. As Ruben Martinez expressed in his novel:

> We are Mexicans in America, Americans in Mexico: we are neither, we are both. Within us, the spirits meld and battle: a quintessential unhappy love affair and, therefore, painful and exhilarating. We cannot love ourselves without hating ourselves; we cannot inhabit one territory without forsaking

---

56. Abdelmalek Sayad, *The Suffering of the Immigrant* (Cambridge: Polity Press, 1999), 59–60. In the Philippines, one town is lined up with Mediterranean style houses (one village was even nicknamed "Little Italy") that are mostly empty or if not, managed by a caretaker. These are owned by overseas contract workers who plan to come back and reside here one day. "Global OFW—a Thriving Entity in a Bad Economy," http://affleap.com/global-ofw-a-thriving-entity-in-a-bad-economy/ (accessed July 2012).

57. Second generation Algerians born in France are granted French citizenship, a benefit given to immigrants from Algeria which was a former French colony. As 2nd generation immigrants, they are quite alienated from Algerian ways but neither are they considered fully French in France, even if they had their education in France. Ibid., 157–58, 251.

the other; we cannot be one, must always be two and more than two: the sum of our parts will always be greater than the whole.[58]

The hyphenated identity "Mexican-American" illustrates this being in-between cultures.

Habitus, as Bourdieu notes, necessarily varies between generations with changes in material conditions and consequent life experiences:

> [G]eneration conflicts oppose not age-classes separated by natural properties, but habitus which have been produced by different *modes of generation*, that is, by conditions of existence which, in imposing different definitions of the impossible, the possible, and the probable, cause one group to experience as natural or reasonable practices or aspirations which another group finds unthinkable or scandalous, and vice versa.[59]

Since they have been reared up in between two cultures, 2nd generation immigrants may adopt practices that differ from those of their parents'.

Psychologically the migrant's identity is constantly challenged. For instance, a migrant who cannot yet speak perfectly the language of their country of immigration, can end up doubting his or her own capacities. It often happens as well that children are able to speak and read faster the new language. Bourdieu noted the importance of early socialization in the formation of habitus. This explains why children of immigrants are able to learn faster a new language with the "proper" accent being inscribed in their bodies. Some parents are thus forced to have their children translate to them official and non-official papers. This can foster a strong feeling of inadequacy, as well as, loss of some authority or control as parent.[60]

Being in betwixt-and-between means to be looked down on for being colored or dark-skinned, in countries where racism has been inscribed in people's minds and bodies. While a migrant can try to learn to speak in the language of the adopted country and appropriate closely their manners and ways, visible minorities can never hide their physical features. Their bodies immediately set them apart socially from the rest.[61] My husband related his experience in Belgium, when as a student he did part-time work in the

---

58. Ruben Martinez, *Crossing Over: A Mexican Family on the Migrant Trail* (New York: Picador, reprint ed., 2002), 223.

59. Bourdieu, *Outline of a Theory of Practice*, 78.

60. Hipólito Tshimanga, "Migration at the Forefront of Political and Theological Reflections," in *Migration and Interculturality: Theological and Philosophical Challenges*, ed. RaúlFornet-Betancourt (Aachen: MWI, 2004), 70.

61. Sayad, *The Suffering of the Immigrant*, 259.

school cafeteria. One Belgian immediately noticed him and shouted: "There is a foreigner here!"

Religious-cultural perspectives on the role of women and men can also be challenged in the migration context. Women's increased consciousness of their rights can become a source of conflict for a migrant couple.⁶² The Catholic Church's complementary anthropology, for instance, is inadequate in helping husbands and wives make sense of and adjust to their new roles, especially in the context of migrant mothers with fathers left-behind in the sending/host country to take care of the children.⁶³

Situated in another setting or field, migrants must acquire a "feel for the game" to survive; they have to re-learn how to act and react in a new context and expand their cultural competence. The migrant is also "challenged to forge a new sense of self out of the resources of the two often conflicting cultural and spiritual traditions."⁶⁴

Migrant as Site of Intercultural Encounters and Reflexivity

While being in betwixt-and-between can cause tension and conflict, this social location can also be a font of creativity. Being in betwixt-and-between is, paradoxically, also being both this and that, both insiders and outsiders. Thus according to Phan, they are in a standpoint that may be able to discern more the strengths, as well as, the weaknesses of both cultures. They are better equipped to contribute to a rethinking of both cultural traditions, the native and the foreign and thus pave the way to the emergence of a new, enriched culture.

This challenge to rethink culture starts within and among the migrants themselves. The migrants especially in highly industrialized countries in

---

62. Ibid., 70–71.

63. Agnes M. Brazal, "Harmonizing Power–Beauty: Gender Fluidity in the Migration Context," Theologies of Migration, 4, no. 2 *Asian Christian Review* (Winter, 2010), 32–46.

64. Phan, "The Experience of Migration as Source of Intercultural Theology in the United States," 9.

Europe and the United States are themselves a site of intercultural encounters—of *tiempos mixtos*—that of the premodern, modern and postmodern.[65]

Many migrants today in Europe and the US oftentimes come from developing countries (with feudal, agricultural economies) and now have to struggle their way in a technologically advanced industrial-capitalist country. Culturally and morally, they may bring with them feudal patriarchal attitudes toward women and children (e.g. the practice of female genital mutilation) but also positive traditional values such as sense of solidarity and community which contrast with the highly individualistic ethos in the countries of destination. Politically, some of them lived in socialist countries (e.g. those from Eastern Europe) where their basic needs were provided by the State while curtailing human rights; now they may have political freedom but they need to find a livelihood in a ruthless and individualistic neo-capitalist system and market economy. Culturally, their countries have been colonized by the Western nations but in a postmodern context of re-appreciation of cultures, the migrants try to recover their cultural traditions which are oftentimes premodern in the context of a modern and postmodern age.

The migrants and their families, in themselves, are thus already a site of intercultural encounters. Intercultural encounters when handled creatively can be very fruitful and productive for both cultures. From being in betwixt-and-between, interculturality moves migrants to "in-beyond," that is, beyond both cultures.

Reflexivity is an important element in Bourdieu's theory of [cultural] practice, as this makes room for changes in cultural practice and the eventual transformation of the habitus. Reflexivity can be developed through socio-analysis or awakening of consciousness, which is a kind of distancing of the self from one's cultural disposition in order to evaluate it.[66] In the migration context, reflexivity allows both nationals and (im)migrants to be transformed

---

65. Premodern societies refer to those that have not undergone industrialization (basically feudal-agricultural economies). Culturally this translates to greater orientation toward the clan and the community against the individual and a slower pace of social change. Modern society was established first in post-feudal Europe and is roughly equivalent to the industrialized world. Culturally, the society is more dynamic. The pace of social change is much faster than in any prior system and this affects profoundly pre-existing social practices and modes of behavior. Examples of modern values are the use of critical individual reason and scientific reasoning. The post-modern condition is modernity which in the 20th cen. has become world historical in its impact. As a philosophical position, postmodernity deconstructs foundationalist accounts of social reality (accounts which identify an underlying base or "foundation" from which patterns of social relationships arise). The new cultural climate is characterized by plurality and fragmentation.

66. Pierre Bourdieu and L. Wacquant, *An Invitation to Reflexive Sociology*, 136, cited by Daniel Franklin Pilario, *Back to the Rough Grounds of Praxis: Exploring Theological Method with Pierre Bourdieu* (Leuven: Peeters, 2005), 237–38.

into the truly human values of each group. This can be an inter-generational process as the habitus of 2nd generation immigrants start to vary from that of the first generation immigrants because of changes in their material conditions and consequent life experiences.

Interculturality asks what new vision of life and ethics, theologies, religious practices, can come about in the encounter between two or more cultures. What values can be learned and appropriated from the migrants by the host community and vice-versa? On the other hand, what disvalues should be rejected? What religious traditions and practices do we maintain, modify and abandon? Rachel Bandung, a 2nd generation Filipina immigrant in the US notes "The trick lies in treating both the cultural store of the past and cultural promise of the present and future with due care and respect, all the while acknowledging honestly and unflinchingly where each has shortcomings and where each can afford compromise and transformation.[67]

The Asian-American Jane Naomi Iwamura notes that this task of intercultural dialogue on the part of the migrants involves three simultaneous processes: retrieval, reexamination and reconstruction.[68] Retrieval is the act of remembering something of value mainly from subtexts of everyday life, which have been passed from generation to generation. A second vital element is critical re-examination of the practice. What has to be kept, what has to be discarded or what has to be modified? Retrieval and reexamination then lead to the reconstruction of something new; a fusion of the native and the foreign, an "in-beyond" religiosity.

Bourdieu's framework will help us to nuance this process of retrieval, re-examination and reconstruction which are not purely conscious phenomena. As site of intercultural encounters, migrants will respond to their situation, neither in a purely voluntaristic way nor simply mechanically determined by their habitus (cultural unconscious) or by rules or norms. Practice is not simply a product of individual decision-making nor determined by supra-individual structures. Pilario clarifies this further by explaining Bordieu's use of the metaphor of the game:

> The metaphor of the game evades both structural objectivism and rational voluntarist subjectivism. One does play a game without necessarily being conscious of its explicit rules all the time. It is not only the rules which determine the player's moves, but more primarily, his/her sense of anticipa-

---

67. Rachel A.R. Bundang, "Home as Memory, Metaphor, and Promise in Asian/Pacific American Religious Experience," *Semeia* 90/91(2002): 102.

68. Jane Naomi Iwamura, "Homage to Ancestors: Exploring the Horizons of Asian American Religious Identity," *Amerasia Journal* (1996): 162–67, cited by ibid., 99.

tion formed by years of physical and psychological training as well as his/her concrete response to the game of the moment ... Never does the player know all the alternative possibilities before passing the ball to a definite direction. Unlike the rational actor, the player's action does not consist of a conscious weighing of all pros and cons made available before his/her eyes at that very moment. A player's move is a skillful spontaneous response always made on-the-spot, typical only of one who has the 'feel for the game.'... [the player] is capable of exercising definitive skills—an inexhaustible capacity for invention and improvisation needed to respond to indefinitely varied situations ... Thus, beyond explicitly obeying 'rules' or executing structures, practice consists of improvisations and inventions at the point of urgency which can anticipate the sense of the future within the present ....[69]

The migrants, therefore, respond to the changed conditions in which they find themselves (field), in a way that they deem promotes best their well-being.[70] Bourdieu would stress the embodied and largely unconscious manner in which these practices get carried out. He, however, recognized as well the need to make people more reflexive in order to transform their habitus. This can be done through socio-analysis or awakening of consciousness, which is a kind of distancing of the self from one's disposition in order to evaluate it:

> The Stoics used to say that what depends upon us is not the first move but only the second one. It is difficult to control the first inclination of habitus, but reflexive analysis, which teaches that we are the ones who endow the situation with part of the potency it has over us, allows us to alter our perception of the situation and thereby our reaction to it. It enables us to monitor up to certain point, some of the determinisms that operate through the relation of immediate complicity between position and dispositions.[71]

The task of reexamination subjects practices to a more conscious critical discernment and evaluation. Intercuturality facilitates such discernment on emerging migrant practices.[72]

---

69. Pilario, *Back to the Rough Grounds of Praxis*, 110.

70. For Bourdieu, all actions are "interested" or have a raison d'être including so-called objective or disinterested endeavors like science or even Christian practice.

71. Pierre Bourdieu, *Paschalian Meditations*, 136, quoted in Pilario, *Back to the Rough Grounds of Praxis*, 204.

72. Upon return, especially after years of stay abroad, migrants come back as changed persons. They have appropriated some of the practices in their host countries. They have gotten use to the "way of life" abroad. To a certain extent, they are "at home but not at home." The family left behind would have to adjust as well to the returning migrant. They encounter the host country's culture via the returning migrant family member.

Synthesis

Using insights from Hall, Bhabha and Bourdieu, we have further explored the concept of interculturality as recognition of a "third space" or a space "in-between" where differences and cultures are reflexively negotiated in fields of power relations and where a collective will that promotes mutual interest may be forged. Interculturality thus involves a politics of constituting-unities-in difference. These differences may not be based solely on ethnicity but also other community-defined relevant identities like gender, race, class. Interculturality is likewise not simply concerned with issues of inter-ethnic justice but also intra-ethnic justice.

Interculturality, in its openness to otherness and engagement, goes beyond binary thinking of "us" and "they," as well as, the exoticization of diversity, in favor of an empowering in-beyond.[73] It respects particularities but also facilitates dialogue between different cultural communities. Interculturality recognizes discontinuities but also highlights continuities and the interanimation of ideas. Because negotiations occur in fields of power relations, it is not enough simply to create opportunities for interaction but it is an imperative to address as well asymmetrical power relations for mutual fecundation to occur. As Raúl Fornet-Betancourt underlines, interculturality seeks "the reorganization of current international relations .... [and] the correction of the asymmetry of power that exists today in the world of international politics."[74] The goal is the affirmation of the rights and dignity of marginalized social groups.

Agnes M. Brazal

---

73. We appropriated the phrase "otherness and engagement" from Fernando Segovia, "Toward a Hermeneutics of the Diaspora: A Hermeneutics of Otherness and Engagement," in *Reading from this Place: Social Location and Biblical Interpretation in the United States*, ed. F.F. Segovia and M.A. Tolbert (Minneapolis: Fortress Press, 1995), 57–73.

74. RaúlFornet-Betancourt, *Filosofar Para NuestroTiempo*, 13, cited by MaríaPilar Aquino, "Feminist Intercultural Theology: Toward a Shared Future of Justice," in *Feminist Intercultural Theology: Latina Explorations for a Just World*, ed. María Pilar Aquino and Maria José Rosado-Nunes (Maryknoll: Orbis, 2007), 16.

4

Cultural Rights of Migrants[1]

We are familiar with the human rights discourse but the concept of cultural rights is largely underdeveloped. This article hopes to help provide some conceptual clarification and theological reflections on the notion of cultural rights, particularly when applied to the case of migrants.

Before the 1960s, migrants were expected to assimilate the dominant culture in the country of migration. Assimilation is the practice where a host country allows individual migrants to join it on the condition that they integrate by giving up their original identity. The image used to describe the integration process is that of the melting pot—whether you are iron, ore or gold—you give up your identity by "melting" and assimilating the identity of the receiving community. This model, however, began to be questioned in the 1970s especially by immigrant groups in favor of a more tolerant and pluralistic policy. This shift in consciousness can be attributed to two trends: 1) the emergence of immigrant transnationalism where migrants, aided by better transportation and instantaneous global communication systems, are able to maintain regular links with their home country; 2) the rise in the ideology of multiculturalism, that is, the notion that immigrants should

---

1. This is a revised and updated version of my article "Cultural Rights of Migrants: A Philosophical and Theological Exploration," in *Faith on the Move: Toward a Theology of Migration in Asia*, ed. Fabio Baggio and Agnes M. Brazal (Quezon City: Ateneo de Manila University Press, 2008), 68–92. The original essay made use of the "Preliminary Draft Declaration of Cultural Rights" produced by a gathering of experts in Fribourg, Switzerland in 1995, whereas this new version is already based on the final document, "Cultural Rights: Fribourg Declaration, 2007."

not forget their customs, traditions, or ethnic identity but should be free to express this publicly.[2]

While the above two trends have been identified by Alan Patten and Will Kymlicka in the context of the situation of immigrants, these are operative or true as well, in the case of migrant workers and refugees. These trends, together with massive migration in today's global context, have led to fears among citizens of host countries of the rise of ghettoes side by side with the dominant cultures. A more developed concept of cultural rights, however, can provide the framework for advocating respect for the cultures of minorities—aliens, indigenous peoples and migrant workers[3]—while at the same time allaying fears of ghettoes and permanent migrant enclaves.

What are Cultural Rights?

As we have noted, the concept of cultural rights is largely undeveloped.[4] This paper aims to contribute to some conceptual clarification of what cultural rights are, through a dialogue with the insights of the French social theorist Pierre Bourdieu and the Canadian liberal theorist of immigrant multiculturalism, Will Kymlicka. Bourdieu can help give light to the notion of cultural rights as basically the right of the individual in social relation, to negotiate between what we can refer to as "the new and the old," "the native and the foreign," "the local and the global." Kymlicka, on the other hand, elaborates on polyethnic [cultural] rights of migrants as a group-defined right. He addresses the fear about the possible clash between an individual cultural identity with a collective identity and group rights. Can a group restrict the freedom of an individual in the name of preserving cultural identity? We posit that the insights of Bourdieu on cultural practice from a post-Marxist

---

2. Will Kymlicka and Alan Patten, ed. "Introduction: Language Rights and Political Theory: Context, Issues, and Approaches," in *Language Rights and Political Theory* (Cambridge: Oxford University, 2003), 8.

3. Halina Niec, "Advocating for Cultural Rights: Cultural Rights at the End of the World Decade for Cultural Development," 7, http://kvc.minbuza.nl/uk/archive/commentary/niec.html (accessed May 2006).

4. Halina Niec refers to its underdevelopment in terms of the following: 1) its legality and enforceability; 2) the possible clash between an individual cultural identity with a collective identity and group rights; 3) the vagueness of what "culture" includes and therefore, which can be considered cultural rights and which rights are not cultural rights but possess cultural dimensions; 4) and the tensions between the universality of human rights and the notion of cultural relativism. On the other hand, the "Preliminary Draft Declaration of Cultural Rights" refers to this "underdevelopment" as due to the neglect of the role of cultural identity when speaking of cultural rights. Ibid., 2–3, 5; see also Laura Reidel, "What are Cultural Rights? Protecting Groups with Individual Rights," in *Economic, Social and Cultural Rights*, ed. Manisuli Ssenyonjo (Surrey: Ashgate, 2011), 411–26.

standpoint can complement Kymlicka's immigrant multiculturalism from a political liberal perspective.

Right to Cultural Expression, Development and Identity

A skeletal catalogue of what can be considered as cultural rights can already be found in international instruments such as the Universal Declarations of Human Rights (1948) and the International Covenant on Economic, Social and Cultural Rights (ICESCR; 1966), and in regional declarations such as the American Declaration on the Rights and Duties of Men (1948), the Additional Protocol to the American Convention on Human Rights in the Area of Economic, Social and Cultural Rights (1988), and in the African Charter on Human and People's Rights (1981). These documents focus on cultural rights as rights of the individual. The notion of cultural rights as "collective right" or "group-specific" right has also been recognized implicitly in the ICESCR and the International Covenant on Civil and Political Rights (ICCPR; 1966). This is explicitly acknowledged in the 1982 World Conference on Cultural Policies, as well as, in the Declaration on the Rights of Persons Belonging to National or Ethnic, Religious and Linguistic Minorities (1992). A number of other documents cataloguing cultural rights have also been produced.[5]

To begin our exploration, we shall take a look at the document "Cultural Rights: Fribourg Declaration," which was initially drafted by a gathering of experts in Fribourg, Switzerland in 1995,[6] revised and adopted in 2007.[7] Before this meeting, the Institute for Interdisciplinary Ethical and Human Rights Studies of Fribourg University had come up with a list of cultural rights that are "unquestionably justifiable" so that those who violate these rights can be sued and tried at the European Court of Human Rights. The 1995 draft and 2007 document seem to have been based on this earlier catalogue of rights but in addition, underline as well the importance of cultural identity when speaking about cultural rights.

---

5. Niec, "Cultural Rights."

6. Groupe de Fribourg in Cooperation with UNESCO, The Council of Europe, and The Swiss National Commission Project, Concerning a Declaration of Cultural Rights (11th version), 1, presented at the General Conference of the United Nations Educational, Scientific and Cultural Organization, September 4, 1996, http://www.americas-society.org/as/events/pdf.d/UNESCO%20Fribourg.pdf#search='Groupe%20de%20Fribourg%20cultural%20right (accessed May 2006).

7. "Cultural Rights: Fribourg Declaration," http://www1.umn.edu/humanrts/instree/Fribourg%20Declaration.pdf (accessed July 2012).

Among the cultural rights the 2007 document lists are respect for cultural identity and the different ways this can be manifested, access to heritages, respect for identification with one or more cultural communities simultaneously regardless of borders, and the right to change this choice. Everyone is likewise entitled to participation in cultural life and policies, education and training in a way that respects the plurality of cultures, right to information, protection of scientific, artistic and creative output and ownership and the right to "respond to erroneous information concerning cultures."[8]

Cultural right in this document can be basically defined as right to cultural expression, development and identity. It is important, however, to identify the document's underlying concept of culture that has become the basis of its list of cultural rights. In anthropological discourses, culture has oftentimes been used as a NOUN. It either refers to some elitist social practice (e.g. music, paintings, theater) or to some communal forms of life, meanings and everyday practices. The notion of culture as VERB, in contrast, stresses that before becoming a NOUN, culture is first a process. The Latin term *cultura* whose root is *colere* means "to cultivate"; thus originally it is a word referring to the cultivation or tending of something (animals and plants).

As the Groupe de Fribourg document itself explicitly states, culture refers to "the values, beliefs, convictions, languages, knowledge and the arts, traditions, institutions and ways of life through which a person or a group express their humanity and the meanings they give to their existence and to their development."[9] This definition may seem to echo a static view of culture, a notion of culture as an already finished product. A careful reading of the list of rights though reveals the document's sensitivity as well to the dimension of culture as continuous process, as practice, such as in the freedom to choose which cultural activities to engage in, or right to education and training to enable one to participate in the development of one's cultural identity. Cultural identity here is also not viewed as something given and fixed but refers to "the sum of all cultural references through which a person, alone or in community with others, defines or constitutes oneself, communicates and wishes

---

8. Ibid. 8.
9. Ibid., 5.

to be recognized in one's dignity."[10] As we have seen, the document's list of rights includes both the right to identify or not with a particular cultural community,[11] and even the freedom to assume multiple cultural identities. The rights this document lists are also basically rights of the person which s/he can exercise alone or together with others.

Appropriating Bourdieu: Culture as Negotiated by an Individual in Social Relation

Bourdieu himself did not speak about cultural rights. His discourse, however, on [cultural] practice as shaped by habitus, capital, and field highlights culture as negotiated by individuals in social relation.[12] Habitus refers to embodied dispositions or the "cultural unconscious." Class distinctions (which for Bourdieu includes, gender, race, ethnicity, place of residence, age) get embodied in the habitus. Thus migrants of the same ethnicity do not necessarily possess similar habitus. Capital for Bourdieu can either be economic (wealth, income, property), social (social connections or network) or cultural (cultivated and embodied dispositions, cultural artifacts, educational credentials). Their interrelation affects one's position in the field (e.g. the receiving society) which is a site of struggle for the right to speak or the power to legitimate. Cultural practice, Bourdieu underlines, possesses logic; it is a strategic response considering one's position in the field of power, that maximizes one's economic, cultural and social capital,[13] or in ordinary lingo, one's well-being.

---

10. "Cultural Rights," Art.2, 5. A commentary on the Fribourg Group draft declaration notes that "cultural identity reveals three kinds of opposition, namely, those between the particular and the universal, the result and the process, and diversification and cohesion. This means that it cannot be understood in a unilateral particularist sense, since identity is also developed by reference to the universal (the ability to be a person) not in a unilateral backward-looking sense, for it is at the same time a process, nor yet as an endless multiplication process, since it also needs unification." Patrice Meyer-Bisch, "The Right to Education in the Context of Cultural Rights," http://www.bayefsky.com/general/e_c.12_1998_17.php (accessed May 2006), 2.

11. The final document defines a cultural community as "a group of persons who share references that constitute a common cultural identity that they intend to preserve and develop." Art. 2, "Cultural Rights: Fribourg Declaration," http://www1.umn.edu/humanrts/instree/Fribourg%20Declaration.pdf (accessed July 2012), 5.

12. See previous essay in chapter 3 for an elaboration of the meaning of habitus, capital and field in Bourdieu.

13. In the field, one form of capital can be converted into another. For example, the social network or capital one acquires in migrant communities can be reconverted into a new or better paying job, thus an increase in economic capital.

Backed up by extensive field work, Bourdieu offers in his book, *Distinction*, the following equation of his general science of practice: [(habitus) (capital) + field] = practice.[14] In Bourdieu's framework therefore, a cultural right, even when exercised by an individual, is always situated within a community in the form of the role of social structures [field], as well as, the community traditions embedded in one's cultural unconscious [habitus]. A right is always exercised by an individual in social relation; an individual embedded in community structures.

In the new field, recent migrants generally possess less social, cultural or economic capital, in the midst of peoples with a different habitus. Transnational migrants, as the Vietnamese-American theologian Peter Phan notes, exist "in a betwixt-and-between situation." They live and move and have their being between two cultures, their own and that of the host country. In this 'in-between' predicament, they belong to neither culture fully yet participate in both."[15]

Being in betwixt-and-between not only can cause tension and conflict, but can also be a font of creativity. As both insiders and outsiders, both this and that, migrants have the potential to discern more the strengths, as well as, the weaknesses of both cultures. In the process of surviving in their new field, they can contribute to a rethinking of both cultural traditions, the native and the foreign and thus pave the way to the emergence of a new, enriched culture.

But this new enriched synthesis cannot develop if the cultural capital of migrants is generally devalued, which is usually the case when power groups use their symbolic capital to inculcate into the migrants a sense of inferiority. Mutual fecundity can only truly happen in the context of a mutually empowering relation. The right to cultural expression and development therefore implies a duty, an obligation on the part of the State, to help enable the practice of such rights through anti-racism policies and some form of accommodation in its institutions.

An attitude of laissez-faire or benign neglect vis-à-vis the cultures on the part of the country of immigration, tantamounts to a policy of assimilation, where in the end, because there is low regard for the cultural capital of the migrants, the latter would indeed either try to survive as ghettoes side by

---

14. Pierre Bourdieu, *Distinction: A Social Critique of the Judgment of Taste* (Cambridge Mass.: Harvard University, 1984), 101.

15. Peter Phan, "The Experience of Migration as Source of Intercultural Theology in the United States," in *Christianity with an Asian Face: Asian American Theology in the Ministry* (Maryknoll, New York: Orbis, 2003), 8–10.

side the dominant culture or the succeeding generations would be forced by circumstances to forget their cultural heritage.

Within the logic of cultural practice as a strategic response to maximize one's capital in a field, the raison d'etre of maintaining or rejecting a traditional cultural practice in the migrant context, is rooted in how this ultimately facilitates the experience of well-being in the new context.

Kymlicka: On Group-Specific Polyethnic [Cultural] Rights

Kymlicka develops the notion of minority rights, particularly in his book, *Multicultural Citizenship*. As a liberal theorist, Kymlicka is interested in showing how minority rights can exist side by side with human rights and the extent to which it is limited by "principles of individual liberty, democracy and social justice."[16] Kymlicka tries to counter those who would contend that liberal philosophy dichotomizes the individual from society by arguing that even if the liberal starting point is the universal value of individual freedom and democracy, these values can in fact be upheld only if they are embodied within the institutions and traditions of particular political communities, and only if citizens have a strong sense of identification with and membership in these particular communities.[17]

Kymlicka distinguishes between two types of minorities: immigrants and national minorities. Immigrants are people who have left their home countries to settle in another country while national minorities constitute historical communities within a country but they have a different language and culture (e.g. aboriginals in Australia, Tamils in Sri Lanka). These two groups, according to Kymlicka, are entitled to a different set of rights.

National minority groups oftentimes aim at maintaining an autonomous societal culture to preserve their cultural identity. Societal culture refers to shared memories, values, practices and institutions (economic, political, religious, etc.) that provide its members with meaningful ways of life. Societal cultures are usually geographically bound and based on a common language.[18] National minority groups therefore, should be able to demand self-government (autonomy) and special representation rights (right of ethnic groups to be represented within the institutions of the larger state).

---

16. Will Kymlicka, *Multicultural Citizenship: A Liberal Theory of Minority Rights* (Oxford: Clarendon Press, 1995), 6.

17. Will Kymlicka and Alan Patten, *Language Rights and Political Theory* (Cambridge, Mass.: OxfordUniversity, 2003), 11.

18. Kymlicka, *Multicultural Citizenship*, 76.

Unlike national minorities, Kymlicka argues that immigrants normally do not wish to set up a parallel societal culture. Having voluntarily decided to leave their home countries, immigrants know that their success and that of their children depends on the extent to which they integrate within the culture of the host country. They have, however, brought with them a shared vocabulary and tradition which continues to function as their spectacles in making sense of the world (in the words of Bourdieu, their matrix of perceptions and actions). Since integration takes time and operates even intergenerationally, immigrants must be assisted in this process. Their rejection of the assimilation model is not a rejection of integration per se but rather a modification in the terms of integration so that while being treated as equal members of the society, their differences as well are respected. It is within this context that Kymlicka speaks of polyethnic rights, which are cultural rights specific to immigrants.

Polyethnic rights are group-differentiated rights which enable "ethnic groups and religious minorities express their cultural particularity without it hampering their success in the economic and political institutions of the dominant society."[19] An example would be the demand for public funding for ethnic art, museums, studies, and associations. Since many Western nations provide state funding for such cultural practices, this demand by immigrants is a way of equalizing recognition and opportunities. But the more controversial polyethnic rights would include "exemptions from laws and regulations that disadvantage immigrants, given their religious practices." An example would be the demand for Muslim girls to be exempted from school dress codes so they can wear the veil.

While polyethnic rights are group-differentiated, it is not helpful, according to Kymlicka, to refer to these as collective rights as some authors would. The term "collective rights" for him connotes a false dichotomy between individual and collective rights. Polyethnic or group-specific rights may be exercised by either an individual or a collective.[20]

Kymlicka also rightly prefers to respond to the fear of a conflict between "collective rights" with "individual rights" by using instead the distinction "internal restrictions" and "external protections."[21] Internal restrictions pertain to a claim of a group to its own members. It is aimed at controlling internal dissent, as when individuals would not follow age-old practices or

---

19. Ibid., 31.
20. Ibid., 46.
21. Ibid., 35–44.

customs. In the name of preserving cultural particularity, an ethnic group may ask the State for a special right to restrict the freedom of its members, for example, to undergo clitoridectomy, or to follow parentally arranged marriages or traditional gender roles. Such internal restrictions can be oppressive to individuals. Kymlicka rejects such internal restrictions which go against the person's right to identify with or reject the cultural community's practices or to revise cultural practices in accordance with the human rights tradition. In reality, very rarely have immigrant groups asked for polyethnic rights to control the members within a group.[22]

External protections, on the other hand, pertain to claims made by a group in relation to the bigger society. While internal restrictions involve intra-group relations, external protections involve inter-group relations. The aim of external protections, posits Kymlicka, is to protect a cultural group's "distinct existence and identity" from the impact of certain political or economic decisions within the larger society.

As with internal restrictions, there are indeed dangers as well that external protections will be used to oppress either another group or individual members of a cultural community. But Kymlicka does not think granting polyethnic rights like funding for immigrant language programs or art associations, or exemptions in dress codes will necessarily lead to the domination of another group. Instead this can even help equalize relationships among groups in the cultural marketplace by placing them on equal footing.[23]

Kymlicka notes that as with self-government rights, "polyethnic rights are not seen as temporary, because the cultural difference they protect are not something we seek to eliminate."[24] Kymlicka seems to be more strongly emphasizing in this instance, the culture of the migrants as a finished product whose distinct identity should be preserved, rather than viewing culture as something which is continuously being negotiated and developed. This also reflects a homogenous concept of culture which, Helder De Schutter

---

22. More than immigrant groups per se, it is religious communities who demand internal restrictions. An example would be the Amish, a Christian sect, which is not required to follow the mandatory education of children in both United States and Canada. Ibid., 41–42.

23. Kymlicka, however, recognizes that certain laws aimed at external protection such as group-libel laws can also be used for internal restrictions. For instance, in the context of the Salman Rushdie affair, some British Muslims wanted similar hate-speech laws that protect blacks and Jews against racist discourse, applied to protect Muslims from the Islamophobia in the West. But these very same laws can also be used to control freedom of expression among the Muslims themselves. Kymlicka, *Multicultural Citizenship*, 43.

24. Ibid., 31.

demonstrates in his article, plagues as well Kymlicka's notion of national minority cultures.[25]

From a feminist perspective, Susan Moller Okin criticized Kymlicka's neglect of the fact that many cultures are patriarchal and thus in the representation of what the "culture" is, it is usually the voice of the men which stands out.[26] For instance, Kymlicka's seemingly unproblematic acceptance of exemptions allowing Moslem women to wear the veil in secular France reveals his monolithic perspective on culture. One Malaysian Muslim woman, according to Okin, remarked that if the ban on the wearing of the veil in schools in France were lifted, her parents would force her to wear the veil against her will. While we are aware of the many meanings that the veil can represent for various Moslem women (e.g. it can be a symbol of defiance of Western culture, it can be a liberating attire because with the veil one can be freer to move around in Moslem places, or it can also be a symbol of subordination),[27] this complexity does not come out in Kymlicka's discussion of polyethnic rights because of his view of cultures as a monolithic bloc.

On the other hand, Kymlicka recognizes too that cultural change can happen in the encounter between the culture of the migrants and the dominant culture. "The liberal view I am defending insists that people can stand back and assess moral values and traditional ways of life." Therefore citizens "should be given not only the legal right to do so, but also the social conditions which enhance this capacity."[28] There thus lurks an ambivalence in Kymlicka's concept of culture in his discourse on immigrants.

In his concept of habitus, Bourdieu is able to integrate more, differences like gender, social class, age. He refers to these as class distinctions which get embodied in the habitus. He defines classes in terms of "'similar positions in social space' that provide 'similar conditions of existence and conditioning' and therefore create 'similar dispositions' which in turn generates similar practices'."[29] Together with economic factors, gender, race, ethnicity, place of residence and age are, for Bourdieu, inseparable features of class habitus. We

---

25. Helder De Schutter, "Nations, Boundaries and Justice: On Will Kymlicka's Theory of Multinationalism," *Ethical Perspectives: Journal of the European Ethics Network* 11, no. 1 (2005): 18, 23–32.

26. Susan Moller Okin, *Is Multiculturalism Bad for Women?* (Princeton, New Jersey: Princeton University, 1999), 23–24.

27. Bahar Davary, "A Matter of Veils: An Islamic Response," in *Ethics and World Religions: Cross-cultural Case Studies*, ed. Regina Wentzel Wolfe and Christine E. Gudorf (Maryknoll, New York: Orbis, 1999), 153–59.

28. Kymlicka, *Multicultural Citizenship*, 92.

29. Pierre Bourdieu, "What Makes a Social Class? On the Theoretical and Practical Existence of Groups," *Berkeley Journal of Sociology* 32 (1987), cited by Schwarz, *Culture and Power*, 153–54.

cannot therefore immediately presuppose a single or homogenous habitus even among migrants of same ethnic grouping. Does this therefore invalidate the need for polyethnic rights?

We posit that external protections are needed primarily for immigrants, not to protect an already established distinct identity, but as Kymlicka underlined as well, to help the members express themselves in their cultural particularity in the process of integrating as full and equal members with those of the majority culture. The choices migrant members themselves will make as well as historical forces, will determine whether this cultural particularity will remain the same, evolve through time, fuse in an in-beyond form with the majority culture or even disappear. This requires further conceptual development in terms of process and member's participation in advocacies for group-specific rights.

Arguments in Favor of Polyethnic [Cultural] Rights

Kymlicka identifies basically two main arguments in support of group-defined rights for immigrants. The equality argument posits that polyethnic rights are needed to ensure that immigrants are treated equally. Such equal treatment entails the accommodation as well of differences. While leaving behind many institutionalized practices, immigrants bring with them a shared vocabulary of tradition and convention. They are thus, in our terms, in-between cultures and learning a new "vocabulary" for life. While not aiming at the recreation of the societal culture they left behind, the immigrants, Kymlicka underlines, should be enabled to integrate in the mainstream culture in a way that respects their difference.[30]

Facilitating integration entails rooting out prejudice and discrimination. This requires re-evaluation of the representation of immigrants in textbooks, official documents and the media, and the recognition of certain group-defined rights. Integration is a long-term inter-generational process so that some accommodations are needed by immigrants to facilitate transition. For instance, some services may be offered in the native tongue of the immigrants.

---

30. Kymlicka, *Multicultural Citizenship*, 92.

"Support should be provided for those groups and organizations within immigrant communities which assist in the settlement/ integration process."[31]

A second argument, the intrinsic value of cultural diversity, posits the value of maintaining cultural diversity in society. This should not be interpreted, according to Kymlicka, as imposing a "duty to maintain one's culture" but simply as a right, if the immigrant so wishes, to maintain his/her culture.[32] The host country, on its part, will be benefited by the new options and perspectives that will make its culture richer and more diverse.[33]

The Discourse of Cultural Rights and the Human Rights Tradition

As we have discussed in earlier sections, cultural rights as human rights have already been acknowledged in several universal and regional declarations, both as individual or group-specific rights. But in general, these documents simply demand the "toleration" of cultural rights. Kymlicka refers to tolerance rights as basically protecting individuals from government interference. For example, the right of migrants to publish their own magazines, to set up their own private schools, to form their own cultural associations, to speak the language they prefer for private conversations in the home, in civic organizations or institutions of civil society, the workplace, can be protected under what UDHR describes as freedom of expression (art.19) and as the right not to be subjected to arbitrary interference with … privacy, family, home or correspondence (art.12). The UDHR also provides a space for accommodations like ensuring a court-appointed interpreter in trials to ensure a migrant's right to a fair trial (art. 10).

In contrast, promotion-oriented rights entails encouraging public institutions to be involved in promoting a cultural right. The UDHR is not clear about promotion rights for immigrant groups, for example, "right to public funding of minority language schools, right to use one's language in dealing with public officials, right to have judicial proceedings in one's language or

---

31. Will Kymlicka, *Politics in the Vernacular: Nationalism, Multiculturalism, and Citizenship* (Oxford: OxfordUniversity, 2001). A history-based argument for a polyethnic right is grounded on a historically backed claim, in particular, by sovereignty treaties or some other form of historical agreement. This is a rare case so that one can treat this more as an anomalous case. An example would be the Hutterites, a Christian sect that had been encouraged by the Canadian government to settle in Canada with the promise that they would be exempted from some education, land ownership, and military service laws. Kymlicka, *Multicultural Citizenship*, 120.

32. Kymlicka, *Multicultural Citizenship*, 217, n.24.

33. Ibid., 78–79.

receive government documents in one's language, right to official language status."[34]

Kymlicka argues also that traditional human rights discourse cannot deal with some crucial questions, such as: "What degree of cultural integration can be required of immigrants and refugees before they acquire citizenship?"[35]

Synthesis: Cultural Rights and Refugees

In the above discussion, we have clarified cultural right as the right to cultural expression, development and identity. Cultural rights are human rights and this has already been acknowledged in universal and regional declarations. Most of these rights focus on the individual as subject of cultural right. Bourdieu's framework underlines that this subject of cultural practice is not the atomistic individual but rather the individual in social relation; the individual possessing a habitus [cultural unconscious] and making decisions in a particular field of power. His model also highlights the fact that cultural practices and cultural identities are negotiated within the new field—the migrant context.

Kymlicka, on the other hand, elaborates on polyethnic rights or cultural rights that are group-specific. Kymlicka argues—on the basis of liberal principles of freedom and equality, and of the intrinsic value of cultural diversity—of immigrants' claim to these group-defined rights. But these rights, he contends, should be used solely for external protections and not to prevent dissent from members of a cultural group. He also notes that while the UDHR protects rights related to cultural expression and development, it does not promote group-specific (polyethnic) rights.

In how far can refugees claim the same type of cultural rights as immigrants? This is a question Kymlicka also broaches. Refugees are different from immigrants in the sense that they did not voluntarily leave their countries and relinquished their national rights. Kymlicka fears that fewer countries would accept these refugees if they are expected to treat them as national minorities and oftentimes, these refugee groups are also too small in number and dispersed to form self-governing communities. He remarks that "the best that refugees can realistically expect is to be treated as immigrants, with the corresponding polyethnic rights, and hope to return to their homeland as quickly as possible."[36] In principle therefore, refugees can also have a claim to polyethnic rights.

---

34. Kymlicka and Patten, *Language Rights and Political Theory*, 26–27.

35. Kymlicka, *Multicultural Citizenship*, 4.

36. Ibid., 97.

Cultural Rights from a Trinitarian Perspective

What can be a theological foundation for speaking of a right to cultural expression, development and identity? The theological foundation of the Church's human rights teaching is our inherent dignity as persons, rooted in our being made in the image and likeness of God. As such, we believe in faith that the law of God is written in our hearts (*Pacem in Terris* 5):

> [T]he Creator of the world has imprinted in man's heart an order which his conscience reveals to him and enjoins him to obey. This shows the obligations of the law are written in their hearts; their conscience utters its own testimony. And how could it be otherwise? For whatever God has made shows forth His infinite wisdom and it is manifested more clearly in the things which have greater perfection.

Jacques Maritain, a personalist philosopher, defends the Church teaching on human rights from a Thomistic perspective, as philosophically based on natural law. Knowledge of this natural law is acquired by "inclination" or "connaturality," that is, it is a practical knowledge, so that even groups with varying ideologies can, on a practical level, agree on a certain list of rights. J. Clague notes how this can explain what is happening within an organization like Amnesty International where members find a shared moral ground even without a common moral theory.

While human rights set a transcultural universal standard, legitimate diversity in the past was also respected via the principle of subsidiarity. The principle of subsidiarity leaves it to individual nation states "how best to maximize human welfare within the bounds of respect for human rights."[37] The principle of subsidiarity, however, presumes first a commonality in the universals and then differentiation on the local level. It seems there is a need to develop other theological metaphors or principles that more dynamically capture sameness and difference.

As we have said, theologically, human rights are grounded in our being made in the image and likeness of God. But the Christian God, in whose image we have been created, is not a unitary but a Trinitarian God characterized by relationality, diversity and creativity. This can be a fertile theological starting point for speaking about the right to cultural expression, development and identity. We shall sketch in broad outlines what such a theology can highlight.

---

[37]. J. Clague. "A Dubious Idiom and Rhetoric: How Problematic is the Language of Human Rights in Catholic Social Thought?" in *Catholic Social Thought: Twilight or Renaissance*, ed. J.S. Boswell, F.P. McHugh and J. Verstraeten (Leuven" Leuven University, 2005), 125–40.

Relationality and Mutuality

At the heart of the various representations of the doctrine of the Trinity is God's relationality. Responding to Arius and Eunomius who posit that the essence of God is in God's unbegottenness, the Cappadocians—Basil, Gregory of Nyssa and Gregory of Nazianzus—underline that the principle of the divine ousia (*loob* or inner self) is inseparable from God's relations.

> According to Greek theology, persons are defined by their "relation of origin," from whence they come. For example, the Son is defined by origin from the Father; the Son is begotten from the Father. The Holy Spirit likewise originates from the Father: the Spirit proceeds from the Father. The identity and unique reality of a person emerges entirely in relation to another person.[38]

Even if for the Cappadocians, the Father is the unoriginate origin, this does not mean the nature of God is in being unrelated or unbegotten as Arius and Eunomius would hold. "[I]t is precisely the economy of Christ and the Spirit that introduces the all-important qualification: the unoriginate God is by nature originating and related."[39]

On the other side, in Latin Trinitarian theology which has shaped much of the Catholic understanding of the Trinity, God is initially one, then three. For example, Augustine's primary model of the Trinity was the individual, instead of the community experience. As created in the image and likeness of God, Augustine propounds that we have within us the vestiges of the Trinity, in our memory, intellect, and will.

It was the 12th cen. monk Richard St. Victor who paved the way for a social instead of a purely psychological approach to the Trinity. He developed a marginal aspect in Augustine's theory of the Trinity and imaged the persons of the Trinity as Lover, the Beloved and the Love between them. Richard St. Victor, living in the 12th century, a period of emerging interest in friendship, was interested in studying how human friendship is related with divine love.

This image of the Trinity in terms of friendship stresses the mutuality of the persons in the Trinity. As Johnson notes:

> Friendship is the most free, the least possessive, the most mutual of relationships, able to cross social barriers in genuine reciprocal regard ... what makes it unique is that friends are fundamentally side-by-side in common interests, common delights, shared responsibilities. Mature friendship is

---

38. Catherine Mowry La Cugna, "God in Communion with Us," in *Freeing Theology: The Essentials of Theology in Feminist Perspective* (New York: Harper Collins, 1993), 87.

39. Ibid., 87.

open to the inclusion of others in the circle, assuming an essential stance of hospitality.[40]

This image of the Trinity as a community of friends does not lead to tritheism because for Richard, humans are basically communal beings, not autonomous selves. In the Divine as well, unlike in finite humans, there is "infinite self-giving and infinite reception of love."[41]

As images of the Trinity, we are likewise persons-in-social relations, not individual isolated subjectivities. Our cultural practices and identities are formed in relation and in dialogue with others. How others perceive and respond to us, whether with hospitality or xenophobia, shapes our self-identity.

The Trinity as community of friends challenges us to be welcoming of "others" who do not initially belong to our "circle" as the migrants and refugees. Mutuality in the Trinity also calls us to recognize the gifts that migrants bring—their contribution to economic development, their cultural capital—and to work toward social reforms that would allow them to have greater access to economic capital. The document of the Pontifical Council for the Pastoral Care of the Migrants and Itinerant People "Starting Afresh from Christ: Towards a Renewed Pastoral Care for Migrants and Refugees" states that "no one, be they migrants, refugees or members of the local population should be looked upon as 'stranger,' but rather as a 'gift,' in parishes and other ecclesial communities."[42]

Equality in Diversity

Equality in diversity is grounded in the sharing of the persons of the same *ousia* (*loob* or inner self).[43] The terms *ousia* or substance has been used to describe what in God is the same always; and persons to refer to what differentiates God. The Greeks used the term *prosopon* to describe what in God is threefold differentiation. *Prosopon* designates a specific individual reality. The Christian God is three *prosopa* (individualities) but what they are like, this term does not really tell us.

---

40. Elizabeth A. Johnson, *She Who Is: The Mystery of God in Feminist Theological Discourse* (New York: Crossroad, 1996), 217.

41. Denis Edwards, *Jesus the Wisdom of God: An Ecological Theology* (Maryknoll, New York: Orbis, 1995), 96.

42. Final Statement, Part II, Pastoral Care, 9, in *People on the Move* 35 (December 2003): 365.

43. *Loob* (a Filipino term) does not refer to the essence of a person as separate from others. As an inner quality, it cannot be separated from its outward manifestation, that is, from the way one relates with others. Rather, the quality of one's *loob* (beautiful, good or bad) precisely depends on the way one relates to others.

While distinct from each other, the three persons are equal because they share the same *ousia* (loob or inner self). We can understand this more clearly in Philippine categories via the term *kapwa* (other or fellow). Virgilio Enriquez, a pioneer in Philippine indigenous psychology propounds that *kapwa* does not only connote the other as distinct from me but more than this, it is the "unity of the self and other." *Kapwa* is generally used to refer to that which is called in English "others." But while referring to a distinct individuality, *kapwa* stresses the shared inner self or shared *loob* with an "other." In this sense, we can speak of the relationality in the Trinity in terms of *pakikipagkapwa* (relating justly with the one who is both similar and different).

Cultural rights can be understood within this Trinitarian social model of equality in diversity. The Trinity is a model for societies and cultural communities, of a relationship without subordination or domination and where difference is allowed to exist. The Church document *Erga Migrantes Caritas Christi* 34 stresses how dialogue with various cultures reflects the unity in diversity in the Trinity:

> Different cultural identities are thus to open up to a universal way of understanding, not abandoning their own positive elements but putting them at the service of the whole of humanity. While this logic engages every particular Church, it highlights and reveals that unity in diversity that is contemplated in the Trinity, which for its part, refers to the communion of all to the fullness of the personal life of each one.

Respect for cultural rights is a manifestation of the Trinitarian *pakikipagkapwa*. *Pakikipagkapwa* in a Philippine perspective, is rooted in our belief in our shared *loob* (inner self) with others. Furthermore, *kapwa* (other or fellow) is the sole Philippine concept that includes both the "insider" and the "outsider"; the "one of us" and the "not one of us," the "similar" and the "different."[44] Thus *pakikipagkapwa* (relating justly with the one who is similar and different) in the form of respect for cultural rights embraces the stranger, the migrant, the alien.

Creativity and Fecundity

The Trinity is also characterized by creativity and fecundity. Here we critically appropriate the Trinitarian theology of St. Bonaventure (thirteenth century).

---

44. Agnes Brazal, "Reinventing *Pakikipagkapwa*: An Exploration of Its Potential for Promoting Respect for Plurality," in *Fundamentalism and Pluralism in the Church*, ed. Dennis Gonzalez (Manila: Dakateo, 2004), 55–61.

Bonaventure underlines that goodness is "self-diffusive." *Ang sankalikasan ay bunga ng pag-uumapaw ng kagandahang-loob ng Diyos.* (Creation is a fruit of the overflowing of God's gracious love.)

From the Fountain Fullness proceeds the Word, the Exemplar, the image of the First Person. The Holy Spirit is Love freely shared between the First and Second Persons and "from this mutual love proceeds the Spirit who is love." This dynamic goodness "explodes into a thousand forms" in the world of creation. Creation is thus the free and creative self-expression of God. This fecundity is at the heart of the Trinitarian reality and is a fruit of the persons' profound and dynamic communion of interdependence and mutuality. Bonaventure used the term *circumincessio* (in Greek, *perichoresis*) to refer to this mutual interpersonal relations and indwelling, which overflows in creation.

For Bonaventure, the Word is given the amazing power to bring the full fecundity of the Father to expression. This may look as if the Word was totally subordinate to the Unoriginate Origin.[45] But this is not the case. The Unoriginate Origin empowers the Word that emanates from Him, to render the Origin's whole depth visible, which without this expressivity would remain hidden and un-communicated. Since the finite entities are created in the image of the Word, they too are endowed with this very theo-expressive force, which allows them to bring the Origin's fecundity to expression within their earthly setting. Applied to the migrant world, this would mean that the migrants, basically, share in the same theo-expressive force as their hosts, and that their cultural creativity (despised as it may be from a sociological standpoint) may enrich the cultural expressions of the receiving country. In this way the riches of the Unoriginate Origin's creative fecundity are disseminated more intensely through the vivid encounter of cultures.[46]

Having emanated from God's goodness, every creature in Bonaventure's theology reflects the Trinitarian presence. In the image of the Trinity, we are inherently creative and fecund. The right to cultural expression, development and identity allows us to actualize this trace of the Trinity in us. Likewise, cultural creativity and fecundity will be a fruit of a process of dynamic communion and interdependence, mutual relations with peoples of other cultures, including that of the migrants.

---

45. See Johnson, *She Who Is*, 219.

46. For the basic idea of (Trinitarian) theo-expressivity, see Hans Urs von Balthasar, *The Glory of the Lord, Clerical Styles* (Edinburgh: Clark, 1984), 300; and Gilles Emery, *La trinité créatrice* (Paris, Vrin, 1995), 183.

The Catholic Bishops Conference of Japan refers to this creative synthesis that can be a fruit of the encounter between the host and the migrant cultures: "This effort to overcome differences between peoples does not mean trying to assimilate the others by imposing one own lifestyle on them, but should be seen as bringing to birth a new society and culture within which we can all live together."[47]

Provisional Conclusion

Our analysis and critical appropriation of the insights of Bourdieu and Kymlicka have helped us clarify some aspects in the notion of cultural rights of migrants. Cultural rights basically refer to rights to cultural expression, development, and identity. These are primarily the rights of the individual in social relation, to negotiate between cultures hopefully toward a new enriched synthesis. Polyethnic rights, a type of cultural rights which is group-specific, should only be claimed for external protections and not to control dissent within a cultural group.

From a theological perspective, we posited that the structure of the triune symbol provides us with a reference point for the values of a society that provides a space for cultural rights to flourish—relationality and mutuality, equality in diversity, creativity and fecundity. This right to self-expression, development, and cultural identity in itself can be viewed, in the light of our faith, as a trace of the Trinity's creativity and fecundity within us.

Agnes M. Brazal

---

47. Catholic Bishops' Conference of Japan, "Seeking the Kingdom of God which Transcends Differences," *Nationality*, 5 November 1992.

III

Toward an Intercultural Church

5

THE CHURCH AS "IMAGINED COMMUNITIES"
Among Differentiated Social Bodies

"Communities," writes anthropologist Benedict Anderson,[1] "are to be distinguished, not of their falsity [or] genuineness, but *by the style in which they are imagined*" (Italics mine). This is to say, notions of community that people construct influence the way they experience each other in actual relationships. In this sense, whether a community is "false" or "genuine" is not the issue, but how social relationships form and inform notions of collective identity. In an interactive experience, people go through a process of imagining or understanding who they are in concrete and changing historical, temporal and social circumstances.

Contrary to its seeming innocence and neutrality, "[d]iscourse plays a powerful role in how we imagine our communities, which in turn shapes and is shaped by our experiences of those communities."[2] Images of collectivity that people make and impose on others are not "objective" but carry certain agenda which others are expected to execute. Conversely, to pursue new or alternative discourse is more than a conceptual exercise but to suggest a different way of looking at things and behaving in the world.

In this essay, I wish to offer some thoughts on what it means to be church among migrants in societies that are ambivalent to the presence of different

---

[1]. Benedict Anderson, *Imagined Communities, Reflections on the Origin and Spread of Nationalism*, rev. ed. (London: Verso, 1991), 6.

[2]. Krista Scott, "Imagined Bodies, Imagined Communities: Feminism, Nationalism, and Body Metaphors," http:// www.stumptuous.com/imagine.html (accessed 25 May 2006).

social bodies or groups. My focus is on how ecclesiological discourses or the self-understanding of the church in the language of images and metaphors describe and prescribe relationships. Suffice to mention here that in the biblical and post-biblical traditions, the church is less defined in technical and doctrinal formulae as it is described in images and metaphors. In particular, I shall examine in the first part the possibilities and limitations of some conventional styles of imagining the church insofar as these reflect both notions and assumptions about what the real and actual things involve, as well as, a paradigm for how members of the church, migrants most especially, are perceived to or should behave. In the second part, I shall retrieve the biblical and post-biblical image of city or city life to open other possibilities of conceiving the church in the migration context. This self-understanding of the church is explored in conversation with a framework from the discipline of social and political science, particularly from the vision of an inclusive participatory society. My thrust is to only sketch a few elements or aspects that can guide us in our search for more inspiring and relevant image of the church that takes into account the struggle of migrants to be recognized and accepted as differentiated social bodies or groups not only in society at large but in the church as well where migrants also seek to be at home in hospitable spaces.

CONVENTIONAL IMAGES AND METAPHORS OF CHURCH IN MIGRATION CONTEXT

In the church, the style through which the church's self-understanding is articulated comes by the language of symbols, images, metaphors, analogies and models. Images and metaphors, as Susan Brooks Thistlethwaite puts it, are thoughts in action.[3] In the New Testament times, for instance, there was no uniform way of defining the church; rather a diversity of images and metaphors were employed by the first-century Jesus' movement to articulate their self-understanding as communities of Jesus' disciples who were struggling with their faith in Christ within the Jewish world.[4] They were primarily interested in following Jesus in their particular worlds, and only then ecclesiological reflections followed or became the expression of their communal identity and mission. Likewise, the Christian church through the

---

3. Susan Brooks Thistlethwaite, *Metaphors for the Contemporary Church* (New York: The Pilgrim Press, 1983), 18.

4. See Paul Minear, *Images of the Church in the New Testament* (Philadelphia: Westminster Press, 1977); Robert Kysar, *Stumbling in the Light: New Testament Images for a Changing Church* (St. Louis, Miss.: Chalice Press, 1999).

medieval times has been less defined in doctrinal formulae as much as it has been described in the language of images and metaphors. Social and political metaphors for the church abound such as the "City of God" and "Perfect Society." The church hierarchy, increasingly closed and authoritarian, used these metaphors or images to emphasize the unequal hierarchical structuring inside the church, as these also describe the church as a ruling political force that identifies itself as set apart from and far above the imperfect world, if not the homeland of evil. The Second Vatican Ecumenical Council, on the other hand, re-rooted the church to the foundational experiences narrated in the Scriptures and recovered the church as a pilgrim people of God, body of Christ and temple of the Spirit, in service to the world.[5]

What follows is an examination of three conventional discourses on the church insofar as they reflect both notions and assumptions about what the real and actual things involve, as well as, a paradigm for how the members should behave. I have chosen these images because they are some of the most familiar in the pastoral field and I suspect that they are widely used in the care for the migrants.

The Church as a Relation of Shepherd and Flock

There are two ways by which the image of the church as a relation of shepherd and flock are used: within the church, shepherd refers to leader and often to the ordained minister, while the flock refers to the members and often to the laity; in the larger human community, the shepherd is the church and the flock is the world, particularly the secular society. The image is derived from a rural context, and as the image suggests, the shepherd tends the flock with utmost care and attention.

In the Fourth Gospel, we read Jesus referring to himself as "good Shepherd" (Jn. 10:7–18). This type of speech is an oxymoron which is intended to jar the readers or listeners to new awareness or to startle them to new understanding.[6] In its original setting of the rural New Testament world, the shepherd was perceived as a person not to be trusted because he gets into contact—even incidentally—with unclean animals like spiders, bugs, rats, and grazes on other's people's lands, thus, pilfering the produce of the land. Far from being a noble profession, the job of the shepherd in first century Palestine was a despised trade, along with gamblers, usurers, and publicans.

---

5. See Joseph A. Komonchak, "Ecclesiology of Vatican II," *Origin* 28 (1999): 763–68.
6. Donald E. Messer, *Images of Contemporary Ministry* (Nashville: Abingdon Press, 1989), 171–74.

True or not, these stereotypes ran in the minds of many Jews in Jesus' time. Yet Jesus is given the title "good shepherd." Note the qualification, "good." By supplying a seemingly incongruous word or thought to the shepherd, the listeners of the first century were being provoked. Unlike the ordinary shepherd who flees the wolves and cares not for the sheep, the good shepherd lays down his life for the sake of the sheep.

The image may have startled the audience, for as John reports, "there was again a division among the Jews because of these words" (Jn.10:19). For the disciples, the "good Shepherd" made a lot of sense. Here was Jesus, a marginal Jew himself, who opted to be an outcast among the least and the lost, to whom he showed compassion and commitment for the sake of their well-being. Take notice also that the christological title applied to Jesus is based on what a good shepherd does. The "good shepherd" is fundamentally praxis, not an honorific title. In its positive sense, the image implies that all the disciples should do as Jesus did; not a few individuals, but all the disciples (the church community) are challenged to become "good shepherds": that is, to offer their lives for others, in an unconditional, disinterested love especially for the lost ones. The image of "good shepherd" challenges people in their way of looking at things, inviting new ways of thinking and acting.

What advantages or benefits do the image has for the church's ministry to the migrants? On the part of the shepherd (the church ministers or the church institution), the image cultivates compassionate response to the migrants who like a sheepfold needs guidance and support as they enter and settle in another place. The migrants can feel that they have a companion and safe haven in the shepherd who is concerned not only with their religious needs but with other aspects of their struggling life as well. The image of "good shepherd" also calls for a person-ability and spirituality of selfless giving, modeled after Christ. It urges the ministers to go beyond the functional roles of preaching, administering, leading worship, and such, and to face the ambiguities and disappointments that come along in the work for and with the migrants. A wandering pastor, the church knows too well what it means to be in exile, in diaspora, and dispersed in foreign lands. Seeking out the "sheepfold," the church goes out of its way to find the migrants wherever they are and to respond to their needs and concerns as they integrate themselves in their host societies.

On the other hand, we may have to ask if the image "shepherd-flock" has become a dead metaphor that has lost its power to inspire and haplessly outdated and rural in economically advanced and modern societies where migrants strive to work and live. Unless the migrants are in places where sheep are common, the image is culturally foreign to them, and thereby lessening the image's impact on their practical living. A harmful ideology could also creep into the image which justifies the ordained minister as above—divinely and hierarchically—the rest of the baptized and amidst the diverse ethnic and cultural groups. In addition, the usage of "shepherd" is exclusively identified with the ordained minister. Rarely is it used for a layperson and nil for a woman. On the moral level, the image of "sheepfold" may also meet resistance from critical lay people, be it among migrants or in the receiving societies. In the real world, the sheep is one of the dumbest and dirtiest animals on earth, not to forget that they stink. To use the "flock of sheep" may offend migrants who have found new freedoms and independence, grown into maturity and responsibility, and in new senses of personhood.[7]

The Church as a Relation of Mother-Teacher and Children-Pupils

Unlike the oxymoron "good shepherd" metaphor, *mater et magistra* is a combination of two matching images. The "mother" image, in particular, is associated with the "bride of Christ" of the letter to the Ephesians. The author likens Christ to a bridegroom and husband and the church to a bride and wife. The personification of the church in "mother" who is also "teacher" is a counterbalance to a concept of church which is dominated by an emphasis on structures, hierarchy and institution. By combining "mother" and "teacher," the church is imagined as gentle and kindhearted yet authoritatively firm in its decisions and commitments. In our times, Pope John XXIII describes the church in this manner:

> Mother and Teacher of all nations—such is the Catholic Church in the mind of her Founder, Jesus Christ; to hold the world in an embrace of love, that men, in every age, should find in her their own completeness in a higher order of living, and their ultimate salvation. She is 'the pillar and ground of the truth.' To her was entrusted by her holy Founder the twofold task of giving life to her children and of teaching them and guiding them—both as individuals and as nations—with maternal care. Great is their dignity, a dignity which she has always guarded most zealously and held in the highest esteem (MM 1).

Behind the image are certain assumptions about motherhood in the real world. According to one adherent of the image, "[t]he teaching role is a

---

7. See Nicole Constable, "At Home but Not at Home: Filipina Narratives of Ambivalent Returns," in *Filipinos in Global Migrations: At Home in the World?*, ed. Filomeno V. Aguilar, Jr. (Manila: Philippine Migration Research Network and Philippine Social Science Council, 2002), 380–412.

natural consequence of motherhood. Not only does a mother share with the child her nature, she also teaches the child how to do those things that will lead it to happiness." The role of a mother is also "to protect her children …. It is known by nature that a mother will protect her children from dangers even to the point of giving her life."[8] Lastly, the mother is a "corrector," for "a good and loving mother never turns away from disciplining her children" so they may grow up as wise adults. What sense does the imagined church as mother and teacher have to the relationship of the church the world? In the view of one bishop, while "the world is a powerful and attractive teacher," it cannot give people what they need, which only the Catholic Church can fully satisfy. In a cosmic scene, the present-day situation is described as a "battle zone" where

> we have two very different teachers struggling for the podium in our hearts. The two teachers are the Church and the world. Each has a map for our lives, but the maps lead in very different directions …. For each of us as a believer, there's no way around Christ's mandate to engage *and convert* the world …. Without the Church, we have only the world, and the world is not enough to feed the hunger in our hearts.[9]

If we accept that the discourse of mother and teacher is informed by a very particular understanding of mothers and teachers, then this same view describes and prescribes the experience of members in the church and the role the church plays in relation to the secular world. Again, it is not whether the kind of church fostered in the image is false or genuine but how the image influences social relationships. On the bright side, the church imagined as *mater et magistra* has helped the church be sensitive to the problems of the secular world, particularly in the light of the reality of human mobility. Like a loving mother, the church sees its role of harmonizing and unifying the diverse, if not conflicting, cultures and religions through programs and activities that give special attention to the human dignity of migrants. As an authoritative teacher, the church particularly the Magisterium through its social doctrines has consistently exhorted governments, business institutions, and international organizations to be humanitarian in their dealings with the people, especially the afflicted and suffering. In addition, the church has been approaching the upper economic classes to help the migrants, as she

---

8. Calloway, Donald, "Mater Ecclesia: An Ecclesiology for the 21ˢᵗ Century," http://ignatiusinsight.org/features2007/dcolloway_matereccl_jun07.asp (accessed 22 June 2010).

9. Charles J. Chaput, "Mater et Magistra: Who the Church is, and Why She Teaches with Authority?" Keynote Address on "Witness, Teach and Educate: Forming Disciples for the New Millennium" 2002 Catechetical Conference, Holiday Inn – DIA, U.S.A.

herself tries to uplift their misery through the many pastoral, educational, and charitable programs.

On the bleak side, the image insinuates that the role of the laity is to be as children to the mother. More concretely, the image would imply that migrants cannot be critical of the teachings of the mother-teacher. They are expected to obey or commit themselves wholly to the words of the church which projects itself as possessing always the right and true judgment. This triumphalist self-image of the church might be counter-productive for the migrants who, because of their encounter with different cultures have become more reflexive of their traditions.

The Church as a Relation of Family in the World

A third metaphor is the church as "family." This organic icon has strong grounding in the bible and in Christian tradition.[10] Several other images cluster around the family: "household of God," "brothers and sisters in Christ," "kinship," "God's building," and "God's temple." The church as family, and in a more fundamental way—the family as church, might prove to be of great value to peoples on the move and in search of home—physically, emotionally, morally, and legally. Such an offer takes into account not only the predicament of many migrant workers of being separated from their families but also the problems of the economically advanced and technology-based societies where the migrants work. The modern economy, according to David Schindler,[11] is favoring a consumerist notion of the human person, as distinct from one which is genuinely communal. To this situation there is an urgent need for the "renewal of home," understood as the "recovery of the primacy of the concrete, constitutive, and intimate—in sum, organic—ways of being and acting, of relating to others, proper to the family (in its nature as communion of persons)."[12] By strengthening familial relations—in the nuclear family or in family-modeled organizations—real time and real space is domesticated through a "community of persons," thereby becoming "the place of (God's) personal community."

---

10. See Carolyn Osiek and David J. Batch, *Families in the New Testament World: Households and House Churches* (Louisville, KY: Westminster/John Knox Press, 1977); Joseph H. Hellerman, *The Ancient Church as Family* (Minneapolis: Augsburg Fortress, 2001).

11. David L. Schindler, "Homelessness and the Modern Condition: The Family, Community, and the Global Economy," *Communio* 27, no. 3 (2000): 411–30.

12. Ibid., 420.

What are the beneficial implications of the church as family? The metaphor enjoins both the guest workers and their hosts to establish a network of humane relationship modeled on the familial community. This thrust can support the idea that the church is for *both* migrants and hosts. Many church representatives argue that migrants are members of God's family and therefore they should not be excluded and discriminated even in the church. The hosts, as siblings too in God's family, are to display their hospitable welcome to the migrants. Rather than ministering migrants and local citizens separately, the church aims toward assimilating and eventually integrating migrants into the "communion of persons." In the church as family of God, people are brothers and sisters in Christ, and then only Chinese, Filipinos, Mexicans, Polish, and Italians. Like a family, the church seeks the harmony of the diverse cultures.

Notwithstanding this noble intention, the metaphor of church as family faces difficulties in today's world of migration. A retrieval of the idyllic home, even if it is couched in the language of "renewal," is impossible given the radically different social milieu the world is in now. As migrants and hosts interact, there is a process of reinvention of their identities and histories. As social processes change, conceptions of family and community evolve as well. Migrants desire for "family" or "home" not anymore in its idyllic past but one which is rethought and reformed in the light of new situations and challenges. The care and obligation for family members are still there but they are lived out differently now and newer forms of family relationships are emerging.[13] As Nicole Constable has also reported, the departure of migrants from and their return to their places of origin have brought about ambivalent responses on the part of both migrants and their families.

> Migration has provided (migrants) with new experiences, desires, options, and visions but with no ready formulas for successfully transplanting them …. And when they return to the place where they were born, they will be, more than likely, in a different space and therefore remain, in a sense, in exile.[14]

---

13. See Elizabeth B. Silva and Carol Smart, eds., *The New Family* (London: Sage Publications, 1999).

14. Constable, "At Home but Not at Home," 404. If the experience of returnees is one of being "home but not at home," children of immigrant families (second-generation youth, especially) struggle with their "hyphenated and hybrid identity." They experience "multiple and contradictory tugs, messages, and pushes and pulls" often occasioned by the gap between subscribing to family ideology and family practices that are traceable to the places of origin of their parents, and the lifestyles, choices and possibilities which their present society offers. See also Diane L. Wolf, "Family Secrets: Transnational Struggles Among Children of Filipino Immigrants," in *Filipinos in Global Migrations*, ed. Filomeno V. Aguilar, Jr., 347–79.

Our concern on the use of the metaphor of family in migration echoes the concern of Carolyn Osiek on how the biblical notion of family can continue to have significance for today:

> If biblical authors can make any contribution to the present debate about 'family values,' perhaps it can be to bring to awareness that the mid-twentieth-century nuclear family is not normative, that the golden age of biblical families was not all it is cracked up to be, but that the family is a very strong structure precisely because it is flexible. It was in fact more flexible in early Christianity than in its contemporary idealized version. Its forms are changing, as they always have been.[15]

What I have attempted is to show how discourses both describe and prescribe certain thinking and practices in the church. The three images and metaphors we scrutinized depict a church whose mission is to hover over the migrants, secure them in its fold, and sees its role as uniting the lost sheep or quarreling children into an unvarying flock, children or family. In short, they are imagined church *for* migrants. To seek other metaphors of the church is to intervene not only in the cognitive level but also in the search for newer or more relevant ways of relationships inside the church and in the secular world. Our concern thus is toward the construction of an imagined church that is not only *for* the migrants but a church *with* and *of* the migrants. How are we to re-imagine the church in which there is a "bringing together (of) persons of different nationalities, ethnic origins and religions into contact (that) contributes to making the true face of the Church visible"? (*Erga Migrantes Caritas Christi* 37)

POINTERS FOR IMAGINING THE CHURCH **WITH** AND **OF** MIGRANTS

In this second part, I shall sketch an ecclesiological search for a church in the context of migration. I am not suggesting another image or metaphor for the imagined church, but I would like to explore what it means to be church in a way which is more germane to the struggles and longings of migrants. We find the life in the city as one that can open a rethinking of the church in migrants' context.

The "city" as an image or a metaphor is not new to Christianity. In the Old Testament, the major reference to the city is Jerusalem. It represents human culture at its best and also at its worst. Instead of a mythical paradise or a wilderness, "God affirms the complexity of human society … and the

---

15. Carolyn Osiek, "The City: Center of Early Christian Life," *The Bible Today* (January 1993): 24.

potential for good in that human structure (the city) is translated ... into a picture of the divine intention."[16]

In the New Testament, the city which is Jerusalem was a focal point of Jesus' prophetic ministry. The cleansing of the temple is a symbolic but direct attack on social and religious structures that had placed the poor, the sick, the outcasts, and women at the margins of society. The city was translated more powerfully into Jesus' praxis of "inclusive wholeness"[17] that was united with the vision of kin-dom or rule of God. Elsewhere I elaborated how Jesus of Nazareth is the bodily carrier of God's universal presence and humanity's compassionate companion.

> Jesus demonstrated God's universal offer of life by being a gracious friend to all, regardless of culture, ethnicity, gender, religion, and social status, but especially the outcasts, poor, sinners, weak, and victims of injustice. This sounds like a value-free or neutral statement, but it is not. In a society characterized by boundaries of differences in terms of social grouping, status and ranking, those who are 'out of place' are treated with apathy if not antagonism. Jesus reached out to the marginals of his time, and many sought him out .... In a society or culture where social relationship and moral norms are strictly bounded, Jesus' hospitality takes a subversive character because it was the socially undervalued people who experienced his power as a restoration of dignity and a sense of recognition. Healing, forgiveness, acceptance, respect, honor—these are the immediate consequences with far-reaching impact on people's lives as they encounter the person, who the disciples on the road to Emmaus call 'a prophet, powerful in word and deed.'[18]

The city is also the site of Christian beginnings and early missionary work in the first century.[19] The city of Antioch, which was among three or four most important cities in the Roman Empire, was the cradle of Gentile

---

16. Donald E. Gowan, *Eschatology in the Old Testament* (Philadelphia: Fortress, 1986), 127–28; see Volkmar Fritz, *The City in Ancient Israel* (Sheffield: Sheffield Academic Press, 1995).

17. Elizabeth Schüssler Fiorenza, *In Memory of Her: A Feminist Theological Reconstruction of Christian Origins* (New York Crossroad, 1994), 118–30.

18. Emmanuel S. de Guzman, "The Laity in the Ministry to the Migrants,"*Exodus Series 6: A Resource Guide for the Migrant Ministry in Asia*, ed. Fabio Baggio (Quezon City: Scalabrini Migration Center, 2006), 21–23.

19. See Wayne Meeks, *The First Urban Christians* (Yale: Yale University Press, 1983); Frederick I. Cwiekosky, *The Beginnings of the Church* (New York: Paulist Press, 1988); Daniel Sperber, *The City in Roman Palestine* (New York: Oxford University Press, 1998).

Christianity[20] and Christian missionary activity. Its cosmopolitanism helped broaden the horizons of the Christian community beyond the narrow confines of Judaism. It was the situation of the gentile converts in Antioch which brought to the forefront the issue of circumcision that was settled in the Council of Jerusalem (Acts 15:1–20).[21] It was in Antioch that the disciples were first referred to as Christians that is a distinct sect of Judaism.[22]

The city has also been represented as the eschatological goal for the church who as alien, exile and in diaspora on earth can find eternal home in God.[23] And of course, we know the neoplatonic imagined church of Augustine of Hippo's "city of God." Responding to critics who viewed the fall of Rome to the Goths was due to the empire's conversion to Christ, Augustine defended Christianity through the contrasting cities of God and man. As the "city of man" or the earthly city lives by love of self, the "city of God" or heavenly city is governed by love of God. Augustine's "city of God" is an experiential reality that is situated in the earthly city. These two cities are different and even with conflicting values, yet Christians, Augustine argued, are to be good citizens and to enjoy the blessings of the "city of man" as they must move on toward eternal peace. For, their ultimate home is in God's city as they journey in the earthly world like strangers traveling in a foreign country. Augustine regards God's city as a place to which people emigrate, being unattached to an earthly city.[24]

We can retrieve the image of "city" in the context of our times and specifically with the search of migrants to have a home in hospitable places. For

---

20. Rodney Stark explains the rise of Christianity in cities like Antioch to its superior capacity to respond to the life marked by poverty, chaos and violence in the urban Graeco-Roman world. "To cities filled with newcomers and strangers, Christianity offered an immediate basis for attachments .... To cities torn by violent ethnic strife, Christianity offered a new basis for social solidarity .... [W]hat they [missionaries] brought was not simply an urban movement, but a new culture capable of making life in Greco-Roman cities more tolerable." *The Rise of Christianity: A Sociologist Reconsiders History* (Princeton, New Jersey: Princeton University Press, 1996), 162.

21. Thus for some time, the Jews and the Gentiles in Antioch gathered together in a common table fellowship. This was, however, short-lived; it stopped when representatives from James came and Peter and all the other Jewish Christians except Paul withdrew from this fellowship (Gal 2:11–13). Meeks, *The First Urban Christians*, 112.

22. Wayne Meeks and Robert L. Wilken, *Jews and Christians in Antioch: In the First Four Centuries of the Common Era* (SBL Sources for Biblical Study 13) (Missoula, Montana: Scholars Press for the Society of Biblical Literature, 1978), 15–16.

23. Kysar, *Stumbling in the Light*, 67–86.

24. V. Grossim, *La pastorale per I migrant al tempo di S. Agostino, dans L'epoca patristica e la pastorale della mobilità umana* (EMP: Padouem, 1989), 177–78, cited by Jean-Pierre Delville, "Migrations and Christianity," paper presented at Omnes Gentes conference on "Migration: Challenges of the Spirit," October 18–20, 2007, Katholieke Universiteit Leuven, Belgium.

this purpose, I shall mainly (though not exclusively) draw insights from Iris Marion Young, a social and political theorist.

Nurturing Relational Difference among Social Groups in Migration

In reconstructing an imagined church in migrants' context, it may be very important, first of all, to understand "difference" between social groups in its relational meaning.[25] While identified among theorists of multiculturalism, Young does not view group difference in an essentialist sense but rather as "ambiguous, relational, shifting, without clear borders."[26] For her, a social group is "a collective of people who have affinity with one another because of a set of practices or way of life; they differentiate themselves from or are differentiated by at least one other group according to these cultural forms."[27] It is an "affinity group" sharing "affective bonding and networking." As such, social group difference is a product of "creation and construction" among group members. These groups are also "fluid; they come into being and fade away." She also recognizes that most have multiple group identifications.[28]

In its relational meaning, difference among social groups is not based on some "given" or "natural" traits that the members collectively possess. Rather difference "comes about," as it were, when groups entertain ideas of being different from each other, and this difference is encountered, discovered and articulated through social interactions.[29]

Several insights flow from taking the relational meaning of difference in our search for appropriate ecclesiological discourse. One insight is that migrants do not have fixed, eternal boundaries defined by their essentially generic background. But so are people in receiving societies. Difference as relational knowledge allows participants to find out their similarities and dissimilarities.[30] In the migrant to migrant and guests to hosts interaction, people discover similarities and dissimilarities, which give them not only a sense of identity but a sense of affinity for one another. By "affinity" it means

---

25. Iris Marion Young, *Justice and the Politics of Difference* (Princeton: Princeton University Press, 1990), 168–73; *Inclusion and Democracy* (Oxford: Oxford University Press, 2000), 87–92.

26. Young, *Justice and the Politics of Difference*, 171.

27. Ibid., 186.

28. Iris Young, "Polity and Group Difference: A Critique of the Ideal of Universal Citizenship," *Ethics* 99 (January 1989): 260.

29. See Thomas Hylland Eriksen, *Ethnicity and Nationalism: Anthropological Perspectives* (London: Pluto Press, 1993), 38.

30. Idem, *Inclusion and Democracy*, 205.

participants recognize their overlapping experiences but it does not mean sameness or uniformity. Boundaries people set up are not cast-ironed because, they can be "somewhat X" and still be "somewhat Y," or they may be "a bit of this and a bit of that" though boundaries are not extended infinitely.[31] Relational difference sees groups as flexible to allow formation of alliances, creative distance, or shifting alliances.

In this light, understanding difference in its relational meaning is crucial in the dealings of diverse social groups in migration, leading to construction of the imagined church. This may mean going beyond the notion of church as a multicultural community, if by "multicultural" this means the peaceful coexistence of various autonomous cultures within one church. We may have to look for ways of conceiving the church as a space of relational difference which recognizes that "[c]ultural conditions today are largely characterized by mixes and permeations."[32]

The church can learn from studies of the social psychology of groups which have shown that individual members of one group evaluate others in another group more favorably when they see certain affinities. "Anthropological evidence also indicates that cross-cutting group loyalties ... seem to be important in reducing internal conflict and maintaining social cohesion."[33] Recognition of social differentiation hence does not break up the church; relational difference can be potent in enriching the life of the church but not at the expense of negating difference.

Attentiveness to Configurations and Dynamics of Power-Relationships

Young encourages "group autonomy" for marginalized social groups so they can develop and represent their group-specific interests and perspectives.[34] For her, "[u]ntil and when group oppression or disadvantages are eliminated, political publics including democratized workplaces and government decision making bodies should include the specific representation of

---

31. Eriksen, *Ethnicity and Nationalism*, 156–57.

32. Wolfgang Welsch, "Transculturality: The Puzzling Form of Cultures Today," in *Spaces of Culture: City, Nation, World*, ed. Mike Featherstone and Scott Lash (London: Sage Publications, 1999), 197.

33. John Duckitt, "Reducing Prejudice: An Historical and Multi-Level Approach," in *Understanding Prejudice, Racism, and Social Conflict*, ed. Martha Augoustinos and Katherine J. Reynolds (London: Sage Publications, 2001), 261; see Nakagawa Akira, "Influence of Migrants upon the Japanese Church." *Japan Mission Journal* 52, no. 3 (1998): 152–60.

34. Young, *Justice and the Politics of Difference*, 168.

those oppressed groups."[35] Young recognizes that social group differentiation partly arises from the experience of oppression and marginalization. The affinity they share is their common experience of oppression. The social group can therefore "melt away" once the group overcomes marginalization. However, there is also a group differentiation resulting from the "freedom of city life"[36] (e.g. cultural or religious group affinities) which necessitates a view of social justice that "requires not the melting away of difference, but institutions that promote the reproduction of and respect for group difference without oppression."[37]

Our imaging of the church has to give room for differentiated social groups to be recognized, to interact, and to form alliances. Acknowledging ethnic differences in the church entail more than tolerance. In tolerance, people are aware of others who are different but they need not relate with each other. I can tolerate the presence of a Hispanic or Chinese sitting beside me in the church but I need not converse with him or her in a meaningful way. Tolerance is another word for "leave them alone." "In social interactions the socially superior group often avoids being close to the lower status group, avoids eye contact, does not keep the body open."[38] Beyond tolerance, respect is required to acknowledge difference. In respect, there is admiration for social groups in their difference. Yet as Young also sharply points out, the rendering of respect may not always be value-free. "The orderliness of respectability means things are under control, everything in its place, not crossing borders."[39] In practice, social groups of migrants in the church are respected so long as they don't do things "out of the ordinary," that is, they have to join and partake in the thinking and practices of the mainstream.

A challenge to dominant groups in the church who are in the privileged position to define the norm—be this based on culture, class, or gender—is to examine their self-projected neutrality as though they are set apart from and far above other social bodies. Social groups who do not belong to the central or dominant social group are considered part of a society, yes, but they fall under odd titles, like "native," "ethnic," "traditional," "indigenous," "provincial," "minorities," "tribal," "mountain people," and the strangest designation of all—"cultural communities." These categories are defined from a particular

---

35. Idem, "Polity and Group Difference," 265.
36. Idem, *Justice and the Politics of Difference*, 238.
37. Ibid., 47.
38. Ibid., 133.
39. Ibid., 136.

social group whose norms serve to evaluate other groups. Accordingly the social group in a position of norm is the opposite of others: they are "not ethnic" and they are "civilized" or "modern." Among overseas migrants, while ethnic background highlights group identity, those coming from the same background distance themselves from one another based on particular class interests and concerns. Migrants of different social classes may interact in church events, but the distance is visible in the circle of friends, professional associations, and the kind of social activities they attend.[40]

Taking cue from Young's "politics of difference,"[41] an imagined church must embody and express "equality as the participation and inclusion of all groups (that) sometimes requires different treatment for oppressed or disadvantaged groups." This would imply that the church allows ways of thinking, lifestyles, and ritual practices other than what has been prescribed by those in the position of norm.

Studies on migration have shown[42] that migrants negotiate power to make sense of their world, subvert the ideology of the dominant groups, and re-invent their lives, relationships and discourses for their own emancipatory interests. What emerges from these researches is the image of migrants who are empowered, ingenious, dynamic and "resisting romances"[43] to confront creatively the harsh realities in societies. Migrant workers skillfully use the conditions of subjugation they are in to create alternative mazeways to survive and even to resist the negation of their social bodies. They have many ways of asserting their own social norms, evaluating their identity as positive and

---

40. Yen Le Espiritu, "Colonial Oppression, Labor Importation, and Group Formation: Filipinos in the United States," in *Filipinos in Global Migrations*, ed. Aguilar, 153.

41. Young, *Justice and the Politics of Difference*, 163–68.

42. See Michael Stewart, "'I can't drink beer, I've just drank water': Alcohol, Bodily Substance and Commensality among Hungarian Rom," in *Alcohol, Gender and Culture*, ed. Dimitra Gefou-Madianou (London: Routledge, 1992), 127–56; Daiva Stasiulis and Abigail Bakan, "Regulation and Resistance: Strategies of Migrant Domestic Workers in Canada and Internationally," *Asian and Pacific Migration Journal* 6, no.1 (1997): 31–57; Neferti Xina M. Tadiar, "Domestic Bodies of the Philippines," in *Filipinos in Global Migrations*, ed. Aguilar, 269–302; Caitríona NíLaoire, Naomi Bush in, Fina Carpena-Méndez, and Allen White, "Negotiating Belonging: Migrant Children and Youth in Ireland," Migrant Children Project Working Paper No. 1, November 2008, http://migration.ucc.ie/children/working%20paper%201.pdf (accessed July 2012); Susan Thieme, *Social Networks and Migration: Far West Nepalese Labour Migrants in Delhi* (Münster: Lit Verlag, 2006); Umut Eril, "Migrating Cultural Capital: Bourdieu in Migration Studies," *Sociology* 44, no. 4 (2010): 642–60; Jane M. Smith, "Identities and Urban Social Spaces in Little Tokyo, Los Angeles: Japanese Americans in Two Ethno-Spiritual Communities," *Geografiska Annaler: Series B, Human Geography* 90, no. 4 (December 2008): 389–408.

43. Julian McAllister Groves and Kimberly A. Chang, "Romancing Resistance and Resisting Romance: Ethnography and the Construction of Power in the Filipina Domestic Worker Community in Hong Kong," in *Filipinos in Global Migrations*, ed. Aguilar, 316–43.

denouncing the false ideology foisted on them by those in position of norm, and declaring their positive difference.

Host societies and local churches might see in these the inability of the migrants to adjust and adapt to new situations. While this may partly be true, there is also the truth that migrants show their pride in being "different," which need not be rejected but acknowledged and celebrated. The imagined church, like a canvas, is brushed with diversity and where group differences are navigated through interweaving strokes.

Dangers of a "Community" that Denies Difference

In Young's view, one of the hindrances for oppressed and disadvantaged groups to experience acceptance in society is the claim for "community" as the ideal of polity or the paradigm of how society works or should work. This is also something that church ministers has left unexamined. To borrow Kenan Osborne's critique of the concept "sacrament,"[44] community has become a "hermeneutical ease" which people use habitually as though the meaning of the word is clear and everyone shares the same meaning. But because it has been used without qualification, it has become obscure, meaningless.

First, the notion of community is highly suggestive of people who are or should be homogeneous in sharing similar beliefs, understandings, priorities and values. The concept expresses a longing for harmony among persons, for consensus and mutual understanding. Young criticizes this notion because it rests on a premise of the social subject as "a relation of unity or mutually composed by identification and symmetry among individuals within a totality." Community as a kind of social relations of "copresence of subjects"[45] tends to deny difference existing among and within social groups.

The desire to bring multiplicity and heterogeneity into unanimity may actually be in fact a way of not facing up to or of erasing difference. In this strategy, the migrant groups are enjoined to participate in religious activities of the church so that they become acceptable members of the community. In these undertakings, only migrant groups are considered different. The members of the local church, notwithstanding the warm hospitality they offer, have already set the rules and standards to which the migrants are to participate and be measured. Respect for differences may not find its visible

---

44. Kenan B. Osborne, *Christian Sacraments in a Postmodern World* (New York: Paulist Press, 1999), 56.

45. Young, *Justice and the Politics of Difference*, 229, 231.

expression in the social relations of "community" which tends to homogenize people rather than be themselves, that is, differentiated with affinity.[46]

The notion of "community" also furthers what I would call "social individualism." For those who find the world chaotic and changes disconcerting, community offers an enclave of security and comfort. Part of the experience of community, however, is people use themselves as the only point of reference and beneficiary of social relations, and thus tends to negate others who are "not-one-of-us." The essentialist approach to defining social groups freezes the experienced fluidity of social relations by setting up rigid inside-outside distinctions among groups."[47] Such rigid conceptualization denies the similarities that group members may have with those not considered in the group. It also denies the fact that there are many shadings and differentiations within and across groups, including gradations of exploitation and marginalization.

Moreover, traditional sociology and ecclesiology regards face-to-face encounter as indispensable requirement for the human collectivity called community. There is value, of course, to a community that fosters intimate relationship in a determinate place and particular time, as it also engenders greater participation of individuals in the life of the church. Particularly in the context of "homelessness" as a modern condition, face-to-face relations can serve as a contrast-cultural response to the alienation produced by the mechanistic structures and technologies. There is no reason though to assume that face-to-face relations found in small communities are more authentic than other forms of human mediations. In a small facial community, there is communication and consensus as much as there is the possibility of division and even violence. Such small communities also tend to be concerned with their "little world," but sometimes at the expense of bigger stakes of justice in society. The church as "a community of communities," in Frank Kirkpatrick's view[48] is not something that is merely concerned with its internal life of fellowship, but must engage in a "radical restructuring of the dominant forms of economic relationship in the larger society." But because the very notion of community requires intimate relationship, it tends to create a ghetto, thereby lessening their impact on larger social issues.

---

46. Ibid., 238.

47. Young, *Justice and the Politics of Difference*, 87–88.

48. Frank Kirkpatrick, *Community: A Trinity of Models* (Washington, DC: Georgetown University Press, 1986), 232.

Small associations are "depoliticizing": they offer friendship and enjoyment but are not predisposed to tackle political, economic, cultural, and gender issues, which the members think only divide the unity of the group.[49] Rather than achieving real unity, the process is a continued justification of exclusion of individuals in the community and differences are reduced to "individual" or "personal differences." Instead of addressing issues of equality and justice in the social order, the community avoids those issues and lives up to its character of mutual sympathy regardless of class, culture and gender. Moreover, by employing the strategic repertoire of "oneness" and "togetherness," any sentiment of protest in the social order (such as exploitation, marginalization, and discrimination) is safely contained. By maintaining that differences are "personal" or "individual," a "state of mind," or that belongs to the "temporal," the repertoire of oneness "has the effect of deflecting attention from political necessity of societal and structural change"[50] which is at the very heart of migrants' struggle to be integrated in the receiving nation-states.

Just exactly how do we imagine the "true face of the Church visible" considering the presence of socially differentiated groups? If we are to let Young speak to us, the theological challenge thrown to the church is the praxis of its twin-fold attributes of unity and catholicity. Would the face that is stained, irregular, blotched—in which the differentiated social bodies have their place—still be church? In an imagined church, there is much room for solidarity that is liberating, not only for one group but to the larger church and the whole of society. Catholicity is not an ideal when all has become the same; catholicity is a praxis through which those who are not yet related to the whole are given privileged spaces in what Jesus calls the *basileia* of God. We hope in the end, we can see their contours, shapes, colors and terrains in the face of the church. And when we look at that portrait, it still will not give us one clear, coherent profile. For in God's *kin-dom*, there is still the positive difference of groups having affinity and in solidarity with each other. The church is one or united, not amidst diversity, but precisely because there is diversity. In the speckled face, we encounter the God who remains unfathomable and whose name ineffable.

---

49. Young, *Inclusion and Democracy*, 162.

50. Amanda Le Couteur and Martha Augoustinos, "The Language of Prejudice and Racism," in *Understanding Prejudice, Racism, and Social Conflict*, ed. Augoustinos and Reynolds, 223.

Ambience of "City Life" in the Imagined Church

It may be argued that the church, for all intents, is a community. It indicates that the church *is* church because it is relational, a peoplehood, a corporate personality, a collective, a solidarity, a mutual accountability. It is hardly conceivable not to think of the church without thinking and talking of it as community. Young's arguments against community are not against those efforts that construct and affirm group identity and relations of group solidarity, as a means of confronting domination, exclusion and discrimination. But "(if) in their zeal to affirm a positive meaning of group specificity people seek or try to enforce a strong sense of mutual identification, they are likely to reproduce exclusions similar to those they confront. Those affirming the specificity of a group affinity should at the same time recognize and affirm the group and individual differences within the group."[51] If we have difficulty of changing our discourse, "community" may still be in use so long as we are aware of the dangers that this concept brings to actual social relationships. It is still possible, however, to imagine the church in other ways or forms of social relations that respect social differentiation. Any imaging of the church has definite politics associated with the image, and as Stanley Hauerwas points out, it is a question whether the image supports or resists the existing body polity;[52] in the context of our discussion, the exclusion and discrimination of migrants.

In imagining the "good society" that affirms and nurtures social group difference, especially the oppressed and disadvantaged groups in society, Young found the ideal polity in city life. In our times, there are certainly unpleasant and horrid experiences of people in cities and towns. Individualism, crass materialism, abandonment, loneliness, exclusion, fast-pace living, crimes and injustices, insecurity, and seeming confusion are some of the common negative experiences. It stands to reason however that cities are meant for the benefit of life which is why residents and state administrations try to do their best to make their cities hospitable spaces for all beings. City life or urbanity characterizes those who live in huge metropolis, as well as, those who reside in suburbs and large towns. These are the same sites where migrants are located and seek a place in hospitable spaces that will affirm their difference.

---

51. Young, *Inclusion and Democracy*, 236.

52. Stanley Hauerwas, *In Good Company: The Church as Polis* (Notre Dame: University of Notre Dame Press, 1995), 23.

Young defines "city life" as a form of social relations of "being together of strangers."⁵³ As imagined society, "city life" is distinct from "being together in oneness or commonness" that characterizes traditional social theories. In "city life," people are strangers to one another, yet they interact within spaces and institutions they all experience themselves as belonging to, but without those interactions dissolving into conformity or uniformity. Beyond familial enclaves, the more open public of politics, commerce and festivals are where strangers meet and interact. Their being together entails some common problems and interests, yet they maintain distance and are critical of domination and imposition. Being strangers does not mean to stand in opposition or contrast to each other. Being stranger is to respect distinctiveness and to show hospitality. In "city life," "there is equality among socially, culturally and sexually differentiated individuals and groups, who mutually respect one another and affirm one another in their differences."⁵⁴

I want to pick up four "virtues" of city life Young has identified in describing the form of social relations among differentiated social groups and bring to light as to how they can guide our search for an imagined church in the context of migration. These virtues can constitute what may be referred to as the *ambience* of a church with and of migrants.⁵⁵ For, to enter and be inside the city, writes Bernd Jager is

> to come to assume a certain stance, to surrender to a certain style of acting upon and of experiencing the surrounding world ... to come under the sway of a certain choreography and at the same time to become the subject of a certain disclosure ... to redraw the limits of our bodily existence to include that place—to come to incorporate it and to live it henceforth as ground of revelation rather than as panorama.⁵⁶

In city life *social differentiation* is manifest. City life is a space where people recognize difference as a reality that they must live with. In a good city life, group distinctions are respected, be it by culture, gender, occupation, and religiosity as well. Individuals and groups do not stand in relations of inclusion and exclusion, but overlap and intermingle without becoming homogenous.

---

53. Young, *Inclusion and Democracy*, 221–28; *Justice and the Politics of Difference*, 227, 237.

54. Idem, *Justice and the Politics of Difference*, 163.

55. For the concept of ambience, I am grateful to the students of St. Vincent School of Theology, Philippines, in the course "The Laity: Theology and Ministry," second semester, academic year 2005–2006. They attempted to draw the faces of the church that are more inclusive and liberating to people of this age.

56. Bernd Jager, "Body, House and City: The Intertwinings of Embodiment, Inhabitation, and Civilization," in *Dwelling, Place and Environment: Towards a Phenomenology of Person and World*, ed. David Seamon and Robert Mugerauer (Dordrecht: Martinus Nijhoff Publishers: 1995), 219–20.

There is mutual respect for difference and where borders of human living are open for people to cross other boundaries and interact.

Another ingredient of the ambience of city life is *variety*. In real cities, suburbs and towns, the interaction of individuals and groups occurs partly because of the multi-use of the social space. The appeal of a city is precisely the diversity of activities it supports. It draws people out in public to those activities and gives people pleasure and excitement. When stores, markets, restaurants, cinemas, malls, parks, offices, and churches and temples are sprinkled with residences, people have a neighborly feeling about their neighborhood, and they go out and encounter one another on the streets and chat. City life offers greater possibilities for variety to come into sight, be noticed for their distinctiveness, and be owned as "our place" or "our spot" by residents and businesses for the novelty their place offers to the passersby.

Moreover, city life is known for its *eroticism*. Young defines eroticism in the sense of "an attraction to the other, the pleasure and excitement of being drawn out of one's secure routine to encounter the novel, strange, and surprising."[57] In city life, one takes pleasure in being drawn out of oneself to understand that there are other meanings, practices, perspectives, lifestyles, and that one could learn or experience as "something more" or different by interacting with them. "A place of many places," the city can fold over on itself in so many layers and relationships that are incomprehensible. One cannot "take it in," so to speak, one never feels as though there are nothing more new and interesting things to explore, no new and interesting people to meet.

Lastly, *publicity* marks city life. By definition a public space is "a place accessible to anyone, where anyone can participate and witness." In entering the public, "one always risks encounter with those who are different, those who identify with different groups and have different opinions or different forms of life." The group diversity of the city is most apparent in public spaces. This helps account for their vitality and excitement. The public is heterogeneous, plural and playful, a place where people witness and appreciate diverse cultural expressions that they do not share and do not fully understand."[58] Public spaces too is the arena where people can manifest their thoughts and feelings, including those concerns, issues and demands that other people would avoid or are not even aware of.

---

57. Young, *Justice and the Politics of Difference*, 239.

58. Ibid., 241.

What are the implications of these virtues or the ambience of city life in our search for images or metaphors of the church *with* and *of* migrants? As an alternative to small communities, the church can be a network where "differentiated solidarity" is experienced. Migrants are affirmed in their difference yet the various migrant groups share responsibly obligations for the well-being of one another, especially in promoting inclusion and justice in the society they all are. Differentiated solidarity does not presume mutual identification or sense of belonging as a condition for respect and inclusion.[59] But because migrant groups interact with one another and with their hosts, they cooperate through events and activities that discourage group-based selfishness, prejudice, or hatred. The basis of people's solidarity with one another is not out of a fellow feeling, but because they find themselves occupying the same place. Strangers in one space, they owe each other a sense of commitment and justice by facing circumstances and problems that potentially affect most of them through collective actions to bring about relations of better living among them.[60]

The imagined church can learn something also from the variety of city life. We may no longer assume that "equality" exists among people when difference in terms of culture, status, and gender are ignored or denied. The reality is people are different, diverse, in plural form. This would imply the promotion of heterogeneous discourses and forms of human organizations which undertake conversation among themselves in order to revise, modify, improve or correct each other's views, beliefs or practices, in a spirit of friendly dialogue.

The experience of Filipino migrants in Tokyo, Japan, for example shows how the construction of an imagined church can be expressed in action through the variety that people undertake to make sense of their selves as a collectivity.[61] Playing the nerve center for the construction of a new ethnic identity is the Catholic chaplaincy and Centro Filipino, a non-government service organization. During Sundays and other holy days, the church provides services to the religious needs of Filipinos, and on regular days of the week, it responds to their "nonreligious" or "secular" needs. What emerges is a church of variety that responds to the diverse needs and concerns of migrants: a "home away from home," "town center," "informal employment network,"

---

59. Young, *Inclusion and Democracy*, 221.

60. Ibid., 223–24.

61. Ibarra Mateo, "The Church's Nonreligious Roles Among Filipino Catholic Migrants in Tokyo," in *Old Ties and New Solidarities: Studies on Philippine Communities*, ed. Charles J-H. Macdonald and Guillermo M. Pesigan (Quezon City: Ateneo de Manila University Press, 2000), 192–204.

"transient boarding house," "information midpoint," "entertainment hub," "refuge shelter"—all rolled into one. While maintaining their group identity, migrants make use of survival and adaptive strategies to reinforce old bonds and build new solidarities, not only among their particular groups but also with other migrant groups.

In addition, two key principles flow from the idea of the church as having features of eroticism and publicity. It means that the church has to go beyond the dichotomy of sacred and secular, spiritual and temporal, soul and body. In the public space that is the church, migrants may discover and affirm the sacred or divine. And second, the public is open in which all participate, and that public must be open and accessible to all. Contrary to the communitarian tradition, the church with city life cannot be conceived as a unity of transcending group differences, or as entailing complete mutual understanding. In public life the differences remain unassimilated, but each participating group acknowledges and is open to collaborate with others.

It may also mean conceding that there is no one way of being church in our times and to acknowledge the value of alternative discourses, structures, rituals and practices that would promote especially the interests of those at the margins of society and of the church. This calls for a kind of solidarity in which the imagined church allows and supports avenues and organizations other than the traditional forms of small communities of face-to-face encounter, of which many are controlled or led by dominant powerful groups. Separate avenues and organizations are probably necessary in order for the marginalized and excluded groups in the church and society to discover and reinforce the positive elements of their life-experiences.

In Young's "politics of difference," "real participatory structures are required in which actual people, with their cultural, social, economic, religious, gender and even occupational differences, assert their perspectives on issues affecting them in institutions that encourage the representation of their distinct voices."[62] In envisioning the church of migrants, there is recognition and acknowledgment of differentiations that exist between participants, including the complexities and conflicting interests in their relationships. Unlike the homogeneous and exclusive tendencies of community, the church that values difference does not only respect and celebrate social group difference but must also try to develop structures and mechanisms that can be liberating especially for those groups who are marginalized or subordinated. As we have mentioned above, among various migrants groups and within each migrant

---

62. Young, *Justice and the Politics of Difference*, 151.

group, there are configurations of power and gradations of domination and oppression. It is not enough thus to approach the migrants' situation only in terms of cultural difference or in projecting the church as a multicultural community. There are also issues revolving around class and gender.

Ministry to migrants has to take into account what Young refers to as "structural difference" that gives space for groups which experience discrimination (those excluded on the basis of class, gender, ability, ethno-linguistic, or caste), to be heard and represented in the organization of the church. Various forms of organizations are encouraged. Some could be directly along religious purposes and others through associational groups that work for the cause of migrants, socially, economically and politically. Especially disadvantaged migrant groups can form separate organizations apart from established groups in the church. They must be given choices whether they want to be part of the institution of the church or remain independent of church influence. This is not to create divisions in the church but to permit other forms of human collectivity that continue to work for the well-being of migrants. As Young asserts, segregation of groups is wrong, but social group distinction is not wrong.[63] "One important way to promote greater inclusion of members of underrepresented social groups is through political and associational institutions designed specifically to increase representation of women, the working class, racial or ethnic minorities, disadvantaged castes, and so on."[64]

Structures of difference also have room for local residents. Due to the intermingling of concerns and interests among social groups, local people can participate in the cause of migrants, perhaps not with religious intention but in actions that are geared toward the social, economic and political inclusion of migrants in civil society. In fact, as ministers to migrants would attest and in my own past experience as migrant and who was into chaplaincy work with migrants, there are citizens of receiving societies who are willing to share their time, expertise and resources for migrants' interest but they do not wish to be bound to church organizations or required to submit to church regulations and rituals. Strangers to one another, migrants and hosts have affinities that propel them to strategies that benefit all. Their relationship may not be inspired by religious faith, but by the fact that they occupy and live the same space in which all become accountable to make their city a hospitable place.

---

63. Young, *Inclusion and Democracy*, 224.
64. Ibid., 141.

PREAMBLE INSTEAD OF A POSTSCRIPT

The problem with some styles of imagined church is not with the biblical imagery from which they find support but with the way in which their underlying ecclesiologies have their practical implications for migrants. In exploring the need to look for other ways of imagining the church, I have put forward the idea that to intervene in images and metaphors is to intervene with the church's self-understanding of its identity and mission with the pains and hopes of migrants as starting point and perspective. This requires a particular way of looking at the reality of migrants' lives, for they possess, at least intuitively, a privilege of insight borne of negativity not experienced by more elite, centrist groups, including those who theologically reflect on their experiences.

Still, one may ask in conversation with the ambience of "city life," what is "the face of the church visible." For one, rather than numerically defined, the church will be a relational church where various migrant groups enjoy their social difference yet fashioning relationship that promotes solidarity with one another, with other migrants of other faiths, with subordinated groups in their host societies, and with God. It will be a church to which accountability falls on the migrant lay people together with other laity in the receiving society, and with the support of the ecclesial hierarchy. It will be a church that is deeply aware and works for the rights of migrants, respects cultural difference and promotes the dignity and equality of women and men. Whether the structural form takes the traditional parish set-up or a "parish or center on the move," it will be a church with the ambience of city life: where social group difference is positively enriched; where multiplicity of life-giving practices and spiritualities are possible; where different spatial moods are encountered in the interactive movement of people and groups; and where its public character takes a political dimension—the critical activity of raising issues and deciding how institutions and social relations should be organized."[65] The church of and with migrants takes seriously its sacramentality in the world—serving as horizon through which the divine presence is made manifest and is acknowledged.

In this paper, I have often used the word "space" in varied shades in reference to a physical place, a cultural category, and a metaphor for social relations and the construction of reality and meanings. Richard Lang in "The

---

65. Ibid., 240.

Dwelling Door: Towards a Phenomenology of Transition" invites us to gaze our attention to doors as spaces that embody our human experience.

> The door is the access to the other, the site of human meeting, the place of dialogue, of judgment. The door is radically *intersubjective*, for it shelters the revelation of self and others .... To be before a door is in its deepest significance to be a sensitive attendant waiting for the manifestation of the other; for the appearance of the real. Our ritual of knocking on the door is the embodiment of respectful waiting or pause; it is not an empty gesture. With this respectful hesitation at a door demarcating difference, we provoke a life of community, of being together with others-in-difference. We celebrate the vital difference between self and other and thereby make possible a meeting. At the doorway, we respectfully wait for the other. In its purest mythic form, the person before the door is the stranger who journeys from afar, who solicits the real, who asks for admission. The dweller offers this stranger hospitality, and the door becomes the meeting place of host and guest, of person and world."[66]

In our strivings to become a church not only for migrants but with and of migrants, it could be that, instead of the migrants, we who work for and with migrants are the strangers who journey from afar, knocking on the door, standing before the door, soliciting the real and asking admission at the doorway—of the migrants. The hospitable door of the migrants stands as benevolent and inviting: "Welcome! We have been waiting for you; come, join us in our meal!" The door ceases to be a surface spectacle; it has turned into a meeting place with lots of surprises to offer.

Emmanuel S. de Guzman

---

66. Richard Lang, "The Dwelling Door: Towards a Phenomenology of Transition," in *Dwelling, Place and Environment: Towards a Phenomenology of Person and World*, ed. David Seamon and Robert Mugerauer (Dordrecht: Martinus Nijhoff Publishers: 1985), 213.

6

MAPPING THE CHURCH ON THE MOVE

While boundaries of territory define commonality as the basis for identity, boundaries of difference highlight issues of particularity. In a shared space, the setting up and strengthening of boundaries of difference can become acute among migrants and hosts, often in strenuous and precarious dynamics. This essay focuses on what it means to be church[1] among peoples of difference who are struggling to find their place in one space.

Through the use of "models," it synthesizes the range of pastoral actions and theological insights of the church in relation to migration[2] Models are attempts to explain and explore actual experiences into conceptual maps or typologies. The models described in this article are gathered from the practices of people ministering to and with the migrants and reflected upon using the disciplines of social anthropology, missiology, and systematic theology. The models are not exclusive of each other, for in doing ministry with migrants, practices overlap. They are also not intended to be exhaustive but are meant to invite further reflections from those who work with migrants.

Four models of church are elaborated, namely: the monocultural host church, the monocultural migrant church, the multiculturalist, and intercultural models. These are clustered into two: models for single cultures and

---

1. "Church" in this paper, refers to the entire church (laity, ordained, and consecrated religious), with institutional features and as a community of persons. The term also covers the global or universal church, although in many instances, speaks of the church in a local place (a diocese, parish, or congregation).

2. For another way of categorizing migrant churches particularly in the Protestant/Pentecostal context in Rotterdam based on their self-identification, see Robert Calvert, "Ecclesial Patterns among Migrant Churches in Rotterdam,"*www.communitas.co.za/artikels/Calvert.doc* (accessed July 2012).

models for multiple cultures. This article also delves more into the intercultural church model which is still in its seminal stage of development but possesses the potential to be a very fruitful way to deal with the diversity of cultures in the migration context.

Single-Culture Models

The single-culture model is anchored on the "one parish, one community" ecclesiology where the unity of the parish is based on parishioners engaging harmoniously in parish life and ethnic-identified ministries are seen as potentially divisive.

Monocultural Host Church

Migrants of varied backgrounds are incorporated into one church (hence, "*mono*"), that is the host church and its culture. In sociality, the monocultural host church is like a "melting pot." Migrants are expected to become "one of them," that of the host society. The model assumes that if a society makes a full effort to incorporate migrants into the mainstream society, they will then naturally work to reciprocate the gesture and adopt new customs, subsequently national unity is retained.

Proponents of this model are committed to the Pauline vision of Christ's community of saints, where there are neither Jews nor Greeks, slaves nor free persons, males nor females, barbarian nor Scythian, for all are now clothed with Christ and Christ is all and in all (Gal 3: 28; Col 3: 11; 1 Cor 12: 13). Translated into social relationships, being a Mexican or Singaporean, Third World or First World, documented or irregular migrant, Christian or Moslem, have no bearing to the foundational truth that all are children of God. But since the faith cannot but be expressed in a particular language/culture, it is the faith practice of the receiving church which remains to be dominant. For example, in response to the memorial regarding national parishes in the US in 1886, the American archbishops stated:

> If the Church of God wishes to make true progress among us [in America], it cannot depend 'exclusively' upon European emigration, but must fix deeply its roots elsewhere than this alone. Therefore, the Church will be neither Irish, nor will it be German, but AMERICAN, and even more,

ROMAN; since there is neither Jew, nor Greek, ... but all are one in Christ Jesus.[3]

The monocultural host church serves therefore as a good vehicle to socialize the migrants into the local Christian culture. This appeals to migrants whose goal is to be accepted by conforming to the local ways of the host culture.

Some monocultural host churches discourage ministries which focus on specific ethnic groups[4] while others offer activities like occasional liturgical celebration in their own language, local tourism, language skills training, professional development modules, and legal, medical and health assistance. These, however, are rendered mainly by members from the host church, who do not necessarily speak the language of the migrants. This may be intentional on the part of the parish/diocese to encourage the migrants to learn the language of the host country while in other cases, this is mainly because there is a lack of qualified staff.

In a parish where there are migrants from several cultures, greater tolerance is needed to ease inter-group tensions and to help them cooperate under the direction of the host community. For instance, in a parish in Taiwan, a Filipino migrant El Shaddai (charismatic) community was relegated to celebrating their liturgies in the parish basement because the usually tolerant Buddhist neighborhood could not understand why they have to use drums and electric guitar in their liturgical celebrations, which is a marked contrast with the usually solemn Chinese liturgical celebrations.

In some monocultural host churches, over-assertion of cultural identities is seen as a threat to the unity of the whole. Migrants can be viewed as needing "purification" from their "superstitious" and "queer" practices that are rooted in some "primitive" worlds or pre-enlightenment beliefs or as some would say "like we believed in the fifties."[5] Mainline churches, for example, may look down or feel uncomfortable with the manner of worship of Pentecostal

---

3. New York 17-12-1886 Corrigan a Simeoni, in S.O.C.G. 1887, vol. 1026, f. 948v (orig. Latin), cited by Stephen M. Di Giovanni, hep, "Historical and Canonical Aspects of the Pastoral Care of Immigrants in Late 19th Cen. America," *People on the Move: A Compendium of Church Documents in the Pastoral Concern for Migrants and Refugees* (Bishops' Committee on Priestly Formation, Bishops' Committee on Migration and National Conference of Catholic Bishops, 1988), 36.

4. Ken Johnson Mondragon, *Ministry in Multicultural and National/Ethnic Parishes: Evaluating the Findings of the Emerging models of Pastoral Leadership Project*, http://emergingmodels.org/files/2012/05/Multicultural-Report.pdf(accessed February 2012), 9.

5. Gerrit Noort, "Emerging Migrant Churches in the Netherlands: Missiological Challenges and Mission Frontiers," *International Review of Mission* 100 (April 2011): 14.

migrant churches.⁶ The host culture sees itself as "cleansing" the migrants to "cloth them with Christ." A similar attitude may or may not be reflected in this church's relation with migrants of other Christian faiths and religions.

The early Christian church in Jerusalem, though bi-cultural—composed of Hebraic and Hellenistic Jewish Christians—is an example of a monocultural host church, as it is characterized by the primacy of the church of the Hebraic Jews and their customs. Although a second tier of Hellenistic Jewish leaders were appointed to take charge of the distribution of food to the widows (Acts 6:5), the highest leadership remained in the hands of the Hebraic Jews.⁷

Monocultural Migrant Church

This refers to a church composed mainly of a single ethnic group of migrants. Some countries have consciously fostered the growth of these "native churches." For example, in the United Kingdom, there are "black majority churches" of migrants from Africa and the Caribbean, which have prospered and now compose majority of the churches.⁸ In other instances, the growth of the monocultural migrant church is a result mainly of the migrants' initiative. In these churches, the migrants worship in the way they did in their home countries, using their own language.

In 19th cen. United States, the monocultural migrant church had taken the form of national churches. Faced with a large number of Catholic immigrants from Europe, 202 language or national parishes were formed in the United States through a structural decision on the diocesan level.⁹ These

---

6. North Star United, one of United Church of Canada congregations, used to cater to Canadian-born members. When Pentecostal migrants joined the congregation, the Canadian-born members eventually left, to be part of another United Church congregation which adopt a more traditional worship style. Samantha Rideout, "Feature: Global Flair," http://www.ucobserver.org/faith/2010/10/global_flair/ (accessed March 2012).

7. See Richmond Paul Boven Williams, "Towards a Strategic Transcultural Model of Leadership that Enhances Koinonia in Urban Southern Africa: Synthesizing Multiple Model of Leadership that Transcends the Sociopolitical Barrier within the Cities of Southern Africa," (PhD in Theology diss., University of Southern Africa, 2006).

8. Doris Pershcke, "The Role of Religion for the Integration of Migrants and Institutional Responses in Europe: Some Reflections," http://findarticles.com/p/articles/mi_m2065/is_4_61/ai_n49577130/pg_5/?tag=content;col1(accessed January 2012).

9. Silvano M. Tomasi, cs "The Response of the Catholic Church in the United States to Immigrants and Refugees," in *People on the Move*, 105; on how Catholic immigrants established ministries for their own respective ethnic groups in the early 20th century, as well as, an evaluation of the impact of national parishes, see Richard M. Linkh, *American Catholicism (1900–1924 European Immigrants)*(New York: Center for Migration Studies, 1975; 2nd printing, 1978).

were non-territorial parishes formed with a priest/pastor who possessed the cultural competence to serve a particular migrant ethnic group. Some ministries were conducted in English to respond to the needs of the second or later generation of immigrants.

The monocultural migrant church model exists today[10] in the form of a religious organization/movement (e.g. charismatic group), a national association of migrants, or a chaplaincy like a "Filipino Catholic center" that is attached to a parish or recognized by the diocesan church leaders. The migrants might be residing in a particular area of a town or city where they have retained their sense of community, rituals and customs, or they can come from various parts of the region and congregate in the center for worship. This church can likewise take the form of a refugee church at the borders of countries (e.g. refugee camp for Sri Lankans run by the Jaffna Diocese of the Church of South India).[11]

The ethnic-based church is different from the previous model in that the ministers are mainly immigrants or "sent by the church" in the originating country. They speak and conduct services in the language of the migrants. This model may be attractive to first generation migrant Christians since it affords a feeling of belonging and of being at home. It can also serve as a platform for integration. Birthe Munck-Fairwood, in her essay on migration and the churches in Denmark notes:

> Many migrants would say that until they started their own church no one noticed them. From being *nobody* they become *somebody*. They could rent facilities and started receiving invitations from Danish churches. Their choirs were invited to give concerts in churches. They found that they were seen and given a voice in a way they would not have been if they had gone to a Danish majority church.[12]

There is the danger, however, of becoming a ghetto church if the relationship with the church of the receiving society is not fostered. For instance, the Vietnamese church in Phnom Penh in the late 1990s conducted their

---

10. Canon 216 of the New Code of Canon Law 1918 prohibited the formation of new national parishes, in order to promote harmony and more rapid assimilation into the US American culture. Ibid., 128.

11. Tom Albinson, "The Church on the Refugee Highway," http://refugeehighway.net/resources/church-on-highway (accessed September 2010).

12. Birthe Munck-Fairwood "Welcome Here? Responses to Migration from Churches in Denmark," in *Together or Apart?: Report from the Nordic Consultation on Migration and Changing Ecclesial Landscapes* (Nordic Ecumenical Working Group on Migration in cooperation with Ecumenism in the Nordic Region [EkumenikiNorden], December 2008), 2418–25.

liturgies solely in Vietnamese, and was thus unable to include the Khmer Catholics.[13]

Underlying this model is the idea that migration is not only an economic phenomenon but significantly a social and cultural experience. When people go to foreign lands, they carry their collective history, their "cultural soul" (if one regards culture as monolithic and static) or "habitus" (if culture is viewed as dynamic). The church is like a "salt" that preserves the culture, if not, the life-giving aspects of the migrants' culture. As salt also enhances the flavor of food, the national or ethnic-based church brings out the individuality of the culture and deepens its flavor.[14] Where there are political restrictions to religious practices, the ethnic-based church provides sanctuary and security for migrants to express their Christian faith in their cultural ways. In many Asian countries, the Christian church is a minority and its members are immigrants from minority cultures. In Thailand and Cambodia, the Catholics are Vietnamese immigrants; in Malaysia, Chinese descent; in Japan, people from Korea, China, Brazil, Peru, the Philippines, and foreign workers. Monocultural migrant churches in these places have given the impression to the locals that Christianity is an alien or foreign religion.

The spirit of this church model can be captured by the image of the church as a migrant on earth—an "alien and exile" (I Pt 2:11),[15] and a "stranger and foreigner seeking a homeland" (Heb 11:13–14). These images are based on the historical conditions of the Jewish diaspora. The audiences of the letters were suffering from actual geographical dislocation, cultural uprootedness,

---

13. Didier Bertrand, "Religious Practices of Vietnamese in Cambodia and Inter-Ethnic Relations," *Asian Migrant* 10, no. 3 (1997): 91.

14. See for instance the study Sharon Kim conducted of twenty-two 2nd-generation Korean-American Reformed churches in Los Angeles. A minority of the pastors of churches wanted to remain mono-ethnic that is predominantly Korean-American to affirm their cultural heritage and develop a distinctive Korean American spirituality. (Though not opposed to a multi-ethnic church, others want to become pan-Asian to include non-Korean Asian-Americans since they believe most parishioners would want to worship with those who are racially similar. Majority, however, want to transform into multi-ethnic churches.) "Shifting Boundaries within Second-Generation Korean American Churches," *Sociology of Religion* 71 (2010): 198–22.

15. John H. Elliott posits that the readers of I Peter are actually Christian migrant workers experiencing socio-cultural alienation and religious harassment. *A Home for the Homeless: A Social-Scientific Criticism of 1 Peter, its Situation and Strategy* with a new introduction (Minneapolis: Fortress Press, 1990). Donald Senior holds that the term "alien and exile" refers more likely to the estrangement Christians experience because of the different values they hold in comparison with the dominant culture. Donald Senior, 1 Peter, *Sacra Pagina* 15 (Collegeville, MN: Liturgical Press, 2003), 8–10. Robert Calvert, in his study of migrant churches in Rotterdam, notes how first generation migrant churches view themselves as "resident aliens" or "new Christian colonies in a space that is foreign." "Ecclesial Patterns among Migrant Churches in Rotterdam." http://communitas.co.za/taakspanne/vbo/konferensies/ecclesial-patterns-among-migrant-churches-in-rotterdam/ (2010) (accessed August 2012).

and estrangement from institutional systems of power. As a wandering people in search of home, the church is in a condition of "now and not yet," whose hope is anchored on the promise of God of a "heavenly home."

MULTIPLE-CULTURE MODELS

The multiple-culture models are premised on the image of the church as "community of communities." In *Ecclesia in America* 41, John Paul II underlines that:

> One way of renewing parishes, especially urgent for parishes in large cities, might be to consider the parish as a community of communities and movements. It seems timely therefore to form ecclesial communities and groups of a size that allows for true human relationships. This will make it possible to live communion more intensely, ensuring that it is fostered not only "ad intra," but also with the parish communities to which such groups belong, and with the entire diocesan and universal Church. In such a human context, it will be easier to gather to hear the word of God, to reflect on the range of human problems in the light of this word, and gradually to make responsible decisions inspired by the all-embracing love of Christ.[16]

Here, the unity of the parish is not based on a common language or regular worship together but on the same ecclesial communion that binds the diocesan and universal church, specifically; the profession of the same faith, the incorporation through the same baptism, and the celebration of the same eucharist (regardless of language). The communities in the parish are gathered together too by a common pastor appointed by a bishop and they celebrate liturgies in the same space, albeit in different times.

---

16. Ken Johnson Mondragon, *Ministry in Multicultural and National/Ethnic Parishes: Evaluating the Findings of the Emerging Models of Pastoral Leadership Project*, http://emergingmodels.org/files/2012/05/Multicultural-Report.pdf (accessed February 2012), 9–10.

Multiculturalist Church

The multiculturalist[17] model assumes that culture is a total way of living shared homogeneously by its members, crafted in a distant past and passed on to generations with minor changes. In this view, the migrants among themselves and the host church are seen as possessing systems of living that are essentially dissimilar to one another. The multiculturalist church encourages ethnic distinctions by facilitating each group of migrants to express their faith in their cultural particularity under the leadership as well of migrants from their own countries. These groups co-exist with one another, where co-existence means permitting migrants to celebrate their own liturgies, programs and activities, with their own leadership, in their own time and with assigned rooms in the parish compound or in the diocese. Once in a while, there will be some interaction among the different migrant groups during special occasions or major liturgical celebrations but groups maintain their relative autonomy. One can thus image the vision of a multiculturalist church as a "salad bowl" consisting of separate ingredients, each with its own taste, shape, and texture. These ingredients (cultures) do not lose their essential identities but in the tossing and mixing of the various ingredients, their taste can blend beautifully.

The multiculturalist church promotes cultural variety by giving each migrant group freedom to develop and grow in their communal life of faith according to their cultural wisdom and resources (e.g. in a diocese, each ethnic community has its own territorial domains such as Chinatown, Korean town, Indian village, Vietnamese street, with their own churches). There is little effort done for the groups to relate with one another, as there

---

17. We have used the term "multiculturalist" instead of multicultural because of the various meanings given to the latter. Some use the terms "multicultural" and "intercultural" interchangeably. See for instance "Characteristics of a Multicultural Church," http://www.baptist.org.uk/justice/racial-justice-resources/doc_view/1026-characteristics-of-a-multicultural-church.html(accessed March 2012). "The word multicultural is being used as a way of talking about diverse and distinct cultures living together and learning to interact with one another. It is not about each culture living separately, so creating self-contained ghettos. It is about valuing diversity, and recognising and respecting the contributions that can be made by different cultures to each other. It is not about each culture claiming a right to be accepted uncritically. It is about all cultures engaging in critical dialogue with each other, so that all can contribute to the building of community and a cohesive society.";Michelle Vu, "Interview: Former Pastor on Segregation in the Church, Cultural Intelligence," http://www.christianpost.com/news/interview-former-pastor-on-segregation-in-the-church-cultural-intelligence-48437/ (accessed March 2012). Others employ the term "multicultural" in a descriptive sense, to refer to the lived reality of diversity as a consequence of migration and "intercultural" to mean the ideal quality of communication or interaction between these groups. See for instance the 2010 World Council of Churches message on migration. "Report of the World Council of Churches (WCC) Consultation on Mission and Ecclesiology of the Migrant Churches," (2010) *International Review of Mission* 100, no. 1 (April 2011): 104–11.

is also less opportunity for communication exchange and common activities. Rather than looking at the group differences as a "problem," migrant groups are sources for invigorating the host church. This becomes urgent particularly in churches that are losing appeal to local citizens, such as in many European churches where non-European migrants are populating and revitalizing the places of worship. Competition and rivalry do arise between the migrant communities in seeking recognition and privileges from the host church, like the use of places, requests for religious services, the attention of ministers, and for financial support as well. In these situations, the host church enforces policies and rules that will respect diversity and promote equal opportunities by separating the various groups as much as possible.

This model may have similarities with the early Christian house churches, some of which may have been organized along ethnic lines. This is very possible as house churches have been established in the immigrant section of cities where migrants settle by ethnic groups. Naturally, Christians would join house churches that are nearer to their place. The house church of Prisca and Aquila may have been a predominantly Jewish Christian church as they themselves are Jewish; the two house congregations referred to in Rom 16:14 and 15 are probably composed mostly of Greek-speaking Gentile converts who are slaves or former slaves.[18]

As there are many *ekklesiae* within Paul's reach, they all are united in the one church of Christ. Though separated by distance and circumstances, each community strives to be faithful to Christ's teachings and to work out their own expression of discipleship that fits their culture's ways. At times Paul praises the efforts of the communities, and at other times, critical and challenging words are spoken, especially when dissensions and factionalism are breaking the church apart. Moreover, the well-being of each community rests on the shoulders of the leaders who Paul thanks for their zeal and commitment. They come from the ranks of their respective churches and they include women, slaves, new converts, former prisoners, husbands and wives, brothers and sisters and relatives, young and elderly (*see* Rom 16: 1–23).

In the multiculturalist model, various cultural practices are respected, thus one can expect that other Christian faiths, religiosities and religions are at the very least tolerated, though initiating dialogue with them may not be a priority. Like in the monocultural migrant church, there is the danger here

---

18. James S. Jeffers, *The Graeco-Roman World of the New Testament Era: Exploring the Background of Early Christianity* (Inter Varsity Press, 1999), 85–86.

of the "ghettoizing of ethnic-identified particularities."¹⁹ As the Presbyterian Cho describes it, as people feel more at home in their ethnic enclave, they feel less need to get out to connect with those outside of one's migrant church. The multiculturalist model may not also be advantageous for women and other minorities within an ethnic group, for in the representation of a culture, it is oftentimes the voice of the male minister or the dominant groups that gets listened to.²⁰

Intercultural Church

The intercultural model takes the multicultural situation a step further by promoting opportunities for meaningful interaction between various cultural groups toward mutual enrichment and positive change in the perspective of the other.²¹ In his address on "Migration and Ecumenism," Cardinal Martini, the head of the Pontifical Council for Migrants and Itinerant Peoples distinguished interculturality from multiculturalism: "We are practically insisting on a concept of intercultural societies, meaning those that are capable of interacting and producing mutual enrichment, going beyond multiculturalism, that can be contented with a mere juxtaposition of cultures."²²

An "in-beyond" or hybrid culture is possible within an intercultural model because it presupposes a concept of culture that is dynamic, heterogeneous, and negotiated within a field of power relations. The sociologist Pierre Bour-

---

19. See Daniel Cho, "Is Multiculturalism Bad for the Church—Part 2: A Reflection on Church and Ethnicity," Presbyterian Record, http://www.presbyterianrecord.ca/2011/07/15/is-multiculturalism-bad-for-the-church-part-2/ (accessed August 2012).

20. See Susan Moller Okin's feminist critique of Will Kymlicka, the Canadian liberal theorist of multiculturalism. *Is Multiculturalism Bad for Women?* (Princeton: New Jersey: Princeton University, 1999), 23–24. See also the critique of multiculturalism in the *White Paper on Intercultural Dialogue "Living Together As Equals in Dignity, "* Launched by the Council of Europe Ministers of Foreign Affairs at their 118th Ministerial Session (Strasbourg, 7 May 2008), http://www.coe.int/t/dg4/intercultural/source/white%20paper_final_revised_en.pdf (accessed July 2012), 18–19.

21. "What is the Intercultural Church?"(Toronto: The United Church of Canada, 2009), http://www.united-church.ca/files/intercultural/what-is.pdf (accessed March 2012); On major features of "interculturality" as identified by the International Network on Cultural Policy, see Annual Ministerial Meetings, "Interculturality Moving Towards a Dialogue Among Nation," International Network on Cultural Policy, http://incp-ripc.org/meetings/2003/theme3_inter_e.shtml (accessed May 2005); see also Bob Rasmussen, "Leading your Church through Intercultural Transformation," http://usmin.onechallenge.org/intercultural-helps/interculturaltransformation (accessed March 2012).

22. "The Church Must Feel Concerned Regarding Immigrants," address given by Cardinal Renato Martino at the Annual Meeting of European National Directors for the Pastoral Care of Migrants, Subiu, Romania, September 3-4, 2007, http://www.piercedhearts.org/heart_church/migration_ecumenism.htm (accessed February 2012). For an example of Protestant churches in the Netherlands poised to move toward interculturality, see Noort, "Emerging Migrant Churches in the Netherlands," 4–16.

dieu's theory of cultural practice as shaped by habitus, field and capital is one framework which may help explain religious/cultural change in the migrant context. The migrant carries his/her habitus (cultural unconscious) into the new field—the host country. What religious and other cultural practices migrants eventually leave behind or appropriate from the host culture is most of the time pre-reflexively chosen depending on what would maximize their well-being that is their economic, social and cultural capital. Race, gender, age, sexuality—which get embodied in the migrant's habitus[23]—can enhance or restrict access to capital. It is therefore difficult for mutual cultural enrichment to happen without the necessary changes in objective conditions such as the dominant societies' recognition of other ethnic groups' cultural capital, as well as, the latter's right to increased access to economic capital.[24] Integral to the ministry of an intercultural church is advocacy to equalize power relations with the country of origin and within the receiving society.

Nonetheless, migrants are not mere pawns, victims, or passive accomplices in structures of global mobility. Cruising intercultural relations, migrants in their "in betwixt-and-between" predicament ("*both* this *and* that, and simultaneously, *neither* this *nor* that")[25] are resourceful actors who find their ways to survive and make sense of their existence. The raison d'être of migrants maintaining or rejecting a traditional cultural practice/identity, is rooted in how this ultimately facilitates their experience of well-being in the new context.

Intercultural Church as Third Space[26]

Interculturality is also "transculturality" which highlights the creation of identities ensuing from the process of cultural negotiation.[27] This does not mean that people lose their identity. On the contrary, interculturality makes people appreciate better the richness of cultures, their own and others. This

---

23. Pierre Bourdieu, "What Makes a Social Class? On the Theoretical and Practical Existence of Groups," *Berkeley Journal of Sociology* 32 (1987), cited by David Schwarz, *Culture and Power*, 153–154.

24. For an elaboration on this from the perspective of Pierre Bourdieu's theory of cultural practice, see chapter 3 of this anthology.

25. Peter Phan, *Christianity with an Asian Face: Asian American Theology in the Making* (Maryknoll, New York: Orbis, 2003), 3–25.

26. "Third space" is an in-between space where cultural meaning and identity beyond binary pairings can be constructed. Homi Bhabha, "Introduction," in *The Location of Culture* (London: Routledge, 1994), 54.

27. Wolfgang Welsch, "Transculturality: The Puzzling Form of Cultures Today," in *Spaces of Culture: City, Nation, World,* ed. Mike Featherstone and Scott Lash (London: Sage, 1999), 194–213.

applies as well when the migrant church dialogues with other faiths/religions. This need not lead to the watering down of the Christian faith but rather to its enrichment. Culture is a synergy of the old and new, past and present, native and foreign, local and global, which people use to enrich their lives and relationships.

In dealing with cultural diversity, some (e.g. the United Church of Canada), have found it useful to identify non-negotiables such as gender equality.[28] In this regard, it is wise to heed the caution of the Council of Europe Ministers of Foreign Affairs against stereotyping or a coded equation between "minority communities" and "gender inequality" as if this issue has already been resolved in the host community.

> Gender equality injects a positive dimension into intercultural dialogue. The complexity of individual identity allows solidarities inconceivable within a stereotyped, communalist perspective. The very fact that gender inequality is a cross-cutting issue means that intercultural projects engaging women from "minority" and "host" backgrounds may be able to build upon shared experiences.[29]

The foregoing discussion suggests that interculturality is more than respecting diversity of cultures. The movement toward in-beyond or transcending identities, participated in by migrants and the receiving local church, makes the intercultural model distinct from other designs. The view of the church as an internally undifferentiated and externally disassociated body is replaced by an embodied church of intersecting multiple heterogeneous bodies that is moving to a new configuration in Christ.

In this process, the church, particularly its hierarchy, is neither supercultural[30] nor exterior to cultures. The entire church is the believers' sustained practice of mutual exchange and cooperation; an in-between space for negotiating religious and other cultural practices. The United Church of Canada notes, "We don't know exactly what an intercultural church will look like. But it's an exciting opportunity. God is calling us to work together to

---

28. See SamanthaRideout, "Feature: Global Flair," http://www.ucobserver.org/faith/2010/10/global_flair/ (accessed March 2012).

29. *White Paper on InterculturalDialogue "Living Together As Equals inDignity,"* Launched by the Council of Europe Ministers of Foreign Affairsat their 118th Ministerial Session(Strasbourg, 7 May 2008), 21.

30. Superculturality propounds a specific culture as the universal culture for all. Superculturality characterizes more the dynamics of cultural encounters in the period of colonization and has gained momentum as well in the current trend towards a one-world "super culture" through the processes of economic globalization. Franz XaverScheuerer, *Interculturality: A Challenge for the Mission of the Church* (Bangalore: Asian Trading Corporation, 2001), 128.

build something new."³¹ A gospel text that has been cited to illustrate the intercultural model is Jesus' encounter with the Syrophoenician woman (Mt 15:21–28 and Mk 7:24–30), where Jesus himself learned to be more inclusive of gentiles in his view of his mission, via his encounter with an other.³²

Indeed, the greatest resources of the intercultural church are the migrants. As *Erga Migrantes Caritas Christi* affirms, migrants are the "hidden providential builders," the "living sign," and an "effective reminder" of the church's identity as communion, characterized by unity, holiness, catholicity, and apostolicity (EMCC, 17, 18, 97, 103).³³

Interculturality in Theological Perspectives

Three complementary motifs from the biblical and theological traditions endorse the obligation to create intercultural Christian communities today.

The first motif is the Pentecost. The narrative of the Pentecost (Acts 2) is a frame of reference for the foundation of an intercultural community (EMCC 18). It reminds the church that the Spirit of God precedes, creates, assists, and completes the church as communion. The church does not possess the Spirit; the Spirit has power over the church. "We cannot dwell in the Spirit, but the Spirit dwells in us, in others, and in the spaces-in-between them and us. The Spirit is the 'Go-Between God'."³⁴ It is the divinity drawing near and passing by; its life-giving power enters and leaves again, constantly moving between-and-betwixt and beyond. This means that God is the only utterly Transcendent.

As the Spirit creates and shrouds the community of fellowship, all are guests in the Spirit-filled home where God is the gracious host. As guests, people of diverse and different identities are to behave properly in God's dwelling by relating with each other with respect. Indifference and division are broken and people are awakened to be sensitive again to the humanness they share with one another. The challenge for the intercultural church is to

---

31. What is the Intercultural Church?, 4.

32. Ibid.

33. Pontifical Council for Migrants and Itinerant People, *Erga Migrantes Caritas Christi: the Love of Christ towards Migrants*, http://www.vatican.va/roman_curia/pontifical_councils/migrants/documents/rc_pc_migrants_doc_20040514_erga-migrantes-caritas-christi_en.html (accessed August 2006); henceforth referred to as EMCC.

34. Sigurd Bergmann, "Revisioning Pneumatology in Transcultural Spaces," in *Spirits of Globalization: The Growth of Pentecostalism and Experiential Spiritualities in a Global Age*, ed. Sturla J. Stålsett (London: SCM Press, 2006), 196.

restore the Spirit-given dignity of each person and group so that all will be empowered "to speak in their own tongues."

The beauty of the Pentecost event is that all use their own language, but they understand each other. "The unity of the church does not come from a common origin or language, but from the Spirit of Pentecost" (EMCC 103). Speech and communication enhance the Spirit's gifts of difference. Breathing with the Spirit (*conspiratio*) in honest relationship, people can speak freely in their cultural ways, express their pains and joys in their own terms, and even talk back to argue or resist. *Koinonia* (fellowship or communion) is less of an end as much as a practice of joint partnership of the believers with the Spirit, in making their community an experience of God's *Kin*-dom of inclusive wholeness. Partnership connotes engagement and distance, whereby believers are given spaces to be themselves and still discover their affinities. In a positive sense, there is truth in the observation that the intercultural community is "filled with new wine" from the Spirit (Acts 2:13).

Another motif for the intercultural church is the pilgrim people of God. The community of the Pentecost is a church *in via*—a people "on the way." This image runs through the New Testament writings under the theme of following Jesus. Discipleship is travelling with Jesus as a community of faith through the way of the cross. The communities of disciples of the Risen Jesus are known as "the Way" (Acts 9:2; 19:9, 23; 22:4; 24:14, 22). The image implies a church that has to go through a process of discovery. "We are left with an openness to change, a willingness always to weigh the possibility that change is one of the progressive discoveries of our life as a church."[35]

The biblical praxis of "the Way" is connected to the image of pilgrimage.[36] The intercultural community is always on the move, not only the migrants but all who belong to that community are, even figuratively, voyagers in life and faith. In a liminal experience, pilgrims go beyond customary norms to try out new ways of thinking and doing. Pilgrimage suggests renewal and regeneration. To be a pilgrim church is to be a transforming church. The followers of Christ go through the process of purification and reform, for in migration there are daily realities of both grace and sin.

Furthermore, there is a sense of egalitarianism in the intercultural church. Rich and poor, male and female, Europeans and Asians, clerical and lay—all

---

35. Robert Kysar, *Stumbling in the Light: New Testament Images for a Changing Church* (St. Louis: Chalice Press, 1999), 65.

36. On the identity of a pilgrim in medieval pilgrimages, see William T. Cavanaugh, "Migrant, Tourist, Pilgrim, Monk." *Theological Studies* 69 (2008): 340–56.

are under the spell of the Spirit of God who directs the pilgrimage. They bring their identities on the road for reciprocal exchange and "to strive for the truth in the perspective of correctly facing differences by dialogue and mutual acceptance" (EMCC 34). Proximity and remoteness, separation and alliance are part of the journey.

How the final goal will look like, depends on how pilgrims make their journey valuable. As the Emmaus story tells us, the two disciples "realized that they are no longer distant foreigners to their own experience. They became aware of their self identity, their status, and this motivates them to begin a new life and change direction (toward Jerusalem)."[37] The destination takes significance not by itself but through the meanings that people have discerned with the "Stranger" in a process of moving beyond their old selves into transformed persons. The vision of Revelation 7:1–12 (cf. Rev 21:22–27) does not negate cultural identities for the sake of unity, but rather, God will be glorified and honored to be in the company of a multiplicity of cultures and other identities.

The Trinity is the third and central motif for the intercultural church. At the heart of the Christian doctrine is the mystery of the one God characterized by relationality, equality in diversity, and creativity.[38] The Trinity speaks of a God who freely initiates friendship, life and love. In the language of the creed, God emerges entirely as a God-in-relation. In the community of friendship, the triune God is animated by mutual partnership and commitment.

The discourse of Father, Son, and Spirit is not a hierarchy of persons. There is no first, second, and third places in the Trinity, and there is no higher, middle, and lower states. Rather, while referring to distinct individualities, the Father, the Son, and the Spirit are at the same time equal, because they all share the same *ousia* or substance. God is one who is both similar and different.

In this diversity, God's gracious love is abundant to flow in the creation of the universe and that same love continually overflows to produce goodness in every creature. This means that all things and persons of whatever identity are potentially or in fact actual bearers of the Trinitarian love.

---

37. Giovanni Zevola, "'What are you Talking About to Each Other, as you Walk Along' (Luke 24:17): Migration in the Bible and Our Journey of Faith," in *Faith on the Move*, 116.

38. Agnes M. Brazal, "Cultural Rights of Migrants: A Philosophical and Theological Exploration," in *Faith on the Move*, 82–86.

For these reasons, the intercultural community welcomes the "others" as equals, with their diverse gifts, to co-create the church into the image of the Trinity. "As in the Trinity, cultural creativity and mutual fecundity is a process of dynamic communion and interdependence, mutual relations with peoples of other cultures, including that of the migrants."[39] This implies also working in the secular world to make it a reflection of the Trinitarian love. Believers are urged to politicize their love that seeks to transform social structures into effective instruments of human liberation and human solidarity.[40] The intercultural church is not for itself, but to serve the greater humanity who moans for equality and solidarity.

Finding the Church a Home in Migration

This article has attempted to draw an itinerary of the church in migration phenomenon. The question has been: what is the shape of the church in the context of diverse and different backgrounds who are struggling to find their places in one space? Four models of church are described, with their pastoral features, premises and assumptions, biblical and theological anchors. The model of intercultural church is offered as an orientation or direction to strive for. A question may still be raised: what is the shape of this church? At hindsight, the models of church have been sketched in the culinary world.

There is a food originating in Mexico, which consists of diced and chopped ingredients from several food groups, such as meat (usually tripe or pork meat), bell pepper, sometimes carrots and tomatoes, as well as, onions, garlic, chili, hominy or beans, herbs and spices. As the ingredients are mixed and slowly stewed for hours, some of their elements melt and blend with the compounds of other ingredients. The ingredients still retain their identities yet their flavors have become opulent because of their commingling with others. Carefully combined, no particular ingredient will be too strong in taste at the expense of other ingredients. The result is a flavorful dish with pleasant aroma and richly hued by the variety of colors. This dish is modestly named "menudo" (small cuts or pieces). It is served in big open bowls brought to the table steaming and fiery. Consumers attest that taking menudo for breakfast stimulates the senses, nourishes the insides, and clears the head.

---

39. Ibid., 86.

40. Anselm Kyongsuk Min, "Migration and Christian Hope: Historical and Eschatological Reflections on Migration," in *Faith on the Move*, 195.

The intercultural church will take a long process of mixing and cooking, of mutual negotiation and exchange, of navigating through betwixt-and-between and moving in-beyond. The taste of this church is yet to be savored, but it is an exciting opportunity to "cook" something new in the cuisine of migratory relations. It is said that because of its spices, menudo has medicinal condiments that replenish vitamins of the body, soothe the stomach, and stimulate the gastric juices to overcome any loss of appetite. This must be delightfully good for the global-wide church! Would this be a foretaste of things to come? In the dining hall, we can only hope that God the Patient Chef will be pleasantly amazed.

Emmanuel S. de Guzman and Agnes M. Brazal

7

BRIDGE OF SOLIDARITY
Ministries in an Intercultural Church

Building on the concepts of an "in-between space" or "third space," one way of imagining an intercultural church—employing a more popular image—is as bridge of solidarity.[1] Having drafted the key concepts and ecclesiological foundations of the intercultural church, this essay posits that the church understood as bridge of solidarity offers signposts to guide pastoral ministries and ministers in the migrant context.

BRIDGE AS IN-BETWEEN SPACE

Bridges are "in-between spaces" which allow us to cross a divide. In everyday life, a bridge is a physical structure built over a river or land that allows people or vehicles to cross from one side to another. It serves as a connecting route between two geographical points or adjacent elements in order to reduce differences of time, distance, or human contexts. Bridges are made for the benefit of people who are traveling from one place to another. On a bridge, there is free flow of movement of objects and human bodies.

In a symbolic way, bridges offer people a means to cross geographical, social, economic, political, cultural and religious boundaries. Bridges can

---

1. Emmanuel S. de Guzman, "The Laity in the Ministry to the Migrants,"Exodus Series 6: A Resource Guide for the Migrant Ministry in Asia, ed. Fabio Baggio (Quezon City: Scalabrini Migration-Center, 2005), 25. This essay is also partly based on Agnes M. Brazal, "Toward an Intercultural Church: Pastoral Implications in the Migration Context," a paper presented at the Omnes Gentes Conference on "Migration: Challenges of the Spirit," October 18–20, 2008, Katholieke Universiteit Leuven, Belgium.

provide a space to talk about differences and to be renewed in our perceptions of the other. In human relationships, the bridge is the person or group who acts as a go-between. When Filipinos, for example, want to communicate with one another, especially between people of different status, they sometimes use a third party who is familiar to the concerned parties. This bridge serves many functions, such as conveying messages, negotiating, facilitating, trouble-shooting, and even settling disputes and reconciling. A go-between is approached not only because of his or her competence to do things, but because he or she possesses appealing and trustworthy qualities which make others to choose him or her as go-between in the first place. Foremost in the desired qualities of an effective go-between are a gracious personality and the ability to persuade in order to influence the course of actions that benefit all parties. Bridges therefore function both as site and as means or medium for social groups separated by a divide to meet or for cultural discourses to be mutually enriched.

Principle of Solidarity

Solidarity, on the other hand, describes—using a theological principle—the nature of the interaction in an intercultural church. Konrad Raiser, former General Secretary of the World Council of Churches, raises the radical demand nowadays to expand our understanding of *oikoumene* to a vision of an "*earth community*, i.e., the sustainable interaction of all life processes." In this context, "solidarity emphasizes the mutual dependency which characterizes the intricate web of life …. Solidarity therefore is more than a moral imperative: it points to that basic feature of mutuality of all human cultures."[2]

In the same line, John Paul II underlines that solidarity is a response to the fact of "radical interdependence" (*Sollicitudo Rei Socialis* 38; henceforth SRS). When applied to the migration context, solidarity refers to a firm commitment to the common good of all individuals and ethnic groups.[3]

---

2. Raiser, Konrad. "Opening Space for a Culture of Dialogue and Solidarity: The Missionary Objectives of the WCC in an Age of Globalization and Religious Plurality," *Sedos Bulletin*, 31, nos. 6–7, (1999): 175.

3. It is important to underline the "freedom" involved in the act of solidarity. In one meeting of the Federation of Asian Bishops' Conference, representatives from Myanmar expressed that they do not like the term "solidarity" because it has always been used by the government to require its people to sacrifice for the sake of the nation. The statement of John Paul II in *Sollicitudo Rei Socialis* (SRS) linking solidarity and freedom in the context of development is thus significant: "In order to be genuine, development must be achieved within the framework of solidarity and freedom, without ever sacrificing either of them under whatever pretext." (SRS 33.8)

Solidarity transforms interpersonal relationships and the relationships between cultural groups and nation-states. It helps us see the other (persons, peoples or nations) not simply as a factor of production that can easily be "discarded when no longer useful, but as our neighbor, a "helper" (see Gn 2:18–20), to be made a sharer, on a par with ourselves, in the banquet of life to which all are equally invited by God." (SRS 39.5) Solidarity allows for the overcoming of distrust and feeling that the others are a "threat" to one's cultural identity and helps us move toward collaboration with them (SRS 39.8) because of our mutual interest. Donal Dorr further adds that solidarity is not just about the strict fulfillment of justice but goes beyond this because it involves as well generosity, care for others, warm friendliness – the practice of the virtues which favor togetherness, and which teach us to live in unity" (SRS 39.10) The experience of solidarity, that is, immersion and actual sharing of life with the other, is important in developing the bonds of affection that link peoples.[4]

Solidarity finds its ultimate inspiration from our being images of the Triune God (SRS 40.3), "the primordial Solidarity of divine Others"[5] which is also the model of a community where equality, difference, mutuality, fecundity and unity are simultaneously recognized and affirmed.[6]

BRIDGE OF SOLIDARITY

The intercultural church as bridge of solidarity facilitates the meeting and alliances of different cultural groups for the common good. In practice, very seldom do we have citizens of host communities mixing with the communities of migrants outside labor relations. Migrants are viewed primarily and simply as a labor force, albeit, a cheap source of labor. In the spirit of true catholicity, the churches in the host countries must promote intercultural encounters beyond the sphere of labor relations. A genuine intercultural exchange can only happen when the receiving communities would be able to look at the migrant not only as a work force, but as human persons or as

---

4. Donal Dorr, "Solidarity and Integral Human Development," in *The Logic of Solidarity: Commentaries on Pope John Paul II's Encyclical 'On Social Concern'*, ed. Gregory Baum and Robert Ellsberg (Maryknoll, New York: Orbis, 1989), 152.

5. Anselm Kyongsuk Min, *The Solidarity of Others in a Divided World: A Postmodern Theology after Postmodernism* (New York: T&T Clark International, 2004).

6. See the discussion on the Trinity in relation to cultural rights in Agnes M. Brazal, "Cultural Rights: A Theological-Pastoral Perspective," in *Faith on the Move: Toward a Theology of Migration in Asia*, ed. Fabio Baggio and Agnes M. Brazal (Quezon City: Ateneo de Manila University Press, 2008), 81–86.

guests, which in ancient times, are believed to be bringing with them gifts or are even mediators of God's self. "An ethic of migration calls for an authentic conversion to the other at the very depth of our societies."[7]

At hindsight, one may interpret Paul's disgust over what happened with the Christian community at Corinth as a rupture in the mission of the church to become Christ's bridge of solidarity (1 Cor. 11:17–34). For Paul, sharing in the same cup, sharing in the same bread means the end of all discrimination between Jew or Greek, man or woman, slave or free in the sphere of mediated real presence. He accuses the Corinthians of "drinking judgment" in their Eucharist, not because they profane the sacral converse of God. On the contrary, Paul is critical of his co-Christians because they have violated the secular, human significance of the meal as a piece of brotherly and sisterly sharing. In a community that declares itself as transcending ethnic and social boundaries, believers with higher status and wealth humiliate the poor. Paul argues that "fellowship" is the concrete form which prevents, and will prevent thanksgiving and praise of God from being lip service. The community is challenged to correct factionalism, expand its small-group boundaries, and share their resources as one "body of Christ."

The Church as bridge of solidarity can function both as the site, as well as, the medium through which conversations can take place. An intercultural church acts as a bridge to link not only the nationals with the different groups of Christian migrants but also provides a space to relate or interact with immigrants from other confessions, faiths or religions.[8] It helps develops affective bonds between members of these groups. An intercultural church is also a site where new identities can be formed; where both the national Christians and the immigrants can forge an in-beyond identity as church.

Incidentally, the English term "Pontiff" which in Christianity technically refers to a "bishop" (and not just the Pope) came from the Latin *pontifex* which is derived from the Latin root word *pons* (bridge) and *facere* (to do, to make). It thus literally means bridge-builder. The pontiff (bishop) and priests sharing in their ministry, together with the laity, are called to be builders of bridges of solidarity in today's world.

---

7. Denis Müller, "A Homeland for Transients: Towards an Ethic of Migrations," *Concilium* (1993/4): 131.

8. Unintentionally perhaps, neo-Pentecostal migrant churches in Germany served as "bridge," between the *Bund freikirchlicher Pfingstgemeinden* (BFP, the alliance of free Pentecostal churches in Germany) of which they are members, and the mainline Protestants in whose buildings they conduct their services. Werner Kahl, "Encounters with Migrant Churches,": Models for Growing Together," *The Ecumenical Review* 61, no. 4 (December 2009): 400–12.

The Church as bridge of solidarity promotes reflexivity and the transformation of habitus of both migrants and nationals through consciousness-raising and discernment. An intercultural perspective asks: what new vision of life and ethics, theologies, religious practices, can come about in the encounter between two or more cultures? What values can be learned and appropriated from the other community and vice-versa? On the other hand, what disvalues should be rejected? What religious traditions and practices do we maintain, modify and abandon?

The Church as bridge of solidarity eschews the rigid separation of communities or churches but rather, promotes a genuine sense of belongingness in a church composed of diverse individuals and communities. In terms of pastoral structures, *Erga Migrantes Caritas Christi* (The Love of Christ towards Migrants) published by the Pontifical Council for the Pastoral Care of Migrants and Itinerant People,[9] envisions two possible types of pastoral structures (EMCC 93), in the line of the interculturality which we envision.[10] First is an interethnic or inter-ritual parish where the parish is the site of pastoral assistance and intercultural encounters of both local and migrant groups, while individual groups maintain a certain autonomy. This may be the case where there is a sizeable immigrant community of a certain ethny or ritual, and newcomers are likely to come in the future. The second type of pastoral structure is the parish providing service to the local population, as well as, one or more migrant groups of the same ethny or rite. The parish serves as the meeting point of these migrant communities, with their chaplains forming part of the parish team. The integration of migrants into the parish can be seen in their incorporation into the parish structures and leadership in other gospel-inspired associations for migrants (EMCC 13).

The above structures are different from national parishes which were set up in the United States from 1833 to 1915.[11] While these helped preserve the vitality of the faith of the immigrants, they are difficult to restructure in the face of the succeeding generations' changing cultural identification. Eventually, children of the immigrants themselves left the national parishes

---

9. Pontifical Council for the Pastoral Care of Migrants and Itinerant People, *ErgaMigrantes Caritas Christi: The Love of Christ Towards Migrants* (Vatican City: 2004); henceforth to be referred to as EMCC or *Erga Migrantes*.

10. This is not to say that the EMCC's vision is totally for an intercultural church.

11. Silvano M. Tomasi, cs, "The Response of the Catholic Church in the United States to Immigrants and Refugees," in *People on the Move: A Compendium of Church Documents on the Pastoral Concern for Migrants and Refugees* (Bishops' Committee on Priestly Formation, Bishops' Committee on Migration and National Conference of Catholic Bishops, 1988), 105.

to join English-speaking or suburban inter-ethnic parishes.[12] Or young people today simply go to the nearest church without caring for its national background. In one German parish, as Andrew Greely recounted, one-fourth of the membership were Irish and one-fourth Polish. Also, where residences had been replaced by highways and industries a number of national parishes in the inner city have virtually become ghost parishes.[13] The pastoral structure of an intercultural church must thus be more flexible than national parishes to the fast pace of social changes and changing cultural identifications of immigrant settlers.

Pastoral Ministries in an Intercultural Church

As bridge of solidarity, Christian communities can escort the migrants to their hospitable places in a variety of ways. Ministry, as Thomas O'Meara recalls, originally was a "verb" before it became a "noun."[14] This means that "ministry" is doing something in public spaces, not as a display of power and prestige, but as service for the sake of the reign of God, especially to the least, the last, and the lost. What kind of "verbs" or eloquent deeds and type of ministers are needed in an intercultural church?

Ministry of Welcome

As bridge of solidarity, an intercultural church can provide a welcoming space for transit migrants, foreign workers and immigrants. In ministries of welcome, a migrant is accepted into a church of mutually influencing cultures and not in just one local culture. The local residents and ministers also are not in their "own" church but in an intercultural space. Correspondingly, the physical setting, the language, gestures, symbols, and leadership are all intercultural, and the gospel is also interpreted through the lens of intercultural experience.

The category of "host and guest" is meaningless in this model. What would be significant are the acts of "hosting and guesting" which are required of all in God's home. Hospitality is creating a free, friendly, and engaging space where the partnership of strangers can develop in a dynamic relationship of making each other find a home and be at home. The intercultural

---

12. Ibid.

13. Andrew Greeley, *The Church, The National Parish and Immigration: Same Old Mistakes* (New York: Center for Migration Studies, 1972), 1–8.

14. Thomas Franklin O'Meara, *Theology of Ministry* (Mahwah, NJ: Paulist Press, 1983).

community is God's graced shelter for friendship and fellowship in a "home away from home."

First welcome can include the provision of assistance to newly arrived migrants and refugees in the form of transit dormitories, canteens, medical/legal/emergency assistance offices, etc. La Casa del Migrante in Tijuana which is located a few miles from the US border offers hospitality to deported male migrants up to a maximum of twelve days every six months regardless of nationality and religion. Ship visitation and opportunities for sound socialization and entertainment can also be provided to seafarers (sea-based migrants) at the port, as what the Apostleship of the Sea,[15] Stella Maris centers, and other Christian maritime organizations are doing.

Initial welcome has to be complemented by efforts toward the gradual integration of im(migrants). Integration in an intercultural church is not a movement from the im(migrant)'s culture to the local culture but rather, a movement toward an in-beyond identity. It is a process of mutual fecundation, which thus changes the face of the Church of arrival itself, following *Erga Migrantes* which underlines that an authentic culture of welcome is receptive to learning from the truly human values of immigrants (EMCC 39). The various ministries we shall discuss below elaborate ways toward this integration that respects and learns from difference.

Ministry of Worship

The celebration of the eucharist oftentimes functions as a central event that gathers Christian immigrants in fellowship. The importance of religion for migrants was affirmed by a study in the United States and Europe that show that migrants tend to be more religious than local non-migrants because this

---

15. Savino Bernardi, "The Pastoral Care of Seafarers," *Exodus Series 8*, 14.

helps them deal with the transition to a new life in a foreign land.[16] Liturgical services in their own language can help keep the faith of the im(migrants) alive as they try to adjust in their new environment.[17] The Church functions as a bridge of solidarity by enabling the immigrants to celebrate their liturgies in their own rite (EMCC 56), language (EMCC 38), and cultural style.[18]

For example, compared to the Japanese liturgies, Brazilian and Filipinos liturgies employ more festive music. Considering the presence of Japanese-Filipino or Brazilian-Filipino families, the preparation of multicultural liturgies can be a rich occasion for an intercultural exchange on symbols and worshipping styles. Felipe Muncada, a Filipino missionary who works with migrants in Japan notes the presence of encouraging initiatives to integrate

---

16. An extensive study comparing the religiosity of first generation immigrants in Europe and the US with the local population in the host country, reveals a significantly higher first-generation immigrants in Europe who are more religious in terms of participation in religious services, as well as, personal prayer. In the US, first-generation immigrants also attend church religious services more than the locals, but do not necessarily engage more in personal prayer. The authors explain the difference between the immigrants in Europe and the US in terms of the function of religion for them. In Europe, it seems religion functions more as a "buffer," a "shock absorber," and a source of comfort for those who are discriminated because of their religion or face harsh social conditions. This is indicated in their higher engagement in personal prayer, more than participation in religious services. But the practice of personal prayer decreases with second generation immigrants who are by this time more integrated in Europe. In the US, religion functions more as a "bridge" facilitating the integration of the migrant through church religious services which are also sites for social support and connections not only within the host country but also the country of origin. Teresa Garcia-Muñoz and ShoshanaNeuman, "Is Religiosity of Immigrants a Bridge or a Bufferin the Process of Integration? A ComparativeStudy of Europe and the United States," IZA DP No. 6384, February 2012, http://ftp.iza.org/dp6384.pdf (accessed July 2012).

17. The St. Joseph Parish in Spring Valley, N.Y., for instance, is a Catholic church which celebrates mass in English and four other languages. Natalie Gott, "Welcoming Immigrants," http://www.faithandleadership.com/features/articles/welcoming-immigrants (accessed July 2012).

18. Edwin Corros, cs, executive secretary of the Philippines Episcopal Commission for Migrants and Itinerant People, relates both stories of exclusion and inclusion when he was still assigned in Taiwan. He notes how some Filipino migrants in Taiwan had to struggle to find a "place" for their liturgical celebrations. In one church, they were initially allowed to gather for worship in the main church. The community immediately grew larger and attracted the attention of police authorities. The police authorities visited several times the parish priest's office, expressing the suspicion that undocumented migrants were among the parishioners frequenting the migrant masses. Without any process of consultation, the parish pastoral council finally decided not to allow anymore the Philippine migrants to celebrate liturgies in the parish.

Corros describes his former parish in Taiwan, St. Christopher, as an example of a church that is striving to be intercultural and welcoming of various groups of migrants that need a place of worship. Initially, St. Christopher parish was composed simply of Taiwanese nationals celebrating Chinese liturgies. When Philippine migrants arrived, the parish started offering a Philippine mass in English. Later on, when Indonesian migrants came, they also organized liturgies in their language and cultural style. All these groups are now integrated and represented in the parish pastoral council.

Hispanic /Filipino /Portuguese mass liturgies with the Japanese liturgy. Different languages are used for the songs and readings.[19]

But simply having different groups perform in their respective cultural ways during a Eucharistic celebration makes the church multicultural and intracultural, but not necessarily intercultural. Interculturation happens when a Sri Lankan migrant in Korea offers a prayer in Vietnamese language or for the Vietnamese people, a Chinese choir of migrants in Japan sings a Malaysian hymn, and an Australian priest reads the gospel in different linguistic versions and renders a homily that is intelligible to a variety of cultural worldviews. The ambience is dramatically festive or contemplatively serene as the calming spirit of the religious traditions of Asia. All this sounds impractical to do but it is actually happening already in some places.

Popular religious festivals and devotional practices have places too in the intercultural church. They bring back a sense of homeland and open the doors to new horizons. In religious performances ordinary believers find the space to touch and be touched by God's goodness and solidarity. Accordingly, such acts subvert the world in which God and God-talk have become possessions of educated elite. Popular devotions are resourceful ways of migrants to navigate through harsh realities of life, and these can be forms of refusal to go along with totalizing systems of thought and speech in migratory relations. Jacqueline Hagan studied how 202 undocumented Catholic migrants from Mexico and the rest of Central America, who are preparing to cross the US border, draw from their religious resources to get strength for the journey.[20] The Catholics, in particular, would seek guidance from the Virgin Mary and other popular saints in the home communities. Most called upon among the Mexicans is the Virgin of Guadalupe. Amira Ahmed's research also reveals how both Christian and Moslem domestic workers in Egypt visit shrines, saints and holy figures to seek for protection and especially in times of crisis and desperation.[21]

---

19. He laments, however, that the popularization of such initiatives are greatly hindered by the lack of priests and open-minded clergy. Felipe Muncada, svd, "Japan and Philippines: Migration Turning Points," in *Faith on the Move: Toward a Theology of Migration in Asia*, ed. Fabio Baggio, cs and Agnes M. Brazal (Quezon City, Philippines: Ateneo de Manila University Press, 2008), 44.

20. "Faith for the Journey: Religion as a Resource for Migrants," in *A Promised Land, A Perilous Journey: Theological Perspectives on Migration*, ed. Daniel G. Groody and GioacchinoCampese (Notre Dame, Indiana: University of Notre Dame, 2008), 8.

21. Amira Ahmed, "'I Need Work': The Multiple Roles of the Church, Ranking and Religious Piety among Domestic Workers in Egypt," *The Asia Pacific Journal of Anthropology*, 11, nos. 3–4 (September–December 2010): 373–74.

The intercultural church ensures that God's Spirit is never possessed but flows freely in productive encounters between people. *Erga Migrantes* underlines the need for "in-depth work of evangelisation and of enabling the local Catholic community to know and appreciate certain forms of devotion of migrants and thus to understand them. From this union of spirit a more participated liturgy can also develop, one that is better integrated and spiritually richer." (EMCC 46)

Popular devotion is to the Catholics as Pentecostalism is to the Protestants (though we also recognize the growth of charismatic communities among Catholics).[22] For many migrants from the impoverished countryside going to the megacities whether in their own country or outside, Pentecostal groups provide communities to displaced peoples, where they can reconstitute their lives. Uprooted from the familiar environment where they grew up, they find in the Pentecostal groups the same belief in the spirits, miracles, camaraderie similar to what their compadres and comadres have provided in their village, the same fiesta atmosphere in the dancing and singing in the prayer sessions. The pastor, in turn, functions as the surrogate patron. By these various means, Pentecostal groups, "enables millions of people to cope with the jarring world of modernity without completely severing their ties to traditional culture."[23]

Valuable as they are, religious expressions contain also conservative, pietistic, dualistic spiritualism, and patriarchal-hierarchical values and assumptions. These will have to be revised in favor of values and styles that interculturality promotes, such as openness to changes and new perspectives, equality and mutual respect of genders[24] and other identities, holistic approach to spirituality, ethic of participation, and involvement in social concerns. By

---

22. Jean-Pierre Bastian, a Mexican religious historian, refers to the Pentecostals as "Catholics without priests." Harvey Cox, "Spirits of Globalization: Pentecostalism and Experiential Spiritualities in a Global Era," in *Spirits of Globalization: the Growth of Pentecostalism and Experiential Spiritualities in a Global Age*, ed. Sturla J. Stålsett (London: SCM Press, 2006), 19.

23. Ibid., 21. See also Caroline Jeannerat's analysis of Nigerian migrants' attraction to Pentecostalism in South Africa, "Of Lizards, Misfortune and Deliverance: Pentecostal Soteriology in the Life of a Migrant," *African Studies* 68, no. 2 (August 2009): 251–71; Rosalina Mira and Lois Ann Lorentzen, "Women, Migration, and the Pentecostal Experience," *Peace Review* 14, no. 4 (2002): 421–25.

24. The United Church of Canada which is striving to become intercultural had to discern about the "non-negotiables" in accepting migrant ethnic churches as members, when a Congolese leader of a congregation that had just joined the United Church delivered a sermon against gays and lesbians. This resulted in three-quarters of the Montreal Presbytery audience to walk out. This African congregation eventually left the United Church over a disagreement regarding same sex marriage. Many leaders would hold that among the non-negotiables is the inclusion of women, gays and lesbians in church leadership. Samantha Rideout, "Feature: Global Flair," http://www.ucobserver.org/faith/2010/10/global_flair/ (accessed March 2012).

integrating these into the religious practices, migrants can fashion new forms of Christian worship.

Ministry of Table Fellowships and Story Telling

Amidst the loneliness, worries and anxieties of migrants and their families, the church as a bridge of solidarity creates spaces for storytelling, as well as, maximizes the potential of table fellowships to be an occasion for interaction and developing friendships.

Shared Meals

Shared meals or the "ministry of food and piñatas"[25] oftentimes follow migrants' Eucharistic celebrations. When held in the parish premises, it can be an occasion for fellowship not only among the migrants themselves but also with the nationals. In many cases however, these table fellowships are hosted in migrants' homes, the plazas or even in public corridors where migrants congregate. These table fellowships are opportunities to listen to the migrants' stories, develop friendships, as well as, expand our "taste" via a sharing of food. Taste, as Pierre Bourdieu notes, is an embodied disposition (part of the cultural unconscious). Sharing a meal and partaking of the food of another cultural group symbolizes openness to the other, on a deep subconscious level. We do not normally eat with people whose company we do not like or with people who we do not consider as equal (not-one-of-us). Shared meals of migrants with nationals can thus be a "liminal" event, an experience of *communitas* that re-lives Jesus' inclusive table fellowships.

Other Spaces for Story-telling

The Church of arrival can also offer counseling services, staffed by people who speak the language of the immigrants and understand their cultural background, as well as, specializing for particular needs such as trauma[26] or intermarriage problems. Such counseling can be done in a center, via the telephone or even online.

---

25. Patrick Murphy, "The Ninety-Nine Sheep and the Mission of the Church," in *A Promised Land*, 152.

26. Robert Schreiter identifies three stages which may call for the ministry of healing among migrants: 1) the departure, especially if this was accompanied by the possible loss of life; 2) the process of arrival; 3) and the settling down. "Migrants and the Ministry of Reconciliation," in *A Promised Land*, 107–23.

When appropriate, an "*e-church*" or a cyber-church[27] can be developed for migrants to get in touch with each other, share their stories of life and faith, seek enlightenment on moral or ethical issues, or to call for urgent assistance in cases of violence.[28] The cyberspace becomes intercultural too when it gives space to those who are not heard or not listened to because they have different visions of life.[29]

A Space for Discernment

As Christians, migrants embody in varying degrees what we may refer to as a "Christian feel for the game," a Christian sense of what is good and bad, right and wrong. What we call Christian virtues are likewise embodied dispositions or good habits[30] which the Christian community views as in accord with the gospel message, and from which individual human actions arise in largely pre-reflective form. One can say Christian virtues and beliefs fuse with the other dispositions of a person arising from his/her ethnicity, gender, class etc. to constitute his/her habitus. Christian faith and practice, shaped by various habitus and fields, thus assume a plurality of expressions. Not all of these practices may be equally valid in the light of the gospel ethic. The church as bridge of solidarity provides a space for reflexivity, guidance and discernment on emerging migrant practices as they struggle to survive in their new context.

Ministry of Dialogue

The migratory phenomena of our times, have multiplied opportunities for ecumenical and inter-religious dialogue. Societies with a Catholic tradition find within their midst people from other faiths/religions while non-Chris-

---

27. From a ministry-based perspective, a cyber-church enables "worship and Christian education, evangelization and community on the World Wide Web." It may or may not be linked to a concrete local church or denomination and may not be engaged in all of the ministries mentioned. It is distinguished from the simple webpages of churches in its being interactive and thrust of forming relationships among the members. A.H. Fjeldstad, "Cyberchurches," 2000, http://www.geocities.com/ResearchTriangle/1541/cybchur.html (accessed April 2014)

28. See *Parokya sa Web* (literally Parish in the Web), the first Philippine virtual parish which aims, among others, to reach out to overseas Filipino workers. http://en.wikipilipinas.org/index.php?title=Robert_Reyes (accessed July 2012) and

29. See for example the Diocese of Partenia, http://www.partenia.org/english/histoire_eng.htm.

30. Bourdieu opted not to use the term "habit" because of its mechanical, repetitive connotations as opposed to the innovative character of habitus. Bourdieu, *Outline of a Theory of Practice*, trans. Richard Nice (Cambridge, Mass.: Cambridge University, 1977; reprint ed. 1998),218 n. 47.

tian societies are increasingly receiving Christian migrants. To what extent are migrants allowed to practice their faiths/religions in these societies? To what extent does prejudice get in the way? The Church as bridge of solidarity can be a space for crossing or healing divides and establishing cultures of solidarity between migrants of different faiths.

Ecumenical Ministry

The Catholic Church in the spirit of ecumenism, states in the document *Erga Migrantes* (EMCC) that "[i]f priests, ministers or communities not in full communion with the Catholic Church do not have a place or the liturgical objects needed for celebrating worthily their religious ceremonies, the diocesan Bishop may allow them to use a church or a Catholic building and also lend them whatever may be necessary for their services (EMCC 56)." When it is not possible for them to celebrate their own rite, they can join the Catholics and partake as well of the Holy Communion.

The World Council of Churches, on its part, stressed the need to work together with the Catholic Church, the World Evangelical Alliance (WEA), Pentecostals and other church world communions in dialogue with migrant churches.[31] They formed the Global Ecumenical Network on Migration (GEM) in 2005 to strengthen inter-faith dialogue and advocacies in solidarity with migrants. Among its projects was to gather the migrant churches in the Gulf region to coordinate their diaconal work for migrants, push forward church–government dialogue and cooperation on the level of local communities, evaluate the situation of contract workers in the Gulf and link the churches in the host with those in the sending country. The World Communion of Reformed Churches[32] has likewise adopted an intercultural thrust, building bridges between ethnic migrant churches and the global ecumenical movement, as well as, with the churches in Switzerland.[33]

---

31. "Report of the World Council of Churches (WCC) Consultation on Mission and Ecclesiology of the Migrant Churches," (2010) *International Review of Mission* 100, no. 1 (April 2011): 104–111.

32. The World Communion of Reformed Churches was born in 2010 when the World Alliance of Reformed Churches (WARC) and the Reformed Ecumenical Council (REC) merged to encompass 230 member churches in 108 countries. These churches are Congregational, Presbyterian, Reformed and United Churches rooted in the 16th-century Reformation led by John Calvin, John Knox, etc.

33. For example in Geneva where there exist 70 ethnic migrant churches which have minimal contact with the global ecumenical movement, efforts to link them have been made through a conference sponsored by the WCC and "Witnessing Together in Geneva," a John Knox International Reformed Centre program. "Witnessing Together in Geneva" also aims to build bridges between the immigrant churches and the churches in Switzerland World Communion of Reformed churches, file:///F:/assissi%202012%20files/World%20Reformed%20Council%20of%20Churches.htm (accessed August 2012).

Inter-religious Dialogue

In the West, inter-religious dialogue has been identified mainly with formal dialogues on the doctrinal level. In Asia, inter-religious dialogue happens both on the formal and informal level. A most basic approach is the dialogue of life where believers from various faiths (especially those living near each other) interact in daily life. Batumalai Sadayandi calls this good neighborology.[34] The dialogue occurs in the context of daily life—in the supermarket, the factory, the hospital, the office—through cordial relations.[35] More organized multi-faith communities can also engage in collaborative projects.

When the need arises, *Erga Migrantes* states that non-Christian immigrants may be allowed to use spaces for social activities in the parish. The activities held therein, can be an opportunity to know each other's faith,[36] as well as, a chance to identify and tap cultural mediators in both sides, who can bridge cultural and religious blocks to promote mutual understanding (EMCC 61). The World Council of Churches, in its 2009 message underlined too the need for inter-religious dialogue and an inter-religious approach in addressing migrants' issues.[37]

The All Saints Cathedral in Egypt is an example of a Church that has functioned—for both Christians and Muslim black African migrants and Sudanese refugees performing domestic work—as a space for emotional sanctuary, as trainer in practical skills and knowledge of Egyptian culture, as recruitment/employment agency which vouchsafes moral virtue, and as provider of "moral" protection.[38]

Orlando Espín notes as well that majority of the migrants come from the more marginalized sector of society, which practice popular religiosity. It is therefore reasonable to assume that with the migration of millions of men and women every year, we have the spread of popular religions. "Popular

---

34. BatumalaiSadayandi, *A Prophetic Christology for Neighbourology: A Theology for a Prophetic Living* (Kuala Lumpur: McHill Litho Center, 1986).

35. See James Kroeger's Dialogue Decalogue Guidelines for Migrants in a Multi-religious context. "Living Faith in a Strange Land: Migration and Interreligious Dialogue," in *Faith on the Move*, 219–51.

36. Chinese Regional Bishops' Conference, "On the Question of Foreign Workers," (6 February 1989) in *Caring for Migrants: A Collection of Church Documents on the Pastoral Care of Migrants* (Strathfield: St. Paul's, 2009), no. 6.

37. Carla Khijoyan, Message of the World Council of Churches, *People on the Move*, no.111, December 2009, file:///F:/assissi%202012%20files/WCC%20Message%20on%20Migration%20and%20Dialogue.htm.

38. Amira Ahmed, "'I Need Work!' The Multiple Roles of the Church, Ranking and Religious Piety among Domestic Workers in Egypt," *The Asia Pacific Journal of Anthropology* 11, nos. 3–4 (September–December 2010): 362–77.

religions are engaged in what could be described as an inter-religious and intercultural dialogue of unprecedented and unforeseen consequences for the religious future of humankind."[39] While much of such exchanges happen on the pre-reflective level and may lead to syncretism, inter-religious dialogues can also be undertaken more reflexively, in order to foster respect for the other religion, as well as, be challenged or enriched by their perspective.

John Paul II emphasized: "If there is a common will to dialogue in spite of being different, it is possible to find a ground of profitable exchange and develop a beneficial and mutual friendship that can also be translated into an effective collaboration towards common objectives in the service of common good."[40] The Interfaith Immigration Coalition is an example of an alliance of various faith-based groups (Protestant, Catholic, Jewish, Islamic, etc.) advocating fair and humane immigration reform in the US.[41]

To facilitate dialogue and harmonious relations with peoples of other faiths, Christian educational institutions should promote in their curriculum mutual understanding of different religions by offering courses for instance about the Islamic faith. They can likewise organize activities for students to have interactions with migrants of other faiths, either in the school, or facilitate inter-cultural immersions for the youth (for example, a Moslem immigrant can live with a Christian immigrant or national for a weekend or a week).

Ministry of Teaching

Formation of Religious Educators

Erga Migrantes also underlines that "[e]piscopal Conferences will likewise entrust to Catholic university faculties in their territories the task of studying

---

39. Orlando O. Espín, "Migration and Human Condition: Theological Considerations on Religious Identities and Unexpected Inter-religious Dialogues," in *Migration and Interculturality: Theological and Philosophical Challenges*, ed. Raúl Fornet-Betancourt (Aachen: MWI, 2004), 183. In his book, *The Faith of the People: Theological Reflection on Popular Catholicism*, Espín speaks of two Afro-Latino religions (Santería and Palo) practiced by the Latino communities in Florida and the Northeast and also some parts of the Midwest and Southern California. These have appropriated symbols of colonial Antillean Catholicism but are more a syncretism of Yoruba, Fon and Kongo African religions which came to the Spanish Antilles during the slave trade. (Maryknoll, New York: Orbis, 1977), 113–14.

40. "Migration and Inter-Religious Dialogue," Message for the 88th World Day of Migration, 2002, http://www.vatican.va/holy_father/john_paul_ii/messages/migration/docume nts/hf_jp-ii_mes_20011018_world-migration-day-2002_en.html (accessed 2006).

41. See Interfaith Immigration Coalition website, http://www.interfaithimmigration.org/ (accessed July 2012).

the various aspects of migration more thoroughly for the benefit of concrete pastoral service for migrants (EMCC 71)." Priests, seminarians and other religious educators must be educated about migration to ensure a quality in the Church's response.[42] Such formation must possess a "global dimension," that is, fostering a vision of a new international economic order where the goods of the earth, from the standpoint of the universal common good, are seen as destined for all (EMCC 8). Ongoing programs or curricula can integrate topics about migration, as well as, information on the language and culture of migrants (EMCC 77), particularly of those groups predominant in one's area.

The Scalabrini International Migration Institute (SIMI) in collaboration with the faculty of theology of the Pontifical Urbanian University in Rome offers a graduate diploma in pastoral care of human mobility.[43] The Scalabrini Migration Center and the Episcopal Commission on Migrants and Itinerant people in the Philippines, has also started in 2007 a Migration Theology program for theological schools. The target students are priests and religious educators in the Philippines and other parts of Asia, who are currently engaged or preparing themselves for a ministry to the migrants/families left-behind. Theological schools and institutes, like St. Vincent School of Theology and Loyola School of Theology, both in the Philippines, have developed their curricula to integrate the experiences of migrants into the formation of future of ministers. Loyola School of Theology offers a diploma and the following degrees in migration theology—Licentiate in Sacred Theology (STL) and Bachelor of Sacred Theology (STB). A Bachelor of Arts (BA) in Intercultural Theology, Migration and Congregational Leadership is also offered at The University of Applied Sciences for Intercultural Theology in close cooperation with the Evangelical Lutheran Mission in Lower Saxony (ELM).[44]

Gradually, the contributions or traditions of other ethnic groups should also be interwoven in the content of various subjects that are taught in school. For instance, with regard Pentecostalism in Canada, Néstor Medina critiques how the Pentecostal story the students receive do not reflect the ethno cultural diversity of Pentecostals now in the country. As of 2001, there were already 120 congregations representing ethno cultural groups from Asia, Africa, and North (Mexico) Central and South America. He notes:

---

42. Cardinal Stephen Fumio Hamao, Message at the Inauguration of the Catholic National Commission for the Pastoral Care of Migration and Tourism in Colombo, Sri Lanka (7 March 2003).

43. http://diplomasimi.org/index.php?cal_m=2&cal_y=2013 (accessed July 2012).

44. http://www.eurodiaconia.org/files/Partners/ITMG_120716_4_englisch_screen.pdf (accessed July 2012).

While the plurality of cultural groups is celebrated, their contributions are kept at arm's length. Their theology is undermined, and their leadership skills are reserved for their own ethno cultural group .... The Pentecostal story students receive is ethno culturally homogeneous and US centered; students of different ethno cultural backgrounds do not find their side of the story in the dominant narratives. While theological literature from these communities may be used, the general methodological framing of theology taught is Eurocentric and preserves the European Enlightenment supremacy of reason. Other sources of knowledge are dismissed as unimportant or secondary. For example, Frank Macchia emphasizes orality as a central aspect of Pentecostal culture, but he points out that the supremacy of reason remains the standard in our Bible colleges. Similarly, the various ways in which the Bible text is approached by different ethno cultural communities is dismissed at best, and silenced at worst.[45]

Formation of the Public

The Church can likewise help raise the bigger public's awareness of migration issues and "the need to oppose baseless suspicions and offensive prejudices against foreigners (EMCC 41)" through the commemoration of National Migrants Sunday.[46] For example, in the 2005 celebration in Taiwan, the occasion focused on the migrants' contribution to Taiwan. For churches which do not have a National Migrants Sunday, they can instead celebrate an International Day that will encourage cooperation between the local community and foreigners. Other occasions for consciousness raising about migrant issues are the International Migrant's Day (18 December) or World Refugee Day (20 June).

Enhancement of Language Skills

Language is an important factor for integration. It is difficult for immigrant parents to get more involved in their children's activities if they do not know the language of the receiving country. It can mean missing out on important school announcements. They also need some basic skills to be able to read, understand and sign official papers. Where the government has failed to facilitate the language training of migrants, the Church or other Christian associations can help provide this much needed formation to facilitate

---

45. Néstor Medina, "Discerning the Spirit in Culture: Toward Pentecostal Interculturality," *Canadian Journal of Pentecostal-Charismatic Christianity* 2 (2011):137–38.
46. It is held in the first Sunday of Lent in the Philippines and last Sunday of September in Taiwan.

their integration into the receiving society and the process of intercultural exchange.[47]

Ministry of Advocacy and Networking

Because of the immense structural and global forces at work in migration, interculturality is attentive to these macro forces that influence the relationships between people. The intercultural way makes possible a reflexive process of vigilance and critique of exploitative relationships.

Advocacy aims at transforming the field of power relations so people are given a voice in the decisions and actions that affect them. This ministry can work to help migrants gain equal access to or recognition of their economic, social and cultural capital, which is necessary if the intercultural exchange will not be marked by relations of domination. This includes exposing structures of inequality in global migration and advocating for the rights of migrants, including their right to reunite with families and to redefine citizenship. Lobbying to shape legislation and policy, mass or protest actions for these causes are just some of the forms of advocacy work.[48] A key concern for advocacy is the protection and the defense of the rights of migrants and their families.

Advocacy work on social justice is indispensable to the prophetic identity of the intercultural church. The intercultural church, while fostering solidarity on the local level, maintains a global outlook by working with international networks of solidarity that advance the causes of the migrants and their families. This can help the intercultural church locate its efforts in a larger scheme of social and ecclesial transformation.

To address migration issues, the Pontifical Commission for the Pastoral care of Migrants and Itinerant People was established in in the Catholic Church in 1970 (under the Congregation of Bishops). In 1988, it became a Pontifical Council. Every five years, the council organizes a World Congress for the Pastoral Care of Migrants and Refugees.[49]

In order to promote the rights of all migrants (registered and unregistered), the Catholic Church has been actively promoting the ratification of

---

47. St. Joseph Parish in Spring Valley, N.Y., is an example of a Church which holds English classes and programs for immigrants. Natalie Gott, "Welcoming Immigrants," http://www.faithandleadership.com/features/articles/welcoming-immigrants (accessed July 2012).

48. Maruja M.B. Asis, "Advocacy and Networking on Migrants' Issues," *Exodus Series 10*, ed. Fabio Baggio (Quezon City: Scalabrini Migration Center, 2005).

49. Ibid., 7.

the UN Convention on the Rights of All Migrant Workers and Members of Their Families. Only 34 countries, all sending nations, have ratified the Migrant Workers' Convention as of October 2005.[50] The document of the World Council of Churches on "Migration and Migrant Workers: Discerning Responses as Churches (2011)," equally supports the ratification of the UN Convention on the Rights of All Migrant Workers and Members of Their Families, as well as, the UN Convention on the Rights of Domestic Workers (June 2011).[51]

The advocacy work of the church can take place on the international, national and local level. Advocacy also involves networking with non-governmental agencies and organizations. The World Council of Churches and the Catholic Church are both members of the International NGO Platform on the Migrant Workers Convention. Several church-related Catholic institutions have historically been engaged as well in advocacy work with the migrants like the Scalabrinian Missionaries, the International Catholic Migration Commission and the Jesuit Refugee Services.

The transnational reach of the church is important in advocacy work. In some countries, NGOs or other international organizations are not allowed and the church is the only institution migrants can turn to for help. It has been suggested that the relatively better protection of Filipino migrants in Asia can be partly attributed to the presence of the Church in most receiving countries. The Church serves as an important social capital for Filipino migrants.[52]

Churches have also engaged in protest actions and one of the more controversial issues today is whether churches can provide sanctuary for undocumented migrants facing deportation and getting separated from their children, who by the fact of their being born in the US are automatically of US citizenship. There are churches that have offered their places as sanctu-

---

50. To date, 42 states have ratified the convention. "Respect Migrants Rights: Ratify the Migrant Workers Convention!," 2014, http://www.fidh.org/en/migrants-rights/Respect-Migrants-Rights-Ratify-the (accessed April 2014).

51. http://www.oikoumene.org/en/resources/documents/wcc-programmes/justice-diakonia-and-responsibility-for-creation/migration/migration-and-migrant-workers-discerning-responses-as-churches.html (accessed July 2012).

52. Ibid., 10.

ary.⁵³ Others however feel that they cannot open the church for sanctuary because their congregation is divided, with advocates of "open borders" on the one hand and those concerned with the law on the other.⁵⁴ Those in favor of opening the churches as sanctuary or as a "space of hope," believe that no law is violated so long as everything is transparent and the Church does not hide undocumented immigrants.

Ministry of Theologizing

Theologies of migration start with a solidarity with the experience of suffering of the migrants and/or the families left behind. Whatever social class they come from, migrants experience uprootedness and of being "in betwixt-and-between" (neither here nor there).⁵⁵ In the theological reflections, it is vital to let the experiences of pain, as well as, resiliency and courage of the migrants, take the center stage and shape the interpretations of the Christian faith.

Migration theology in the host country necessarily has to take an intercultural approach.⁵⁶ It analyzes the situation of the migrants including their everyday (*lo cotidiano*) and faith discourses,⁵⁷ in relation to related discourses of other socio-cultural-religious groups in the receiving society, using the tools of the social and the human sciences, but textured with a preference for the interests of those in the margins.⁵⁸ The product of this reflection is

---

53. John Paul II affirmed: "In the Church no one is a stranger, and the Church is not foreign to anyone, anywhere. As a sacrament of unity and thus a sign and a binding force for the whole human race, the Church is the place where illegal immigrants are also recognized and accepted as brothers and sisters. It is the task of the various Dioceses actively to ensure that these people, who are obliged to live outside the safety net of civil society, may find a sense of brotherhood in the Christian community. (no. 5)" "Undocumented Migrants," Message of John Paul II for the World Migration Day, 1995, http://www.vatican.va/holy_father/john_paul_ii/messages/migration/documents/hf_jp-ii_mes_25071995_undocumented_migrants_en.html (accessed April 2014).

54. Angie Chuang and Nancy Haught, "Churches Face Dilemma over Sheltering Migrants," http://www.bennyhinn.org/yourlife/In TheNews-Religion-News/Sheltering-Migrants.html (accessed August 2007).

55. Peter Phan, "The Experience of Migration as Source of Intercultural Theology in the United States," in *Christianity with an Asian Face: Asian-American Theology in the Ministry* (Maryknoll, New York: Orbis, 2003), 15–18.

56. Ibid.; Jorge E. Castillo Guerra, "A Theology of Migration: Toward an Intercultural Methodology," in *A Promised Land*, 254–59.

57. As tool for analysis, see my approach which systematized Stuart Hall's method of discourse analysis for use in theology and, integrated some more insights he appropriated from Michel Foucault. It blends a semiotic and discursive approach to a cultural text. Agnes Brazal, "Redeeming the Vernacular: Doing Postcolonial-Intercultural Theological Ethics," *Asian Horizons* 4, no. 1 (June 2010): 50–66.

58. Among Indians, for instance, the distinction between "good" and "low" caste remains and Dalits continue to be discriminated by fellow Indians in North America and Europe. Knut Jacobsen and Selva Raj, *South Asian Christian Diaspora* (Cornwall: Ashgate, 2008).

then discerned from the perspective of the Christian tradition and allowed to question or re-articulate our understanding of the tradition.[59] Intercultural theologizing recognizes that the Christian tradition and the gospel in particular, is not a monolithic whole and therefore the dialogue is occurring between multiple cultural orientations. The fruit of this process is hopefully a theology that inspires and helps transform the unjust socio-economic-political context of migration.

Three hermeneutical approaches, guided by the effective history of the Gospels, are employed in the process of analyzing the social and faith discourses on migration: hermeneutics of suspicion, appreciation (or retrieval), and reconstruction.[60] A hermeneutics of suspicion critiques the manner in which a discourse (a way of speaking about something) has been used to promote the interest of dominant (colonial/metropolitan) groups and thus serve to marginalize those on the periphery as the migrants. For example, it analyzes the effects of assimilationist stance of dominant groups, and how minority groups have appropriated, resisted or negotiated with these cultural impositions. A feminist standpoint would focus in particular on the perspectives of/impact on women. When applied to the faith tradition, suspicion may be cast not only on the interpretations of the text (world in front of the text) but also on the world behind and world of the text itself.

A hermeneutics of appreciation (retrieval), on the other hand, will focus on how a discourse has been used by migrants or in favor of migrants to resist colonial/metropolitan discourses. It appreciates the minority groups' culture and religious traditions as myths and rituals, not out of a romantic nostalgia of the past, but to rediscover the wisdom in their culture which can help them in their struggle for full humanization. The majority groups as well need to reinvent resources from their culture that promote dialogue with and solidarity with other cultures and marginalized groups.

A hermeneutics of reconstruction is sensitive to how the resources of the migrants' cultural practice in its encounter with other cultures in the host

---

59. Phan notes how complex the inter-(multi-) cultural dialogue can be. In Bourdieu's concept of cultural practice, this will not be purely a conscious phenomena as well. For a bibliography on the employment of interfaith/multi-faith hermeneutics in the African context, see Musa W. Dube, "Intercultural Biblical Interpretations," *Swedish Missiological Themes* 98, no. 3 (2010): 380. See also Jaume Flaquer Garcia, sj, *Itinerant Lives: Notes on an Inter-religious Theology of Migration*, for an example of a multifaith hermeneutics comparing the attitude toward the stranger in Judaism, Christianity, and Islam. http://www.migrastudium.org/doc/Vidas%20Itinerantes%20Vides%20Itinerants%20yo%20Cuaderno%20en128.pdf (accessed July 2012).

60. Phan, "The Experience of Migration as Source of Intercultural Theology in the United States," 157–60.

society is shaping a new culture; an in-beyond culture. Life-giving or humanizing discourses are re-articulated within the Christian faith in a reconstructive activity that integrates liberation concerns and the active agency of the sub-altern or marginalized groups.[61]

Understanding the relationship of Christianity and ethnicity (a way of marking difference based on a shared culture) in this manner is in line with what *Gaudium et Spes* propounds:

> [T]he Church sent to all peoples of every time and place, is not bound exclusively and indissolubly to any race or nation, nor to any particular way of life or any customary pattern of living, ancient or recent .... she can enter into communion with various cultural modes to her own enrichment and theirs too. (GS 58)

Ministers for an Intercultural Church[62]

An intercultural Church requires ministers (ordained and lay) who can function as cultural mediators. Such a big task needs a team of ministers who think, feel, and act intercultural. The best model is the inclusion of migrants, former migrants, or children of migrants who grew up living in several cultural worlds. For example, some second-generation Korean American churches see themselves as "strategically positioned" to act as bridge between various groups in a multi-ethnic church.[63] They are acquainted with the subtleties and complexities of living in-betwixt-and-between, and hence might be able to expedite processes for in-beyond experiences. The team of ministers has to be committed, as well as, competent, psycho-emotionally, spiritually, relationally, and intellectually. A certain maturity in person-ability is desired to escort the mutually enriching cultures in their communal search for God.

---

61. Gerrit Noort observes though that even if a lot of academic research has been focused on migrant churches since 1997 in Europe, and intercultural hermeneutics has been recognized as important in theological discussions, these have not translated into theologies from the global South or from migrant churches changing the face of systematic theology. He sees the need to learn "how to theologize together, without reducing such practices as healing and exorcism to superstition and without declaring Western styles of believing as unbelief." This for him "requires an intercultural hermeneutic that doesn't equate an intercultural approach to theology with relativism, but that supports the student to identify and strengthen identity in the context of migration." "Emerging Migrant Churches in the Netherlands: Missiological Challenges and Mission Frontiers," *International Review of Mission* 100, no. 1 (April 2011): 13, 15.

62. On how leaders can transform a monocultural church to an intercultural church, see Michael J. Morris, "The Role of Leaders in the Development of an Intercultural Church," (A Major Project, Doctor in Ministry, Trinity Evangelical Divinity School, Deerfield, Illinois, May 2010). See also the experience of St. Mary/St. Anthony Church, Kansas City in Murphy, "The Ninety-Nine Sheep and the Mission of the Church," 154–57.

63. Sharon Kim, "Shifting Boundaries within Second-Generation Korean American Churches," *Sociology of Religion* 71 (2010):117.

To be effective cultural mediators, the ministers must be grounded in their own cultural and religious identity which they bring as a gift in the dialogue with peoples of difference. The minister ideally must know the language and culture both of the migrants and the receiving society in order that he or she can truly function as a "bridge, linking the community of migrants to the host community" (EMCC 77).

As mediators of relationships, ministers exercise evocative leadership to engender mutual empowerment. This involves appreciating acts of collaboration, trusting people and accompanying them even in learning from mistakes, nurturing personal and group confidence, as well as, challenging harmful thinking and behaviors that obstruct intercultural respect. It is equally important for ministers to accept their limitations, to ask help from migrants, and to be evangelized by the migrants.

Regarding migrant chaplaincy, it is better if the chaplain works in a team partnership with a local priest, if not the parish priest himself. He must have a grasp of the dynamics of migration and formation in intercultural communication (EMCC 78). In relation to the choice of a chaplain for the migrants, there is a need for mutual collaboration between the church in the sending and the receiving countries.[64] Churches in the sending countries should avoid sending problematic priests or those with questionable orientations to minister to the migrants. In the Philippines, while the Episcopal Commission for Migrants and Itinerant People prescribes that priests sent to be chaplains abroad must be approved first by the Commission, many times this has not been strictly observed. Ministers from sending countries must receive too a pre-training or orientation about the culture and the politics in the host country. In Britain, they use the term "easy jet priests" to refer to Polish Catholic priests who are flown to minister to the migrants, without any preparation or orientation regarding the cultural habitus of the Catholics in the host country.[65]

Ministers also need to be critical of the use of biblical narratives that tend to monopolize the truth about God and give legitimacy to an ideology of supremacy and exclusion. To offer a liberating message to migrants, they have

---

64. See for instance, *United States Conference of Catholic Bishops, Inc. and Conferencia del Episcopado Mexicano* "Strangers No Longer Together on the Journey of Hope," A Pastoral Letter Concerning Migration from the Catholic Bishops of Mexico and the United States, no. 50-51, 2003, http://www.usccb.org/issues-and-action/human-life-and-dignity/immigration/strangers-no-longer-together-on-the-journey-of-hope.cfm (accessed April 2014).

65. Jocelyn Cesari, "Religion and Diasporas: Challenges of the Emigration Countries," *INTERACT Research Report* 2013/01, http://interact-project.eu/docs/publications/Research%20Report/INTERACT-RR-2013-01.pdf (accessed May 2014).

to read the bible from the perspective of the "others" whose voices are hidden, suppressed, or distorted in the written texts. It is envisioned in the intercultural church that theological reflections will be about experiences of God and Jesus "from the margins," from the underside," "from the Canaanites," "from the borderland," "from the outcasts," and "from the belly of the empire." And where faiths/religions intersect, Christians are obligated to explicitly share their story of God-in-Jesus as a saving story for humanity, yet with openness that their story is not the whole story as there are also other narratives of redemption in their midst.[66]

The African Theological Training in Germany (ATTiG), a program of the Academy of Mission conducts intercultural bible studies in providing theological training to African migrant church leaders who may come from different faith confessions.[67] The participants are mostly neo-Pentecostal or charismatic "mainline" Christians. These bible studies combine on the one hand, Gerald West's method which he developed in the 1990 South African post-apartheid context, which bring together "ordinary" and academic readers of Scripture, and on the other hand, a Catholic method of Bible sharing that also originated in South Africa.[68] In line with West's approach, these "avoid a paternalistic 'reading for' as well as an uncritical 'listening to' the migrants' voice." The moderator makes sure that nobody dominates the sharing. Biblical texts are chosen equally in cases when participants from two distinct churches are involved, e.g. from the German Lutheran and Ghanaian Pentecostal traditions. The intercultural bible study serves to correct problematic readings on both sides, as well as, enriches the participants through their encounter with different theological predisposition and culturally-bound hermeneutical keys. An example is the West African Pentecostal reading of Matthew 6:33 "Seek you first the kingdom of God and his righteousness and all these things shall be added unto you." The West African Pentecostal interpretation of this in the extreme sense of the granting of a wish for individual prosperity and success can rightly be critiqued. Europeans, on the other hand, who take "eternal life" to mean life after death can be critiqued and enriched by the West African Christians' interpretation of "eternal life" in John 3:16 as focused on the life here and now. This interpretation is more

---

66. See Garcia, "Itinerant Lives."

67. Werner Kahl, "Encounters with Migrant Churches: Models for Growing Together," *The Ecumenical Review* 61, no. 4 (December 2009): 400–12.

68. Gerald O. West and M.W. Dube, eds., "'Reading With': An Exploration of the Interface between Critical and Ordinary Readings of the Bible, African Overtures," *Semeia* 73 (Atlanta: Scholars Press, 1996).

faithful to the *zoen aionion* (life for the believer from now till eternity) in John's Greek gospel.[69]

The African Theological Training migrant church leaders are also empowered and motivated to be more actively engaged in German church life at the local level, bringing with them the African and Pentecostal heritage as an asset in transforming the Church in Germany.

Ministries in the Sending Countries

Even churches in sending countries are likewise called to become intercultural. First, some sending countries are also multi-ethnic in themselves. The Philippines for instance is the 5th most multi-ethnic nation in the world, and encounters between various local cultures are reinforced by migration from the countryside to the megacities. Secondly, return migrants come back no longer as they were before, but bringing with them some cultural practices from the countries where they worked. Not only they but the family left behind has to re-adjust in the encounter with new cultural practices via the return migrant. Thirdly, "culture" is not synonymous solely with ethnicity; there can be other factors in the formation of a sub-culture within an ethnic group such as age, social class, sexual orientation. It is therefore possible to view the encounter of the traditional cultural practice and the new cultural practices emerging from migration in the sending country as an encounter of two cultures, the "contact zone" that an intercultural church needs to address.

What are some facets of the above ministries in the sending countries? In the ministry of welcome, both sending and receiving churches can lend support to migrants in celebrating their return, focusing on their in-beyond experiences, and paving ways for them to enter again another "in betwixt-and-between" phase with their families and neighbors. In the ministry of story-telling, various opportunities can be made available to address the concerns of the families left-behind, like dealing with separation, coping with sexual needs, communicating effectively with spouses and children through cyberspace, proper investment of money sent home, and constructively sorting out changes and expectations in gender roles, orientations, and behaviors. Counseling may be offered as well for returning migrants who find it difficult to re-adjust in their return, those who have contracted HIV or those who have faced traumatic experiences abroad. In the ministry of teaching, some private schools in the Philippines conduct special gatherings for students left

---

69. See Kahl, "Encounters with Migrant Churches," 400–12, for an example of an intercultural bible study.

behind, who are increasingly becoming the majority of their school population. The Episcopal Commission for Migrants and Itinerant People conduct programs for the sons and daughters of overseas Filipino workers.

Migrant workers are not just objects of evangelization but are, as Pope John Paul II affirmed referring to Filipinos in particular, "evangelizers and missionaries" themselves.[70] No systematic study has been done as to the extent migrant workers are invigorating the churches abroad. The Philippine bishops however note: "Many are the stories of the positive effects of their faith witness on others."[71] In order to harness this potential, an appropriate catechesis should be given to migrants before they go abroad.[72] As the Taiwanese bishops affirmed, foreign workers can indeed be messengers of the good news of God's reign, noting how "[t]he Roman empire was converted by foreign workers, slaves, soldiers and merchants who were believers in Christ."[73]

The ministry of advocacy and networking evidently requires the collaboration of institutions and peoples from both sending and receiving countries. As for the ministry of theologizing in the sending countries, among the various topics this can focus on are: how the families left-behind articulate their faith to deal with the separation from loved ones; the virtues that must be developed in relation to the management of sexuality and emotions, family life and finances; a renewed theological anthropology in the context of migrant mothers and father left-behind[74]; transnationalism and the nation, and so on.

---

70. Catholic Bishops Conference of the Philippines (henceforth CBCP), "On the Occasion of National Migration Day," 1988, no. 3, in *Caring for Migrants: A Collection of Church Documents on the Pastoral Care of Migrants*, ed. Fabio Baggio, cs and Maurizio Pettena, cs. Strathfield: St. Paul's, 2009).

71. CBCP, Acts and Decrees, Second Plenary Council of the Philippines, 1991. Many African Pentecostal churches in Germany and the Netherlands are more self-conscious of their sense of mission, viewing themselves as churches whose task is to re-evangelize Europe. Noort, "Emerging Migrant Churches in the Netherlands," 12.

72. Ibid., Art. 56, no. 1. In the host country, catechesis can be given in the migrants' own language. Catholic Bishop Conference of Japan, "Seeking the Kingdom of God," 1992, in *Caring for Migrants*.

73. Chinese Regional Bishops' Conference, "On the Question of Foreign Workers," no. 6., in *Caring for Migrants*. See also Jean-Pierre Delville, "Migrations and Christianity," paper presented at Omnes Gentes conference on "Migration: Challenges of the Spirit," October 18–20, 2007, Katholieke Universiteit Leuven, Belgium.

74. See Agnes M. Brazal, "Harmonizing Power–Beauty: Gender Fluidity in the Migration Context," 4, no. 2 *Theologies of Migration, Asian Christian Review* (Winter, 2010), 32–46.

AN OPENING RATHER THAN A CLOSING

The ministry of individual Christians and of Christian communities as bridges of solidarity must ultimately be rooted in spirituality. In this connection, there is a mystery in what Christians call "Black Saturday." This day is when the Christian household is silently and prayerfully commemorating the death of the Galilean Jew because of his words and deeds that broke boundaries of differences and reconciled people to their bodies, to one another, and to God. This day is also the moment, theologically, when the dead compassionate companion of humanity "descended to the dead." An irony! While Christianity's ecclesial body is in deep pensive mood and its sacred places are closed to the public, here is the crucified humane body of God continuing solidarity work with the departed, offering them God's comforting embrace, extending the hope of life in its fullness, and promising to vindicate their forsaken bodies in God's name. Even in death, he crosses boundaries of differences. Indeed, "Holy Saturday" is the bridge between the crucified Jesus on Good Friday and the anticipation of the Risen Christ on Easter Sunday.

The drama taking place on this day of mourning is a message compelling enough to the Christian church that it has a commitment to live up to the millions of "people on the move" who are suffering and dying in ways more than one. Raised up by God, Christ is alive and remains in the world through the befriending Spirit, who breathes life to the migrants. This vision "rests in the conviction that the life, breath, and power of God in and through the Spirit resides at the heart of all creation, even and especially the wounded and the weak, the most vulnerable. Its most pressing mandate is to let life continue, rather than to harness, control, and master it. Its most compelling exercise is in letting life be instead of forcing itself in the name of good order."[75]

Happy are those who love the world for God, for they shall find their place in God's space!

Agnes M. Brazal and Emmanuel S. de Guzman

---

75. Michael Downey, "Looking to the Last and the Least: A Spirituality of Empowerment," in *That They Might Live: Power, Engagement, and Leadership in the Church*, ed. Michael Downey (New York: Crossroad, 1991).

BIBLIOGRAPHY

Aguilar Jr., Filomeno V. ed. *Filipinos in Global Migrations: At Home in the World?* Manila: Philippine Migration Research Network and Philippine Social Science Council, 2002.

Ahn, Ilsup. "Economy of 'Invisible Debt' and Ethics of 'Radical Hospitality': Toward a Paradigm Change of Hospitality from 'Gift' to 'Forgiveness.'" *Journal of Religious Ethics* 38 (2010): 243–67.

Ahmed, Amira. "'I Need Work!': The Multiple Roles of the Church, Ranking and Religious Piety Among Domestic Workers in Egypt." *The Asia Pacific Journal of Anthropology*, 11, nos. 3 and 4 (September–December 2010): 362–77.

Akira, Nakagawa. "Influence of Migrants upon the Japanese Church." *Japan Mission Journal* 52, no. 3 (1998): 152–160.

Andall, Jacqueline. "Hierarchy and Interdependence: The Emergence of a Service Caste in Europe." In *Gender and Ethnicity in Contemporary Europe*, ed. Andall. Oxford: Berg, 2003.

Anderson, Benedict. *Imagined Communities, Reflections on the Origin and Spread of Nationalism.* Revised ed. London: Verso., 1991.

Annual Ministerial Meetings. "Interculturality Moving Towards a Dialogue Among Nation." International Network on Cultural Policy, http://incp-ripc.org/meetings/2003/theme3_inter_e.shtml (accessed May 2005).

Aquino, María Pilar. "Feminist Intercultural Theology: Toward a Shared Future of Justice." In *Feminist Intercultural Theology: Latina Explorations for a Just World*, ed. María Pilar Aquino and Maria José Rosado-Nunes, 9–28. Maryknoll: Orbis, 2007.

Asis, Maruja M.B. "Advocacy and Networking on Migrants' Issues." *Exodus Series 10* (2005), ed. Fabio Baggio.

Asis, Maruja. *Hearts Apart: Migration in the Eyes of Filipino Children*. Manila: ECMI–CBCP, Scalabrini Migration Center and Overseas Workers Welfare Administration, 2004.

Baggio, Fabio, cs and Maurizio Pettena, cs, eds. *Caring for Migrants: A Collection of Church Documents on the Pastoral Care of Migrants*. Strathfield: St. Paul's, 2009.

Baggio, Fabio. "The Migration–Development Disconnect in the Philippines." In *Moving Out, Back and Up: International Migration and Development Prospects in the Philippines*, ed. Maruja M.B. Asis and Fabio Baggio, 109–26. Quezon City: Scalabrini Migration Center, 2008.

Baggio, Fabio. "Migration Politics and Ethics in East and Southeast Asia." In *Migration Management and Ethics: Envisioning a Different Approach*, ed. Fabio Baggio and Laura Zanfrini, 27–50. Corso Milano: Polimetrica, 2006.

Baggio, Fabio, ed. *Exodus Series 1–13: A Resource Guide for the Migrant Ministry in Asia*. Quezon City: Scalabrini Migration Center, 2005/2012.

Baggio, Fabio. "History of the Pastoral Care of Migrants." *Exodus Series* 5 (2005), ed. Fabio Baggio.

Battistella, Graziano. "The Human Rights of Migrants." *Exodus Series* 11 (2005).

Bateson, Gregory. *Steps to an Ecology of Mind: Collected Essays in Anthropology, Psychiatry, Evolution, and Epistemology*. Chicago: University of Chicago Press, 1972.

Bauman, Zygmunt. "From Pilgrim to Tourist—or a Short History of Identity." In *Questions of Cultural Identity*, ed. Hall and du Guy, 18–36.

Bernardi, Savino. "The Pastoral Care of Seafarers." *Exodus Series 8* (2005), ed. Baggio.

Bergant, Diane, csa. "Ruth: The Migrant who Saved the People." In *Migration, Religious Experience and Globalization*, ed. Gioacchino Campese, cs and Pietro Ciallella, cs, 49–61. New York: Center for Migration Studies, 2003.

Bergmann, Sigurd. "Revisioning Pneumatology in Transcultural Spaces." In *Spirits of Globalization: The Growth of Pentecostalism and Experiential Spiritualities in a Global Age*, ed. Sturla J. Stålsett. London: SCM Press, 2006.

Bertrand, Didier. "Religious Practices of Vietnamese in Cambodia and Inter-Ethnic Relations." *Asian Migrant* 10, no. 3 (1997): 90–93.

Bhabha, Homi K. "Introduction." In *The Location of Culture*. London/New York: Routledge, 1994; reprint 2010.
Bonacich, Edna and Lucie Cheng, eds.*Labor Immigration Under Capitalism: Asian Women in the United States Before World War II*. Berkeley: University of California, 1984.
Borg, Marcus J. *Meeting Jesus Again for the First Time: The Historical Jesus and the Heart of Contemporary Faith*. San Francisco, CA: HarperSanFrancisco, 1995.
Borg Marcus J. and N.T. Wright. *The Meaning of Jesus: Two Visions*. San Francisco, C.A.: HarperSanFrancisco, 1989.
Borg, Marcus J. *Jesus, A New Vision: Spirit, Culture, and The Life of Discipleship*. San Francisco, CA: HarperSanFrancisco, 1987.
Bosniak, Linda. "Citizenship, Noncitizenship, and the Transnationalism of Domestic Work." In *Migrations and Mobilities: Citizenship, Borders and Gender*, ed. Seyla Benhabib and Judith Resnik, 127–56. New York: New York University Press, 2009.
Bouma, Gary. "Religion and Migrant Settlement." *Asian Migrant* 18, no. 2 (April–June 1995): 38–41.
Bourdieu, Pierre. *Masculine Domination*, trans. Richard Nice. Stanford, California: Stanford University Press, 2001.
Bourdieu, Pierre. *Outline of a Theory of Practice*, trans. Richard Nice.Cambridge, Mass.: Cambridge University, 1977; reprint ed. 1998.
Bourdieu, Pierre. *Distinction: A Social Critique of the Judgment of Taste*. Cambridge, Mass.: Harvard University, 1984.
Bourdieu, Pierre and Loïc J. D. Wacquant. *An Invitation to Reflexive Sociology*. Chicago: The University of Chicago Press, 1992.
Brazal, Agnes. "Harmonizing Power–Beauty: Gender Fluidity in the Migration Context." *Theologies of Migration. Asian Christian Review* 4, no. 2 (Winter, 2010), 32–46.
Brazal, Agnes."Redeeming the Vernacular: Doing Postcolonial–Intercultural Theological Ethics." *Asian Horizons* 4, no. 1 (June 2010): 50–66.
Brazal, Agnes M. "Cultural Rights of Migrants: Philosophical and Theological Exploration." In *Faith on the Move: Toward a Theology of Migration in Asia*, ed. Baggio and Brazal, 68–92.
Brazal, Agnes M. "Beyond the Religious and Social Divide: The Emerging Mindanawon Identity." *Chakana* 2, no. 3 (2004): 7–26.

Brazal, Agnes M. "Reinventing Pakikipagkapwa: An Exploration of Its Potential for Promoting Respect for Plurality." In *Fundamentalism and Pluralism in the Church*, ed. Dennis Gonzalez, 50–70. Manila: Dakateo, 2004.

Brown, Karen McCarthy. *Mama Lola: A Vodou Priestess in Brooklyn*. Berkeley: University of California Press, 1991.

Bundang, Rachel A.R. "Home as Memory, Metaphor, and Promise in Asian/Pacific American Religious Experience." *Semeia* 90/91 (2002): 87–104.

Brooker, Peter. *A Glossary of Cultural Theory*. 2nd ed. London/New York: Oxford University Press, 2002.

Calloway, Donald. "Mater Ecclesia: An Ecclesiology for the 21st Century." http://www.catholic.net/rcc/Periodicals/ Homiletic/ 2001-11/calloway.html (accessed 22 June 2006).

Calvert, Robert. "Ecclesial Patterns among Migrant Churches in Rotterdam." www.communitas.co.za/artikels/Calvert.doc (accessed July 2012).

Castells, Manuel. "Immigrant Workers and Class Struggles in Advanced Capitalism: The Western European Experience." *Politics and Society* 5, no. 1 (1975): 33–66.

Castles, Stephen. *Ethnicity and Globalization: From Migrant Worker to Transnational Citizen*. London: Sage Publications, 2000.

Catholic Bishops' Conference of Japan. "Seeking the Kingdom of God which Transcends Differences." *Nationality*, 5 Nov. 1992.

Catholic Bishops Conference of the Philippines. "On the Occasion of National Migration Day." 1988. In *Caring for Migrants*, ed. Baggio and Pettena.

Cavanaugh, William T. "Migrant, Tourist, Pilgrim, Monk." *Theological Studies* 69 (2008): 340–56.

Chan Yiu Sing, Lucas. "A Model of Hospitality for Our Times." *Budhi: A Journal of Ideas and Culture* 10, no. 3 (2006): 1–30.

Chaput, Charles J. "Mater et Magistra: Who the Church is, and why she Teaches with Authority?" Keynote Address on "Witness, Teach and Educate: Forming Disciples for the New Millennium." 2002 Catechetical Conference, Holiday Inn – DIA, U.S.A.

"Characteristics of a Multicultural Church." http://www.baptist.org.uk/justice/racial-justice-resources/doc_view/1026-characteristics-of-a-multicultural-church.html (accessed March 2012).

Chinese Regional Bishops' Conference, "On the Question of Foreign Workers." no. 6. In *Caring for Migrants*, ed. Baggio and Pettena.

Cho, Daniel. "Is Multiculturalism Bad for the Church—Part 2: A Reflection on Church and Ethnicity." Presbyterian Record, http://www.presbyterianrecord.ca/2011/07/15/is-multiculturalism-bad-for-the-church-part-2/ (accessed March 2012).

Chuang, Angie and Nancy Haught. "Churches Face Dilemma over Sheltering Migrants." http://www.bennyhinn.org/yourlife/In TheNews-Religion-News/Sheltering-Migrants.html (accessed August 2007).

Cesari, Jocelyn. "Religion and Diasporas: Challenges of the Emigration Countries." *INTERACT Research Report* 2013/01, http://interact-project.eu/docs/publications/Research%20Report/INTERACT-RR-2013-01.pdf (accessed May 2014).

Classen, Constance, David Howes, and Anthony Synnott. *Aroma: The Cultural History of Smell*. London/New York: Routledge, 1994).

Clague, J. "A Dubious Idiom and Rhetoric: How Problematic is the Language of Human Rights in Catholic Social Thought?" In *Catholic Social Thought: Twilight or Renaissance*, ed. J.S. Boswell, F.P. McHugh and J. Verstraeten, 125–40. Leuven: Leuven University, 2000.

Constable, Nicole. "At Home but Not at Home: Filipina Narratives of Ambivalent Returns." In *Filipinos in Global Migrations*, ed. Aguilar, 380–412.

Council of Europe Ministers of Foreign Affairs. *White Paper on Intercultural Dialogue "Living Together As Equals in Dignity."* Launched by the Council of Europe Ministers of Foreign Affairs at their 118th Ministerial Session(Strasbourg, 7 May 2008). http://www.coe.int/t/dg4/intercultural/source/white%20paper_final_revised_en.pdf (accessed July 2012).

Cox, Harvey. "Spirits of Globalization: Pentecostalism and Experiential Spiritualities in a Global Era." In *Spirits of Globalization: the Growth of Pentecostalism and Experiential Spiritualities in a Global Age*, ed. Sturla J. Stålsett, 11–22. London: SCM Press, 2006.

Crossan, John Dominic. *The Historical Jesus: The Life of a Mediterranean Jewish Peasant*. San Francisco, CA: HarperSanFrancisco, 1992.

Crüsemann, Frank. "'You Know the Heart of a Stranger' (Exodus 23:9): A Recollection of the Torah in the Face of New Nationalism and Xenophobia." In *Migrants and Refugees*, ed. Dietmar Mieth and Lisa Sowle Cahill, *Concilium* (1993/4) (London: SCM, 1993), 95–109.

Cruz, Gemma Tulud. *An Intercultural Theology of Migration: Pilgrims in the Wilderness*. Leiden: Brill, 2010.

"Cultural Rights: Fribourg Declaration." http://www1.umn.edu/humanrts/instree/Fribourg%20Declaration.pdf (accessed July 2012).

Cwiekosky, Frederick I. *The Beginnings of the Church*. New York: Paulist Press, 1988.

Davary, Bahar. "A Matter of Veils: An Islamic Response." In *Ethics and World Religions: Cross–cultural Case Studies*, ed. Regina Wentzel Wolfe and Christine E. Gudorf, 153–59. Maryknoll, New York: Orbis, 1999.

deCerteau, Michel. *The Practice of Everyday Life*, trans. Steven F. Rendail. Berkeley: University of California Press, 1984.

de Guzman, Emmanuel S. "Mapping the Church on the Move." *Exodus Series 12* (2012), ed. Baggio.

de Guzman, Emmanuel S. "The Church as 'Imagined Communities' Among Differentiated Social Bodies." In *Faith on the Move*, ed. Baggio and Brazal, 118–54.

de Guzman, Emmanuel S. "The Laity in the Ministry to the Migrants." *Exodus Series 6* (2005), ed. Baggio.

de Guzman, Emmanuel S. "Fundamentalism and Multi-Contextuality in Classrooms of Theology." In *Fundamentalism and Pluralism in the Church*, ed. Dennis T. Gonzalez, 126–58. Manila: DaKaTeo, 2004.

Delville, Jean-Pierre. "Migrations and Christianity." paper presented at Omnes Gentes conference on "Migration: Challenges of the Spirit." October 18–20, 2007, Katholieke Universiteit Leuven, Belgium.

De Schutter, Helder. "Nations, Boundaries and Justice: On Will Kymlicka's Theory of Multinationalism." *Ethical Perspectives: Journal of the European Ethics Network* 11, no. 1 (2005): 17–40.

Di Giovanni, Stephen M. "Historical and Canonical Aspects of the Pastoral Care of Immigrants in Late 19th Cen. America." *People on the Move: A Compendium of Church Documents in the Pastoral Concern for Migrants and Refugees*. Bishops' Committee on Priestly Formation, Bishops' Committee on Migration and National Conference of Catholic Bishops, 1988.

Dirlik, Arif. "The Postcolonial Aura: Third World Criticism in the Age of Global Capitalism." In *Dangerous Liaisons: Gender, Nation, and Postcolonial Perspective*, ed. Anne McClintock, Aamir Mufti and Ella Shohat, 501–28. London: University of Minnesota Press, 1997.

Dizon-Añonuevo, Mai. "Migrant Returnees, Return Migration and Reintegration." In *Coming Home: Women, Migration and Reintegration*, ed. Estrella DizonAñonuevo and Augusto T. Añonuevo, 136–51. Manila: BalikbayanFoundation, Inc., 2002.

Dorr, Donal. "Solidarity and Integral Human Development." In *The Logic of Solidarity: Commentaries on Pope John Paul II's Encyclical 'On Social Concern'*, ed. Gregory Baum and Robert Ellsberg, 143–54. Maryknoll, New York: Orbis, 1989.

Douglas, Mary. *In the Active Voice*. London: Routledge & Kegan Paul, 1982.

Downey, Michael. "Looking to the Last and the Least: A Spirituality of Empowerment." In *That They Might Live: Power, Engagement, and Leadership in the Church*, ed. Michael Downey, 176–92. New York: Crossroad, 1991.

Dreyfus, H. and P. Rabinow, *Michel Foucault: Beyond Structuralism and Hermeneutics*. Brighton: Harvester Press, 1982.

Dube, Musa W. "Intercultural Biblical Interpretations." *Swedish Missiological Themes* 98, no. 3 (2010): 361–88.

Dube, Musa. "Postcolonialism and Liberation." In *Handbook of U.S. Theologies of Liberation*, ed. Miguel de la Torre, 288–94. St. Louis, Missouri: Chalice Press, 2004.

du Gay, Paul, Stuart Hall, Linda Janes, Hugh Mackay and Keith Negus. *Doing Cultural Studies: The Story of the Sony Walkman*. Keynes: The Open University, 1997.

Duckitt, John. "Reducing Prejudice: An Historical and Multi-Level Approach." In *Understanding Prejudice, Racism, and Social Conflict*, ed. Martha Augoustinos and Katherine J. Reynolds, 253–72. London: Sage Publications, 2001.

Eagleton, Terry. *The Idea of Culture*. Oxford: Blackwell, 2000.

Edwards, Denis. *Jesus the Wisdom of God: An Ecological Theology*. Maryknoll, New York: Orbis, 1995.

Elliott, John H. *A Home for the Homeless: A Social-Scientific Criticism of 1 Peter, its Situation and Strategy* with a new introduction. Minneapolis: Fortress Press, 1990.

Emmer, Pieter. "'We are Here, Because You were There:' European Colonialism and Intercontinental Migration." *Concilium* (1993/4): 42–51.

Emery, Gilles. *La trinitécréatrice*. Paris, Vrin, 1995.

Eriksen, Thomas Hylland. *Ethnicity and Nationalism, Anthropological Perspectives*. London: Pluto Press, 1993.

Espín, Orlando O. "Migration and Human Condition: Theological Considerations on Religious Identities and Unexpected Inter-religious Dialogues." In *Migration and Interculturality: Theological and Philosophical Challenges*, ed. Raúl Fornet-Betancourt. Aachen: MWI, 2004.

Espín, Orlando O. *The Faith of the People: Theological Reflection on Popular Catholicism* (Maryknoll, New York: Orbis, 1977).

Espiritu, Yen Le. "The Intersection of Race, Ethnicity and Class: The Multiple Identities of Second-Generation Filipinos. In *Filipinos in Global Migrations*, ed. Aguilar, 144–175.

"The FEAR of Smell – the Smell of FEAR." http://www.grandarts.com/exhibits/STolaas.html (September 2007).

Fernandez, Eleazar S. "From Babel to Pentecost: Finding a Home in the Belly of the Empire." *Semeia* 90–91 (2002): 29–50.

Fiorenza, Elizabeth Schüssler. *In Memory of Her: A Feminist Theological Reconstruction of Christian Origins*. New York Crossroad, 1994.

Fiske, John. "Opening the Hallway: Some Remarks on the Fertility of Stuart Hall's Contribution to Critical Theory." In *Stuart Hall: Critical Dialogues*, ed. David Morley and Kuan-Hsing Chen, 212–20. London: Routledge, 1996.

Fornet-Betancourt, Raúl."Philosophical Presuppositions of Intercultural Dialogue." http://them.polylog.org/1/ffr-en.htm (accessed July 2012).

Fornet-Betancourt, Raúl. "Hermeneutics and Politics of Strangers: A Philosophical Contribution on the Challenge of Convivencia in Multicultural Societies." In *A Promised Land*, ed. Groody and Campese, 210–24.

Fox, Kate. "The Smell Report: An Overview of Facts and Findings." http://www.sirc.org/publik/smell.pdf (accessed September 2007).

Francis (Pope). Chrism Mass: Homily of Pope Francis. Saint Peter's Basilica. Holy Thursday, 28 March 2013. http://w2.vatican.va/content/francesco/en/homilies/2013/documents/papa-francesco_20130328_messa-crismale.html (accessed April 2014).

Fritz, Volkmar. *The City in Ancient Israel*. Sheffield: Sheffield Academic Press, 1995.

Garcia, JaumeFlaquer, sj. *Itinerant Lives: Notes on an Inter-religious Theology of Migration*. http://www.migrastudium.org/doc/Vidas%20Itinerantes%20Vides%20Itinerants%20yo%20Cuaderno%20en128.pdf (accessed July 2012).

Garcia-Muñoz, Teresa and Shoshana Neuman, "Is Religiosity of Immigrants a Bridge or a Buffer in the Process of Integration? A Comparative Study of Europe and the United States." IZA DP No. 6384, February 2012. http://ftp.iza.org/dp6384.pdf (accessed July 2012).

"Global OFW—a Thriving Entity in a Bad Economy." http://affleap.com/global-ofw-a-thriving-entity-in-a-bad-economy/ (accessed July 2012).

Gott, Natalie. "Welcoming Immigrants." http://www.faithandleadership.com/features/articles/welcoming-immigrants (accessed July 2012).

Gowan, Donald E. *Eschatology in the Old Testament*. Philadelphia: Fortress, 1986.

Graham, Wade. "The French Immigration Debate: The Short, Hot Summer of '91." http://www.thesocialcontract.com/pdf/two-one/Wade.pdf (accessed September 2007).

Greeley, Andrew. *The Church, The National Parish and Immigration: Same Old Mistakes*. New York: Center for Migration Studies, 1972.

Groody, Daniel and Gioacchino Campese, eds. *A Promised Land, A Perilous Journey: Theological Perspectives on Migration*. Notre Dame, Indiana: University of Notre Dame, 2008.

Grossberg, Lawrence. "Identity and Cultural Studies: Is that All there Is?" In *Questions of Cultural Identity*, ed. Hall and du Gay, 87–107.

Grossberg, Lawrence. "History, Politics and Postmodernism." In *Critical Dialogues*, ed. Morley and Chen.

Groupe de Fribourg in Cooperation with UNESCO, The Council of Europe, and The Swiss National Commission Project Concerning a Declaration of Cultural Rights (11th version). Presented at the General Conference of the United Nations Educational, Scientific and Cultural Organization, September 4, 1996. http://www.americas-society.org/as/events/pdf.d/UNESCO%20Fribourg.pdf#search='Groupe%20de%20Fribourg%20cultural%20right (May 2006).

Groves, Julian McAllister and Kimberly A. Chang. "Romancing Resistance and Resisting Romance: Ethnography and the Construction of Power in the Filipina Domestic Worker Community in Hong Kong." In *Filipinos in Global Migrations*, ed. Aguilar, 316-43.

Gudorf, Christine. "A Matter of Veils: A Case Study." In *Ethics and World Religions: Cross-cultural Case Studies*, ed. Christine Gudorf and Regina Wentzel Wolfe. Maryknoll, N.Y.: Orbis Books, 1999.

Guerra, Jorge E. Castillo. "A Theology of Migration: Toward an Intercultural Methodology." In *A Promised Land*, ed. Groody and Campese, 254–59.

Hagan, Jacqueline. "Faith for the Journey: Religion as a Resource for Migrants." In *A Promised Land*, ed. Groody and Campese, 3–19.

Hall, Edward Twitchell. *Beyond Culture*. New York: Anchor Books, 1976.

Hall, Stuart. "Introduction." In *Representation: Cultural and Signifying Practices*, ed. Stuart Hall, 1–12. London: Sage, 1997.

Hall, Stuart. "Introduction: Who Needs Identity?" In *Questions of Cultural Identity*, ed. Hall and Du Gay, 1–17.

Hall, Stuart. "The Question of Cultural Identity." In *Modernity and its Futures*, ed. Stuart Hall, Tony McGrew, and David Held, 274–316. Polity Press, in association with Open University, 1992.

Hall, Stuart. "Old and New Identities, Old and New Ethnicities." In *Culture, Globalization and the World System*, ed. Anthony D. King, 41–68. London: Macmillan, 1991; reprint ed., 1993.

Hall, Stuart. "Cultural Identity and Diaspora." In *Identity: Community, Culture, Difference*, ed. Jonathan Rutherford, 222–37. London: Lawrence and Wishart, 1990.

Hall, Stuart. "Cultural Studies: Two Paradigms." *Media Culture and Society* 2, no. 1 (January 1980).

Hall, Stuart. "The Problem of Ideology: Marxism without Guarantees." In *Critical Dialogues*, ed. David Morley and Kuan-Hsing Chen, 27–46. London: Routledge, 1996.

Hall, Stuart. "On Postmodernism and Articulation: An Interview with Stuart Hall." In *Critical Dialogues*, ed. Morley and Chen.

Hall, Stuart and Paul du Gay, *Questions of Cultural Identity*. London: Sage Publications, 1996.

Hamao, Stephen Fumio (Cardinal). Message at the Inauguration of the Catholic National Commission for the Pastoral Care of Migration and Tourism in Colombo, Sri Lanka (7 March 2003).

Hammar, Tomas. "The Civil Rights of Aliens." In *The Political Rights of Migrant Workers in Western Europe*, ed. Zig Layton-Henry. London: Sage Publications, 1990.

Harkin, Michael E. "Things the Nose Knows." http://www.chass.utoronto.ca/epc/srb/srb/nose.htm (accessed September 2007).

Harper, Dean. *Living in Two Cultures: The Socio-Cultural Situation of Migrants and their Families*. Aldershot, UK: Gower and the UNESCO, 1982.

Hauerwas, Stanley. *In Good Company: The Church as Polis*. Notre Dame: University of Notre Dame Press, 1995.

Hellerman, Joseph H. *The Ancient Church as Family*. Minneapolis: Augsburg Fortress, 2001.

Heyer, Kristin. "Reframing Displacement and Membership: Ethics of Migration." *Theological Studies* 73 (2012): 188–206.

Heyward, Carter. "Mutuality." In *A–Z of Feminist Theology*, ed. L. Isherwood and D. McEwan, 155–56. Sheffield: Sheffield Academic Press, 1996.

Ikas, Karin. "Crossing into a Mexifornian Third Space." In *Communicating in the Third Space*, ed. Karin Ikas and Gerhard Wagner, 123–45. New York: Routledge, 2009.

Iwabuchi, Koichi. *Recentering Globalization: Popular Culture and Japanese Transnationalism*. Durham, NC: Duke University Press, 2002.

Jacobsen, Knut and Selva Raj, *South Asian Christian Diaspora*. Cornwall: Ashgate, 2008.

Jager, Bernd. "Body, House and City: The Intertwinings of Embodiment, Inhabitation, and Civilization." In *Dwelling, Place and Environment: Towards a Phenomenology of Person and World*, ed. David Seamon and Robert Mugerauer, 214–25. Dordrecht: Martinus Nijhoff Publishers, 1985.

Jeannerat, Caroline. "Of Lizards, Misfortune and Deliverance: Pentecostal Soteriology in the Life of a Migrant." *African Studies* 68, no. 2 (August 2009): 251–71.

Jeffers, James S. *The Graeco-Roman World of the New Testament Era: Exploring the Background of Early Christianity*. Inter Varsity Press, 1999.

John Paul II (Pope). "Migration and Inter-Religious Dialogue." *Boletin Eclesiastico de Filipinas* 78, no. 833 (November-December, 2002): 600–605.

John Paul II (Pope). *Sollicitudo Rei Socialis*. December 30, 1987.

John Paul II (Pope). "Undocumented Migrants." Message of John Paul II for the World Migration Day, 1995. http://www.vatican.va/holy_father/john_paul_ii/messages/migration/documents/hf_jp-ii_mes_25071995_undocumented_migrants_en.html (accessed April 2014).

Johnson, Elizabeth A. *She Who Is: The Mystery of God in Feminist Theological Discourse*. New York: Crossroad, 1996.

Jolly, Susie with Hazel Reeves. "Gender and Migration: Overview Report." BRIDGE, 16. http://www.bridge.ids.ac.uk/reports/CEP-Mig-OR.pdf (accessed July 2012).

Kahl, Werner. "Encounters with Migrant Churches: Models for Growing Together." *The Ecumenical Review* 61, no. 4 (December 2009): 400-12.

Kalscheuer, Britta. "Encounters in the Third Space: Links Between Intercultural Communication Theories and Postcolonial Approaches." In *Communicating in the Third Space*, ed. Karin Ikas and Gerhard Wagner, 26–46. New York: Routledge, 2009.

Kalscheuer, Britta and Lars Allolio-Näcke. "Why does the Current Debate on Interculturality Prevent the Development of Intercultural Communication?: A Critical Note on the Interculturality Discourse." http://sietarcongress.wu-wien.ac.at/docs/T6_Kalscheuer.pdf (accessed July 2012).

Kim, Sharon. "Shifting Boundaries within Second-Generation Korean American Churches." *Sociology of Religion* 71 (2010): 98–22.

Kirkpatrick, Frank. *Community: A Trinity of Models*. Washington, DC: Georgetown University Press, 1986.

Kohl, James Vaughn and Robert T. Francoeur. *The Scent of Eros: Mysteries of Odor in Human Sexuality*. New York: Continuum, 1995.

Komonchak, Joseph A. "Ecclesiology of Vatican II." *Origin* 28 (1999): 763–68.

Kroeger, James. "Living Faith in a Strange Land: Migration and Interreligious Dialogue." In *Faith on the Move*, ed. Baggio and Brazal, 219–51.

Küster, Volker. "The Project of an Intercultural Theology." *Swedish Missiological Themes* 93, no. 3 (2005): 417–32.

Kymlicka, Will and Alan Patten. *Language Rights and Political Theory*. Cambridge: Oxford University, 2003.

Kymlicka, Will. *Politics in the Vernacular: Nationalism, Multiculturalism, and Citizenship*. Oxford: Oxford University, 2001.

Kymlicka, Will. *Multicultural Citizenship: A Liberal Theory of Minority Rights*. Oxford: Clarendon Press, 1995.

La Cugna, Catherine Mowry. "God in Communion with Us: Trinity." In *Freeing Theology: The Essentials of Theology in Feminist Perspective*, ed. La Cugna, 83-114. New York: Harper Collins, 1993.

"Labor Export Policy of Developing Countries: The Case of the Philippines and Indonesia." http://edm.iboninternational.org/component/content/article/413–special-features/250-labor-export-policy-of-developing-countries-the-case-of-the-philippines-and-indonesia (accessed July 2012).

Lang, Richard. "The Dwelling Door: Towards a Phenomenology of Transition." In *Dwelling, Place and Environment: Towards a Phenomenology of Person and World*, ed. David Seamon and Robert Mugerauer, 201-14. Dordrecht: Martinus Nijhoff Publishers, 1985.

Layton-Henry, Zig. "Citizenship or Denizenship for Migrant Workers?" In *The Political Rights of Migrant Workers in Western Europe*, ed. Layton-Henry, 186-95. London: Sage, 1990.

LeCouteur, Amanda and Martha Augoustinos. "The Language of Prejudice and Racism." In *Understanding Prejudice, Racism, and Social Conflict*, ed. Martha Augoustinos and Katherine J. Reynolds. 215–30. London: Sage Publications, 2001.

Lee, Jung Young. *Marginality: The Key to Multicultural Theology*. Minneapolis: Fortress Press, 1995.

Letter to Diognetus." http://www.crossroadsinitiative.com/library_article/344/Letter_to_Diognetus.html (accessed August 2007).

Lindsay, Robert. "Do the Races Smell Different?" July 3, 2009. http://robertlindsay.wordpress.com/2009/07/03/do-the-races-smell-different/ (accessed July 2012).

Linkh, Richard M. *American Catholicism (1900–1924 European Immigrants)* New York: Center for Migration Studies, 1975; 2nd printing, 1978.

Loomba, Ania. *Colonialism/Postcolonialism: the New Critical Idiom*. London: Routledge, 1998.

Mall, Ram Adhar. *Intercultural Philosophy*. Lanham, Maryland: Rowman and Littlefield Publishers, 2000.

Martinez, Ruben. *Crossing Over: A Mexican Family on the Migrant Trail*. New York: Picador, reprint ed., 2002.

Martino, Renato (Cardinal). "The Church Must Feel Concerned Regarding Immigrants." Annual Meeting of European National Directors for the Pastoral Care of Migrants, Subiu, Romania, September 3-4, 2007. http://www.piercedhearts.org/heart_church/migration_ecumenism.htm (accessed February 2012).

Marynovych, Miroslav. "Citizenship." In *Catholic Theological Ethics: Past, Present and Future. The Trento Conference*, ed. James F. Keenan, 267–74. Quezon City: Ateneo de Manila University Press, 2013.

Marx, Karl. *Capital: A Critique of Political Economy*. Vol. 1: *The Process of Production Capital*, ed. Frederick Engels, trans. Samuel Moore and Edward Aveling. Moscow: Progress Publishers, reprint ed., 1984.

Mateo, Ibarra. "The Church's Nonreligious Roles among Filipino Catholic Migrants in Tokyo." In *Old Ties and New Solidarities: Studies on Philippine Communities*, ed. Charles J-H. Macdonald and Guillermo M. Pesigan, 192–204. Quezon City: Ateneo de Manila University Press, 2002.

McKenna, Thomas. *Muslim Rulers and Rebels: Everyday Politics and Armed Separatism in the Southern Philippines*. Berkeley: University of California Press, 1998.

Medina, Néstor. "Discerning the Spirit in Culture: Toward Pentecostal Interculturality." *Canadian Journal of Pentecostal-Charismatic Christianity* 2 (2011): 137–38.

Meeks, Wayne A. *The First Urban Christians: The Social World of the Apostle Paul.* Yale University Press, 1983.

Meeks, Wayne and Robert L. Wilken. *Jews and Christians in Antioch: In the First Four Centuries of the Common Era.* SBL Sources for Biblical Study 13. Missoula, Montana: Scholars Press for the Society of Biblical Literature, 1978.

Messer, Donald E. *Images of Contemporary Ministry.* Nashville: Abingdon Press, 1989.

Metz, Johann Baptist. *Faith in History and Society,* trans. David Smith. New York: Seabury Press, 1980.

Metz, Johannes B. "The Future in the Memory of Suffering." *Concilium* 6, no. 8 (June 1972): 9–25.

Meyer-Bische, Patricia. "The Right to Education in the Context of Cultural Rights." http://www.bayefsky.com/general/e_c.12_1998_17.php (accessed May 2006).

"Migration to Latin America." http://www.let.leidenuniv.nl/history/migration/chapter53.html (accessed August 2007).

"Migration to North America." http://www.let.leidenuniv.nl/history/migration/chapter52.html (accessed August 2007).

Miike, Yoshitaka. "Beyond Eurocentrism in the Intercultural field: Searching for an Asiacentric Paradigm." In *Ferment in the Intercultural Field: Axiology, Value, Praxis.* International and Intercultural Communication Annual, vol. 26, ed. William J. Starosta and Guo-Ming Chen, 243–76. London: Sage, 2003.

Min, Anselm Kyongsuk. "Migration and Christian Hope: Historical and Eschatological Reflections on Migration." In *Faith on the Move,* ed. Baggio and Brazal, 177–202.

Min, Anselm Kyongsuk. *The Solidarity of Others in a Divided World: A Postmodern Theology after Postmodernism.* New York: T&T Clark International, 2004.

Minear, Paul. *Images of the Church in the New Testament.* Philadelphia: Westminster Press, 1977.

Mira, Rosalina and Lois Ann Lorentzen. "Women, Migration, and the Pentecostal Experience." *Peace Review* 14, no. 4 (2002): 421–25.

Mondragon, Ken Johnson. *Ministry in Multicultural and National/Ethnic Parishes: Evaluating the Findings of the Emerging Models of Pastoral Leadership Project.* http://emergingmodels.org/files/2012/05/Multicultural-Report.pdf (accessed February 2012).

Morley, David and Kuan-Hsing Chen. *Stuart Hall: Critical Dialogues.* London: Routledge, 1996.

Morris, Michael J. "The Role of Leaders in the Development of an Intercultural Church." A Major Project, Doctor in Ministry, Trinity Evangelical Divinity School, Deerfield, Illinois, May 2010.

Müller, Denis. "A Homeland for Transients: Towards an Ethic of Migrations." *Concilium* (1993/4): 130–36.

Multiculturalism in the Netherlands and the Murder of Theo Van Gogh." http://findarticles.com/p/articles/mi_m2242/is_1669_286/ai_n13661901 (accessed August 2007).

Muncada, Felipe, svd. "Japan and Philippines: Migration Turning Points." In *Faith on the Move*, ed. Baggio and Brazal, 20–48.

Munck-Fairwood, Birthe. "Welcome Here? Responses to Migration from Churches in Denmark." In *Together or Apart?: Report from the Nordic Consultation on Migration and Changing Ecclesial Landscapes*, 2418–25. Nordic Ecumenical Working Group on Migration in cooperation with Ecumenism in the Nordic Region (EkumenikiNorden), December 2008.

Murphy, Nathan W. "Origins of Colonial Chesapeake Indentured Servants: American and English Sources." http://pricegen.com/immigrantservants/origins.htm#intro (accessed November 2009); originally published in the *National Genealogical Society Quarterly* 93, no. 1 (March 2005): 5–24.

Murphy, Patrick. "The Ninety-Nine Sheep and the Mission of the Church." In *A Promised Land*, ed. Groody and Campese, 141–59.

Niec, Halina. "Advocating for Cultural Rights: Cultural Rights at the End of the World Decade for Cultural Development." http://kvc.minbuza.nl/uk/archive/commentary/niec.html (accessed May 2006).

Nirenberg, David. *Communities of Violence: Persecution of Minorities in the Middle Ages.* Princeton: Princeton University Press, 1996.

Noort, Gerrit. "Emerging Migrant Churches in the Netherlands: Missiological Challenges and Mission Frontiers." *International Review of Mission* 100 (April 2011): 4–16.

Okin, Susan Moller. *Is Multiculturalism Bad for Women?* Princeton, New Jersey: Princeton University, 1999.

O'Meara, Thomas Franklin. *Theology of Ministry*. Mahwah, NJ: Paulist Press, 1983.

O'Neill, William. "Christian Hospitality and Solidarity with the Stranger." In *And You Welcomed Me: Migration and Catholic Social Teaching*, ed. Donald Kerwin and Jill Marie Gerschultz, 149–56. New York, NY: Lexington Books, 2009.

Osborne, Kenan B. *Christian Sacraments in a Postmodern World*. New York: Paulist Press, 1999.

Osiek, Carolyn. "The City: Center of Early Christian Life." *The Bible Today* (January 1993): 17–21.

Osiek, Carolyn and David J. Batch. *Families in the New Testament World: Households and House Churches*. Louisville, KY: Westminster/John Knox Press, 1977.

Parr, Joy. "Smells Like?: Sources of Uncertainty in the History of the Great Lakes Environment." http://www.historycooperative.org/journals/eh/11.2/parr.html (accessed September 2007).

Phan, Peter C. "Migration in the Patristic Era: History and Theology." In *A Promised Land*, ed. Groody and Campese, 35–61.

Panikkar, Raimund. "Religion, Philosophy and Culture." http://them.polylog.org/1/fpr.en.htm (accessed May 2005).

Parrenas, Rhacel Salazar. "Transgressing the Nation-State: The Partial Citizenship of 'Imagined (Global) Community' of Migrant Filipina Domestic Workers." http://www.iuoui.edu/-anthkb/a104/philippines/migrationfilipinas.htm (accessed September 2007).

Parry, Benita. "The Postcolonial: Conceptual Category or Chimera?" *The Yearbook of English Studies* 27 (1997): 3–21.

Pershcke, Doris. "The Role of Religion for the Integration of Migrants and Institutional Responses in Europe: Some Reflections." http://findarticles.com/p/articles/mi_m2065/is_4_61/ai_n49577130/pg_5/?tag=content;col1 (accessed January 2012).

Pertierra, Raul et al. *Txt-ing Selves: Cellphones and Philippine Modernity*. Manila: De La Salle University Press, 2002.

Pettaná, Maurizio. "Migration in the Bible: The Commandment of Hospitality." *Exodus Series 6*, ed. Baggio.

Phan, Peter. "The Experience of Migration as a Source of Intercultural Theology in the United States." In *Migration, Religious Experience, and Globalization*, ed. Gioacchino Campese, cs and Pietro Ciallella, cs, 143–69. New York: Center for Migration Studies, 2003; also in Phan, *Christianity with an Asian Face: Asian American Theology in the Ministry.* Maryknoll, NY: Orbis, 2003.

Pilario, Daniel Franklin. *Back to the Rough Grounds of Praxis: Exploring Theological Method with Pierre Bourdieu.* Leuven: Peeters, 2005.

Pistone, Michele R. and John J. Hoeffner. *Stepping Out of the Brain Drain: Applying Catholic Social Teaching in a New Era of Migration.* New York: Rowman and Littlefield, 2007.

Pohl, Christine D. Responding to Strangers: Insights from the Christian Tradition." *Studies in Christian Ethics* 19 (2006): 81–110.

Pohl, Christine D. *Making Room: Recovering Hospitality as a Christian Tradition.* Grand Rapids, Mich.: Eerdmans, 1999.

Pontifical Council for the Pastoral Care of Migrants and Itinerant People. *Erga Migrantes Caritas Christi* (The Love of Christ towards Migrants), 1 May 2004. http://www.vatican.va/roman_curia/pontifical_councils/migrants/documents/rc_pc_migrants_doc_20040514_erga-migrantes-caritas-christi_en.html (accessed August 2006),

Pontifical Council for the Pastoral Care of Migrants and Itinerant People "Starting Afresh from Christ: Towards a Renewed Pastoral Care for Migrants and Refugees." Final Statement, Part II, Pastoral Care, *People on the Move* 35 (December 2003).

Portes, Alejandro."Migration and Underdevelopment."*Politics and Society* 8, no. 1 (1978): 1–48.

Puwar, Nirmal. "'Postcolonial Bourdieu': Notes on the Oxymoron." http://eipcp.net/transversal/0308/puwar/en (accessed June 2012).

Raghuram, Parvati. "Caring about the Brain Drain Migration in a Postcolonial World." *Geoforum* 40, no. 1 (January 2009): 25–53.

Rasmussen, Bob. "Leading your Church through Intercultural Transformation." http://usmin.onechallenge.org/intercultural-helps/intercultural-transformation (accessed March 2012).

Reidel, Laura."What are Cultural Rights? Protecting Groups with Individual Rights." In *Economic, Social and Cultural Rights*, ed. Manisuli Ssenyonjo, 411–26. Surrey: Ashgate, 2011.

"Respect Migrants Rights: Ratify the Migrant Workers Convention! 2014." http://www.fidh.org/en/migrants-rights/Respect-Migrants-Rights-Ratify-the (accessed April 2014).

Rideout, Samantha."Feature: Global Flair." http://www.ucobserver.org/faith/2010/10/global_flair/ (accessed March 2012).

Rorty, Richard. *Contingency, Irony and Solidarity*. Cambridge: Cambridge University Press, 1989.

Sadayandi, Batumalai. *A Prophetic Christology for Neighbourology: A Theology for a Prophetic Living*. Kuala Lumpur: McHill Litho Center, 1986.

Salazar-Parrenas, Rhacel. "Transgressing the Nation-State: The Partial Citizenship and 'Imagined (Global) Community' of Migrant Filipina Domestic Workers (2001)." http://www.iupui.edu/~anthkb/ a104/philippines/ migrationfilipinas.htm (accessed 12 Feb 2006).

Sanders, E.P. *The Historical Figure of Jesus*. London: Allen Lane, The Penguin Press, 1993.

Sarangi, Srikant. "Intercultural or Not? Beyond Celebration of Cultural Differences in Miscommunication Analysis." *Pragmatics* 4, no.3 (1994): 409-27.

Sassen, Saskia. *Globalization and its Discontents: Essays in the New Mobility of People and Money*. New York: The New Press, 1998.

Sayad, Abdelmalek. *The Suffering of the Immigrant*, trans. David Macy. Cambridge: Polity, 2004.

"Scent and Emotion Linked through Learning." http://www.jyi.org/news/nb.php?id=110 (accessed September 2007).

Scheuerer, Franz Xaver. *Interculturality: A Challenge for the Mission of the Church*. Bangalore: Asian Trading Corporation, 2001.

Schindler, David L. "Homelessness and the Modern Condition: The Family, Community, and the Global Economy." *Communio* 27, no. 3 (2000): 411–30.

Schreiter, Robert."Migrants and the Ministry of Reconciliation." In *A Promised Land*, ed. Groody and Campese, 107–23.

Schreiter, Robert. "Communication and Interpretation Across Cultures." *International Review of Mission* 85 (1996): 227–40.

Schüssler Fiorenza, Elizabeth. *In Memory of Her: A Feminist Theological Reconstruction of Christian Origins*. New York: Crossroads, 1992.

Schwarz, David. *Culture and Power*. Chicago: University of Chicago, 1997.

Scott, Krista. "Imagined Bodies, Imagined Communities: Feminism, Nationalism, and Body Metaphors (1999)." http://www.stumptuous.com/imagine.html (accessed 25 May 2006).

Segovia, Fernando. "Toward a Hermeneutics of the Diaspora: A Hermeneutics of Otherness and Engagement." In *Reading from this Place: Social Location and Biblical Interpretation in the United States*, ed. F.F. Segovia and M.A. Tolbert, 57–73. Minneapolis: Fortress Press, 1995.

Segundo, Juan Luis. *The Historical Jesus of the Synoptics*. Maryknoll, N.Y.: Orbis, 1985.

Senior, Donald. "Beloved Aliens and Exiles: New Testament Perspectives on Migration." In *A Promised Land, A Perilous Journey: Theological Perspectives on Migration*, ed. Daniel G. Groody and Gioacchino Campese, 20–34. Notre Dame, Indiana, University of Notre Dame, 2008.

Senior, Donald. 1 Peter, *Sacra Pagina* 15. Collegeville, MN: Liturgical Press, 2003.

Senior, Donald. *Jesus: A Gospel Portrait*. Mahwah, N.J.: St. Paul's Publication, 1997.

Shapiro, Michael J. "Triumphalist Geographies." In *Spaces of Culture: City, Nation, World*, ed. Mike Featherstone and Scott Lash. London: Sage Publications, 1999.

Sheldrake, Philip. *Spaces for the Sacred*. London: SCM Press, 2001.

Sherzer, Joel. "A Discourse-Centered Approach to Language and Culture." *American Anthropologist* 89 (1987): 295–309.

Silva, Elizabeth B. and Carol Smart, eds. *The New Family*. London: Sage Publications, 1999.

"Smell: Early Research & Culture: Early Odour Research in the West." nicks.com.au/admin/externalviewer/.../file/file_20079291640545471.pdf (accessed September 2007).

Smith, Jane M. "Identities and Urban Social Spaces in Little Tokyo, Los Angeles: Japanese Americans in Two Ethno-Spiritual Communities." *Geografiska Annaler: Series B, Human Geography* 90, no. 4 (December 2008): 389–408.

Sperber, Daniel. *The City in Roman Palestine*. New York: Oxford University Press, 1998.

Sriskandarajah, Dhananjayan. "Migration Madness: Five Policy Dilemmas." *Studies in Christian Ethics* 19, no. 1 (2006): 21–37.

Stark, Rodney. *The Rise of Christianity: A Sociologist Reconsiders History*. Princeton, New Jersey: Princeton University Press, 1996.

Stasiulis, Daiva and Abigail Bakan. "Regulation and Resistance: Strategies of Migrant Domestic Workers in Canada and Internationally." *Asian and Pacific Migration Journal* 6 no. 1 (1997): 31–57.

Staubli, Thomas and Silvia Schroer. *Body Symbolism in the Bible*. Collegeville, Minn.: The Liturgical Press, 2001.

Stewart, Michael. "'I can't drink beer, I've just drank water': Alcohol, Bodily Substance and Commensality among Hungarian Rom." In *Alcohol, Gender and Culture*, ed. Dimitra Gefou-Madianou, 127–156. London: Routledge, 1992.

Sugirtharajah, R. S. "Postcolonial Biblical Interpretation." In *The Modern Theologians: An Introduction to Christian Theology since 1918*, ed. David F. Ford with Rachel Muers, 535–52. Oxford: Blackwell Publishing, 2005.

Tadiar, Neferti Xina M. "Domestic Bodies of the Philippines." In *Filipinos in Global Migrations*, ed. Aguilar, 269–302.

Tat-Siong Benny Liew, ed., *Postcolonial Interventions: Essays in Honor of R. S. Sugirtharajah, The Bible in the Modern World* 23. Sheffield: Sheffield Phoenix Press, 2009. Review by Erin Runions. *Journal of Postcolonial Theory and Theology*. http://postcolonialjournal.com/Resources/Review%20Postcolonial%20Interventions.pdf (accessed July 2012).

Thieme, Susan. *Social Networks and Migration: Far West Nepalese Labour Migrants in Delhi*. Münster: Lit Verlag, 2006.

Thistlethwaite, Susan Brooks. *Metaphors for the Contemporary Church*. New York: The Pilgrim Press, 1983.

Thomas, Rebekah. "Biometrics, Migrants, and Human Rights." www.migrationinformation.org/Feature/print (accessed September 2007).

Thompson, John B. "Introduction to Bourdieu's Language and Symbolic Power." In *Pierre Bourdieu*, vol. 3, ed. Derek Robbins, 183–96. London: Sage, 2000.

Tomasi, Silvano M., cs. "The Response of the Catholic Church in the United States to Immigrants and Refugees." In *People on the Move: A Compendium of Church Documents on the Pastoral Concern for Migrants and Refugees*. Bishops' Committee on Priestly Formation, Bishops' Committee on Migration and National Conference of Catholic Bishops, 1988.

Tshimanga, Hipólito. "Migration at the Forefront of Political and Theological Reflections." In *Migration and Interculturality: Theological and Philosophical Challenges*, ed. Raúl Fornet-Betancourt, 55–74. Aachen: MWI, 2004.

Umut Eril. "Migrating Cultural Capital: Bourdieu in Migration Studies." *Sociology* 44, no. 4 (2010): 642–60.

United Church of Canada, "What is the Intercultural Church? (Toronto: The United Church of Canada, 2009), http://www.united-church.ca/files/intercultural/what-is.pdf (accessed March 2012).

United States Conference of Catholic Bishops, Inc. and Conferencia del Episcopado Mexicano. "Strangers No Longer Together on the Journey of Hope." A Pastoral Letter Concerning Migration from the Catholic Bishops of Mexico and the United States, no. 50–51, 2003. http://www.usccb.org/issues-and-action/human-life-and-dignity/immigration/strangers-no-longer-together-on-the-journey-of-hope.cfm (accessed April 2014).

Von Balthasar, Hans Urs. *The Glory of the Lord, Clerical Styles*. Edinburgh: Clark, 1984.

Vu, Michelle. "Interview: Former Pastor on Segregation in the Church, Cultural Intelligence." http://www.christianpost.com/news/interview-former-pastor-on-segregation-in-the-church-cultural-intelligence-48437/ (accessed March 2012).

Welsch, Wolfgang. "Transculturality: The Puzzling Form of Cultures Today." In *Spaces of Culture: City-Nation-World*, ed. Mike Featherstone and Scott Lash, 194 - 213. London: Sage, 1999.

West, Gerald. "Doing Postcolonial Biblical Interpretation@Home: Ten Years of (South) African Ambivalence." http://neotestamentica.files.wordpress.com/2009/10/421ggwest-sample.pdf (accessed July 2012).

West, Gerald O. and M.W. Dube, eds. "'Reading With': An Exploration of the Interface between Critical and Ordinary Readings of the Bible, African Overtures." *Semeia* 73 (Atlanta: Scholars Press, 1996).

Whatmore, Sarah. *Hybrid Geographies: Natures, Cultures, Spaces*. London: Sage Publications, 2002.

Wijsen, Frans. "'The Future of the Church is in our Hands': Christian Migrants in the Netherlands." In *Postcolonial Europe in the Crucible of Cultures: Reckoning with God in a World of Conflicts*, ed. Jacques Haers, sj, Norbert Hintersteiner and Georges De Schrijver, sj. Amsterdam: Rodopi, 2005.

Williams, Richmond Paul Boven. "Towards a Strategic Transcultural Model of Leadership that Enhances Koinonia in Urban Southern Africa: Synthesizing Multiple Model of Leadership that Transcends the Sociopolitical Barrier within the Cities of Southern Africa." PhD in Theology diss., University of Southern Africa, 2006.

Wimmer, Franz. "Is Intercultural Philosophy a New Branch or a New Orientation in Philosophy?" http://homepage.univie.ac.at/franz.martin. wimmer/intpheng95.pdf (accessed July 2012)

Wolf, Diane L. "Family Secrets: Transnational Struggles Among Children of Filipino Immigrants. In *Filipinos in Global Migrations*, ed. Aguilar, 347–79.

World Council of Churches, "Report of the World Council of Churches (WCC) Consultation on Mission and Ecclesiology of the Migrant Churches." (2010) *International Review of Mission* 100, no. 1 (April 2011): 104–11.

Wright, N. Thomas. *Jesus and the Victory of God*. Minneapolis: Fortress, 1996.

Young, Iris Marion. *Inclusion and Democracy*. Oxford: Oxford University Press, 1990.

Young, Iris Marion. *Justice and the Politics of Difference*. Princeton: Princeton University Press.

Young, Robert. *Colonial Desire: Hybridity in Theory, Culture and Race*. London: Routledge, 1995.

Zanfrini, Laura. "The Ethics of Migration: Reflections on Recent Migration Policies and 'Non-policies' in Italy and Europe." In *Migration Management and Ethics: Envisioning a Different Approach*, ed. 61–100. Corso Milano: Polimetrica, 2006.

Zevola, Giovani. "What are you Talking about to Each Other as you Walk Along?" (Lk 24: 17): Migration in the Bible and our Journey of Faith" in *Faith on the Move*, ed. Baggio and Brazal, 93–117.

INDEX

Althusser, Louis, 51
Anderson, Benedict, 91
Apostleship of the Sea, 141
Assimilation, 60, 69, 74, 76, 121n 10

Bhabha, Homi, xvii, 54–56
Bourdieu, Pierre xvii–xviii, xx, 56–60, 62, 126–27, 145, 146n 30, 155n 59; social classes, 57
Brain: drain, 11, 14n 45, 15; waste, 11, 12n 40: gain (reverse brain drain), 14; circulation, 15–16

Capital, according to Bourdieu, xviii, 35, 56, 58–59, 73–74: transformation, 58n 49, 50, 73n 13; maximization, 60, 75; symbolic, 59; and Trinity, 84; and ministry, 152

Capitalism, xix, 7–11: and colonial migration, 2
Castles, Stephen, 9
Catholicity, 108, 129
Church, early, 100–101, 120, 125, 138
Church structures: chaplaincy, 112–13, 121, 157; cyber, 146; inter-ritual parish, 139; national, 118, 120–21, 139–40; refugee, 121
Church metaphors: alien and exile, 122; bridge, 135–39, 140, 142n 16, 156,; city, xx–xi, 99–101, 109–115; community of communities, 107, 123; family, 97–99; mother-teacher and children-pupils, 95–97; pilgrim, 6, 93, 130–31; sanctuary, 122, 148, 154; shepherd and flock, 93–95

Church metaphors, culinary: melting pot, 69, 118; menudo chowder, 56, 132–33; salad bowl, 124; salt, 122

Citizenship: partial, 34n 39; denizen, 60n 55

Classen, Constance, 20

Constable, Nicole, 98

Culture: culturalism, 49, 50n 10, 54; discourse-centered, xvn 14, xvii; in-beyond, 34, 55–58, 64–65, 67, 79, 126–29, 138, 141, 156

Cultural practice, xvii, xviii, 56, 58, 64, 70, 73, 75, 81, 127–28, 155n 59

Cultural rights: "Cultural Rights: Fribourg Declaration," 70–73; as human rights, 71–72, 80; polyethnic rights, 76–81, 87; toleration vs promotion, 80–81

Dangerous memory, xix, 2, 4, 42–43

De Certeau, Michel, 35

Difference: and community, 106–108; relational meaning, 102–103; "Unities-in-difference," 52, 67; and Trinity, 85

Domestic work, 143, 148, 153

Douglas, Mary, 25

Ecclesia in America, 123

Ecumenism, 147

Erga Migrantes Caritas Cristi, 5, 85, 99, 129, 139, 141, 144, 147–48, 150

Emmer, Pieter, 2

Espín, Orlando, 149

Family, 12: extended, 13; generation conflicts, 62; left-behind, 66n 72, 159–60; reunification, 11

"Feel for the game," 56–57, 63, 66, 146

Field, 56, 58, 60–61, 63, 66–67, 74, 81

Foreigner, Bible, 36n 44

Fornet-Betancourt, Raúl, xv, xvii, 67

Foucault, Michel, xvn 14, xvii–xviii, 31

Gender, 12n 38, 13, 24, 59n 51, 63

Ghettoes or cultural enclaves, 70, 74

Gramsci, Antonio, 49

Global Ecumenical Network on Migration, 147

Habitus, 56–58, 64–66, 73–74, 78–79, 81, 127, 139, 146; generation conflicts, 62

INDEX

Hall, Stuart, xvii–xviii, 49–52; theory of articulation, xviii, 53–54

Hospitality, 7n 21

Hybridity, xvii, 55–56

Identity, xvii, xx: cultural, 50–52, 70, 72, 73n 10, 75, 87; hyphenated, 55, 62, 98n 14; interpellation, 51

Intercultural: bible studies, 158–59; church, 126–33

Interculturality, xv–xvii, 47–49, 52, 64–65, 67, 126, 139, 144; See also transculturality

Immigrants vs national minorities, 75–76

In betwixt-and-between, xvii, 60–64, 74, 127, 154, 157, 159

Indentured servants, 3

Interfaith Immigration Coalition, 149

Inter-religious dialogue, 148–49

John Paul II, Pope, 7, 123

Johnson, Elizabeth, 83

Kymlicka, Will, xx, 70, 75–80

Labor force quotas, 10, 14

Letter to Diognetus, 16

Marx, Karl, 9, 50n 10, 57

Metz, Johannes Baptist, 1–2, 4, 42

Migrants: and biometric technology, 28–29; evangelizers and missionaries, 160; guest worker, 9, 11–13; highly skilled, 8n 22, 13–14; new industrial reserve army, 9–11; irregular, 10, 12, 154n 53

Migration: colonial, 3, 7–8; development strategy, xiii; mentality, 13; Third world debt crisis, 8–9

Migration theology, 154–56: teaching, 150–51

Ministers, 156–59

Moller Okin, Susan, 78

Monocultural: host church, 118–20; migrant church, 120–23

Multicultural vs multiculturalist, 124n17

Multicultural Citizenship, 75

Multiculturalism, xxn 27, 47 ; feminist critique, 78

Multiculturalist church, 124–26

Mutuality, 15, 48, 59–60, 83–84, 86–87, 136–37

National Migrants Sunday, 151

Odor: cultural, 26, 33; racial, xix, 151; cultural fragrance, 33; "odor of sanctity," 42–43; "odor of sheep," 43

Popular devotions or religiosity, 57–58, 143, 149

Postcolonial, xx: criticism, xvii–xviii; theorists, 48, 55; post-colonialism, xvi; liberation-postcolonial, xvin 19

Pentecost, 129–30

Pentecostal migrant church, 155, 117n 2, 119–20, 120n 6, 138n 8, 144, 147, 151, 158–60

Phan, Peter, 63, 74

Pontifical Commission for the Pastoral Care of Migrants and Itinerant People, 153

Power: and culture, xv, xiv, xvii–xviii; field of power relations, 58; at the margins, 30–31; and mutuality, 59–60, 67

Racism, 10, 26, 28, 52–53, 62, 74

Redemptioners, 3

Reflexivity, 64–66, 139, 146

Refugees, 81, 121

Reproduction cost, 9, 15

Resistance. xvi–xix, 35, 52

Sayad, Abdelmalek, 61

Scalabrini Migration Center, xi, xiv, 13, 150

Stella Maris centers, xii–xiii, 29–30, 141

Solidarity, 7, 16, 112, 115, 136–40

Supercultural, 128n 30

Symbolic violence, 59

Third space, 54–56, 67

Tolerance, 80, 104, 119

Transculturality, 48, 127

Transnationalism, 13, 69, 161

Twitchell Hall, Edward, xiv

Trinity: model of intercultural relation, 13, 82–87, 131–32; and pakikipag-kapwa, 85

UN Convention on the Rights of All Migrant Workers and Members of Their Families, 153

World Communion of Reformed Churches, 147

World Council of Churches, 136, 147–48, 153

World Evangelical Alliance, 147

Young, Iris, xx, 102–114

www.ingramcontent.com/pod-product-compliance
Lightning Source LLC
Chambersburg PA
CBHW050109170426
43198CB00014B/2505